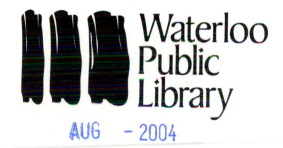

How It Works®

Science and Technology

Third Edition

Marshall Cavendish
99 White Plains Road
Tarrytown, NY 10591

Website: www.marshallcavendish.com

Third edition updated by Brown Reference Group plc.

Library of Congress Cataloging-in-Publication Data
How it works: science and technology.—3rd ed.
p. cm.
Includes index.
ISBN 0-7614-7314-9 (set)   ISBN 0-7614-7328-9 (Vol. 14)
1. Technology—Encyclopedias. 2. Science—Encyclopedias.
[1. Technology—Encyclopedias. 2. Science—Encyclopedias.]
T9 .H738 2003
603—dc21   2001028771

Consultant: Donald R. Franceschetti, Ph.D., University of Memphis

Brown Reference Group
Editor: Wendy Horobin
Associate Editors: Paul Thompson, Martin Clowes, Lis Stedman
Managing Editor: Tim Cooke
Design: Alison Gardner
Picture Research: Becky Cox
Illustrations: Mark Walker, Darren Awuah

Marshall Cavendish
Project Editor: Peter Mavrikis
Production Manager: Alan Tsai
Editorial Director: Paul Bernabeo

Printed in Malaysia
Bound in the United States of America
08 07 06 05 04   6 5 4 3 2

Title picture: Robot kicking a ball, see *Robotics*

How It Works®

Science and Technology

Volume 14

Quality Management
Salt Production

Marshall Cavendish
New York • London • Toronto • Sydney

Contents

Volume 14

Quality Management

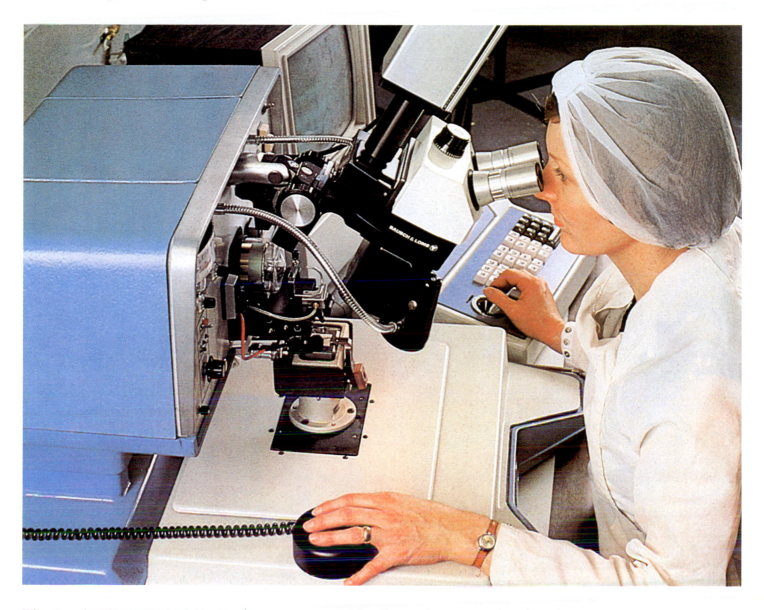

The aim of quality control is to ensure that manufactured items are satisfactory to the customer and at the same time to keep costs as low as possible and meet production deadlines. The aim is not necessarily to produce items of the highest possible quality, since this aim generally involves additional costs or time, which may not be acceptable to the customer.

Quality control is essentially a statistical technique in which samples of the product are tested, and the results compared to preset limits to judge the acceptability of the batch the sample came from. The required standard is laid down in the product specification, which should include limits of acceptability. In many cases, national or international standards are used—such as those issued by the American Standards Association (ASA) or the British Standards Institute (BSI).

The parameters specified fall into two main types—variables and attributes. Variables are quantities that can be measured, such as dimensions, weights, and electric resistance. Attributes are those properties that cannot be measured, such as flavor or visual appearance, and are more difficult to specify, although frequently they are significant in determining the acceptability of a product. Normally, attributes can be assessed only on a pass or fail basis, while the measurement of variables can yield information about the performance of the manufacturing process.

For example, consider a machining process in which a piece of metal is ground down to a thickness of 0.5 in. (12.7 mm). The tolerance or variation allowed in the specification is ±0.005 in. (0.127 mm), and thus, any pieces in the thickness range of 0.495 to 0.505 in. (12.57–12.83 mm) would be acceptable. With an accurate machine, the actual production would be more precise, and a series of parts might average out at, say, 0.502 in. (12.75 mm).

▲ Examining electronic components for conformity with the product specification. The sample is viewed through a microscope and can be recorded on videotape.

ULTRASONIC TEST CAR

EQUIPMENT DESIGNED
BY WELLS – KRAUTH

If the next set of measurements gave a slightly larger mean value of 0.503 in. (12.78 mm), still well within tolerance, it could be assumed that the machine is starting to move out of tolerance, and appropriate adjustments might be made before any out-of-tolerance work is produced.

Sampling

In most cases measurements and any other checks are made on a sample of the product taken from the production batches, or run. The sample size depends on a number of factors, such as the batch size, nature of the product, the repeatability of the manufacturing process, and the quality required, and can be set in a number of ways. A common method, adopted by major users, such as the U.S. government, relies on setting an Acceptable Quality Level (AQL). This level is defined as the proportion of defective products that is acceptable to the customer. Standard tables then give the sample sizes to suit the batch size and the AQL together with limits for the numbers of faulty components found in the sample. If the number of faulty parts found during testing is less than or equal to the lower (acceptance) limit, the batch is accepted, and if the upper (rejection) limit is reached during testing, the batch is rejected. When the number of faults reaches the acceptance number partway through the sample, testing is continued until the rejection number is reached or until all the sample is tested and thus passed.

When a decision to accept or reject a batch of parts is made on the basis of testing one sample, the technique is known as single sampling. This procedure can be refined by the use of more than one test sample. In double sampling, the first sample is tested and the number of defective parts checked against the preset acceptance and rejec-

▲ An automatic trolley for testing railway tracks. This ultrasonic car has six eyes, which examine the tracks for defects; it can record data at up to 25 mph (40 km/h). Just one of these cars is able to check up to 100 miles (161 km) of track in a working day.

tion limits, which are more rigorous than for single sampling. Particularly good or bad batches would meet or exceed these limits and thus be immediately accepted or rejected, but average batches would lie somewhere between the limits. In such cases, a second sample is taken and tested, and the total number of defective parts from both samples is compared to a new set of limits. The rapid acceptance of good batches—and rejection of bad ones—with this system reduces the total amount of testing and thus helps reduce costs.

This basic principle can be extended to multiple sampling, where a series of samples is taken and tested in turn, and to sequential sampling, in which the samples are tested one at a time. After each part has been inspected, the cumulative results obtained from the parts tested so far are examined using an appropriate sampling plan to see if the results justify either accepting or rejecting the batch. If the decision is not conclusive in either way, the process is repeated with another part. This sequential approach is more complex than straightforward batch testing but generally involves the testing of fewer components.

Inspection and testing

Various forms of inspection and testing are used to establish whether products conform to specifications and to control the manufacturing process to ensure that acceptable items are produced. Generally, it is easier to check variables, which can be measured, than attributes, which cannot. Often attributes are checked by visual inspection or comparison to a set standard, but this method can be difficult with an attributes such as flavor, which tends to vary with a tester's perceptions.

The simplest way of testing variables is by the use of gauges to check a part's critical dimensions. Such tests are often carried out by a machine operator as part of the production process, but automatic gauging techniques are also widespread. Continuous testing methods with X rays and gamma rays are used to check the thickness of sheet products, such as paper, and of coatings, such as tin.

Nondestructive test methods use X rays or ultrasonics. Ultrasonic techniques, for example, can be used to check the quality of welds in pipework intended for nuclear power plants, giving a readout that indicates the size, nature, and position of any defects.

Testing for quality control can be carried out at various stages during the manufacturing process, starting with the incoming materials. Inspection and measurement are normally separate from the manufacturing process and sometimes carried out by a separate inspectorate.

A connection disk used to check the circuit of a microchip. Precisely aligned wires make contact with the chip to measure voltages and currents. The microchip can be tested at several stages during its manufacture, and the results are then compared against a preset acceptance level.

ISO 9000 and 14000

One important development in quality management is the increasing use of a set of standards provided by the International Organization for Standardization (known as ISO) in Switzerland. This organization was established in 1947, and the standards it sets are now used by more than 100 countries around the world. The revised standards of 1994 are known as ISO 9000, and they attempt to provide guidelines for products and procedures that facilitate international trade. ISO 9000 covers a broad range of industrial processes, from airplane manufacture and software development to horticulture and accounting, and is used where organizations wish to improve the general quality of their procedures and products or where a law stipulates that ISO standards be used. When a manufacturer or organization has changed its standards to make them compliant with ISO, an independent audit is carried out to check that these new standards have been reached. The auditor then grants the organization certification or registration. ISO, however, does not itself carry out these checks or grant certificates. This process is carried out by a number of different bodies in different countries set up independently of ISO in order to encourage confidence in the system.

Businesses benefit from this form of quality management by increased efficiency and the ability to compete in world markets. If a business needs to purchase screws, for example, any screw manufacturer around the world that produces screws to ISO standards may be used with the assurance that their products will be made to certain exact criteria. In this way, businesses are able to purchase the cheapest screws from anywhere in the world and therefore make less expensive products. Customers benefit because of the standardization and therefore compatibility of technology as well as the increased competition between businesses that results in lower prices. In the field of emerging technologies, international standards ensure that the same technologies are used throughout the world, thus preventing a situation where competing alternative technologies occur, such as was the case in the early development of domestic video recorders, when betamax systems competed with VHS.

Another set of standards developed by ISO is ISO 14000. These standards relate to environmental management and include environmental auditing, labelling, and product standards. ISO 14000 helps to assess the effects of business on the quality of air, soil, and water.

 SEE ALSO: Ergonomics • Mass production • Statistics • Ultrasonics

Quantum Theory

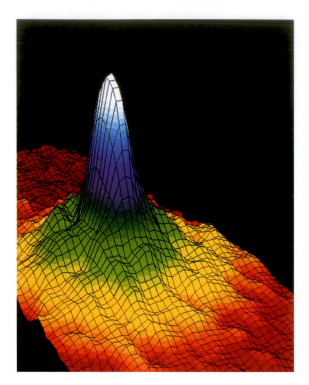

◀ This graph shows the density of low-velocity rubidium atoms forming a Bose–Einstein condensate (BEC), in which all of the atoms are in the same quantum state. This form of matter occurs when certain atoms are cooled to a temperature close to that of absolute zero.

Quantum theory was developed by physicists in the 20th century as a means to describe the behavior of light, atoms, and subatomic particles. This theory evolved from attempts to explain certain physical phenomena that could not be understood using the prevailing theories of classical physics. Classical physics describes a world in which, given enough information regarding the velocity, position, and mass of objects, it would be possible to exactly predict their future behavior. Quantum physics, however, refutes this claim and states that the behavior of matter at an atomic and subatomic level can be described only in terms of probability. In addition, quantum theory unites three of the four fundamental forces of nature: the strong force, the weak force, and the electromagnetic force. The force that is not included is gravity. Finding a unification theory capable of explaining the relationship of all four forces is an important area of research in theoretical physics.

The nature of light

In the 17th century, the Dutch physicist Christiaan Huygens proposed that light was a kind of wave. Around the same time, however, the British physicist Sir Isaac Newton proposed that light was made up of particles called corpuscles, and it was this theory that prevailed until the 19th century, when physicists once more began to investigate the wavelike properties of light. One experimental observation that caused physicists to reassess their understanding of light was devised by the British physicist Thomas Young and is called Young's double-slit experiment.

In water, if a series of wave fronts passes through two narrow openings in a wall, the waves emerge from the openings as two series of concentric waves. When the waves from each hole merge with one another, the peaks of the waves join together forming constructive interference while the troughs merge forming destructive interference. Where a trough meets a peak, however, the two cancel each other out. Young's experiment uses a single source of light shining through two slits onto a screen. The light emerging from the two slits interferes, leaving a series of light and dark bands on the screen. This phenomenon is explainable only if light is a wave.

The limitations of classical physics

In 1900, problems with the wave theory of light led the German physicist Max Planck to present a theory proposing that atoms produce packets of energy called quanta. Planck arrived at this theory by studying the behavior of blackbody radiation—an ideal blackbody is one that absorbs all radiation. In practice, an ideal blackbody is approximated by a cavity with a tiny opening through which radiation can pass. Conversely, a blackbody is also an ideal emitter of radiation, and it is in understanding the intensity of wavelengths emitted from a blackbody that physicists began to notice the limitations of classical physics. Classical physics, relying on a theory of light as a wave, predicts a much larger amount of radiation at high frequencies than actually occurs, a phenomenon that perplexed and worried physicists and consequently became known as the ultraviolet catastrophe. This discovery led Planck to his conclusion that "oscillators" in atoms could produce packets of energy only in certain quantities that he called quanta (singular, quantum). The energy carried by each quantum is proportional to the frequency of the radiation, so that

Energy = Frequency x Constant

The constant, written h, soon became known as the Planck constant. Planck assumed that quanta of radiation spread out like waves on the surface of a pond after leaving their source, allowing the long-established wavelike behavior of radiation to be explained. Planck did not suggest, however, that light itself was quantized, merely that something inside the atom permitted the absorption or emission of only certain quantities of energy.

Photoelectric effect

Einstein's study of the photoelectric effect soon confirmed the quantum nature of light. In the photoelectric effect, some metals lose negative charge, later found to be electrons, when exposed to ultraviolet light, which has a higher frequency (and therefore higher energy) than visible light. As the intensity of the light increases, more electrons leave the metal, but there is a certain limiting threshold frequency of the incident light below which no electrons are emitted.

These facts were very difficult to account for using the classical wave theory of light, but in 1905, Einstein was able to explain it by extending Planck's ideas and proposing that quanta of radiation (called photons in the case of light quanta) do not spread out like waves after leaving the source but maintain their character as discrete bundles of energy. Thus, the high-energy photons of ultraviolet light are able to eject electrons when they strike the surface of a metal. An increase in the light intensity simply means that a larger number of photons hit the surface and consequently eject more electrons, but these photons must be sufficiently energetic. If the frequency of the light falls below the threshold frequency, the photons will not have enough energy to eject any electrons. Einstein later argued that a full understanding of light needed to take account of both its wave- and particlelike behavior. Despite its paradoxical nature, this theory, known as the wave–particle duality, is now the accepted explanation for the behavior of light.

The Bohr model of the atom

In addition to the breakthroughs made in understanding the wave and particle nature of light, a model of the atom became established that enabled physicists to extend their understanding of the quantum world. This model, developed in 1913 by the Danish physicist Neils Bohr, provided an explanation for the dark Fraunhofer lines observed in the spectrum of the Sun. These lines result from the presence of absorbing elements in the Sun's atmosphere, and although they had been discovered more than a century before by the German researcher Joseph Fraunhofer, there was no ready explanation for them. Bohr produced a model of the atom that describes a central nucleus surrounded by orbiting electrons that exist at specific quantized energy levels. The absorption or emission of radiation is explained as the movement of an electron up or down an energy level. In this way, Bohr avoided a problem of classical physics; that is, a normally orbiting electron should emit radiation by Maxwell's laws, lose energy, and spiral into the nucleus. Bohr was also able to explain spectral lines as being caused by radiation emitted or absorbed when an electron jumps between two energy levels. Bohr's

◀ This electronic display, produced at Fermilab near Chicago, shows a top quark event resulting from a proton–antiproton collision. A top quark and an antitop quark are produced and decay into two muons, shown by the blue tracks. A neutrino is also produced but leaves no trace in the detector. It does, however, carry away energy from the collision, the amount of which can be determined by the size of the pink block (right). The top quark was discovered by the Fermilab detectors in 1995.

DOUBLE-SLIT EXPERIMENT

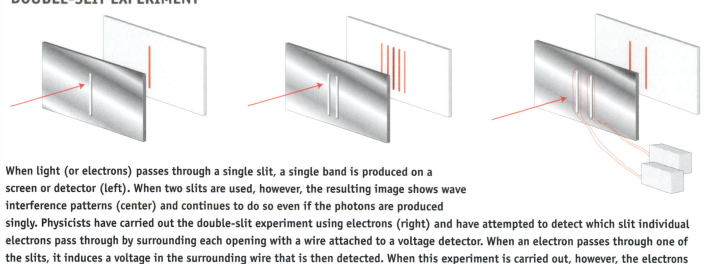

When light (or electrons) passes through a single slit, a single band is produced on a screen or detector (left). When two slits are used, however, the resulting image shows wave interference patterns (center) and continues to do so even if the photons are produced singly. Physicists have carried out the double-slit experiment using electrons (right) and have attempted to detect which slit individual electrons pass through by surrounding each opening with a wire attached to a voltage detector. When an electron passes through one of the slits, it induces a voltage in the surrounding wire that is then detected. When this experiment is carried out, however, the electrons cease to act like a wave, and the interference patterns are lost, resulting in an image showing two single bands of the same intensity.

work consequently paved the way for the far-reaching conceptual advances that were to put the quantum theory on a firm mathematical basis almost ten years later.

Electron waves

In 1924, the French physicist Prince Louis de Broglie extended the Bohr model by working from the postulates of quantum theory. De Broglie proposed that matter must also possess wavelike properties and that the Bohr model could be more easily explained by considering the electron as a wave. Many experiments have since confirmed this theory, one of which was carried out in 1989 by a group of physicists in Japan who performed the classic two-slit interference experiment with a beam of electrons.

The experiment is carried out in a similar way to Young's double-slit experiment, but here electrons are used instead of photons. According to the wave theory of matter, the incident waves on the second screen (in this case, electron detectors) should form interference patterns, and this phenomenon is in fact what is observed. If the experiment is slowed down so that only one electron is emitted at a time, the initial pattern appears as a random series of dots. After 70,000 electrons have been emitted, however, the familiar interference pattern emerges that can be accounted for only if the electrons were each passing through both slits at the same time as if the electrons "knew" there were two slits and not one.

To try to understand this strange behavior, physicists have devised methods for detecting whether an electron has passed through a particular slit. A loop of wire is placed around each slit so that if the electron passes through one of the loops, a small current is induced that can then be detected. The results, however, for this experiment are even more strange. The photons are found to pass through a particular slit, but they now behave like particles—the interference pattern is lost. The state of the electron, whether it is a wave or a particle, depends upon which aspect of its nature is being measured.

Pauli exclusion principle

A year after de Broglie presented his matter-wave theory, the Austrian physicist Wolfgang Pauli provided an explanation (known as the Pauli exclusion principle) for the pattern of light emission from atoms by proving that each electron in an atom must exist in a different state to any other electron. The state of the electron includes a characteristic that physicists call spin and which can take on only one of two values, plus or minus one-half. It was later discovered that the Pauli exclusion principle applies to other particles, known collectively as fermions. Fermions are all particles with half-number spin and include electrons, protons, and neutrons. The Pauli principle places no such restriction on particles such as photons, pions, and kaons, which have whole-number spin and are called bosons. It is the exclusivity of the fermions' states that prevents matter from collapsing in on itself. This principle also explains the way that electrons build up around the nucleus in successive energy levels.

Quantum mechanics

With a description of the atoms and an understanding of matter existing as both a wave and a particle, the groundwork was in place for the development of quantum theory. Prior to 1925, physicists relied on the framework of classical physics to explain the quantum world. This approach essentially involved making clumsy calculations that could be adjusted to produce the correct results, but it was not satisfactory to physicists. A new approach was supplied by the German physicist Werner Karl Heisenberg and the Austrian physicist Erwin Schrödinger. Heisenberg developed a form of matrix mathematics called quantum mechanics to explain quantum behavior. Around the same time Schrödinger developed an alternative system of wave mechanics that was easier to use and produced the same results. Both of these systems used mathematics to calculate the probability that an electron would be at a particular position at a particular time.

The Heisenberg uncertainty principle

In 1927, Heisenberg developed one of the most important consequences of the new quantum formalism, a result now known as the Heisenberg uncertainty principle. This principle states that you can never know both the position and velocity of a particle at the same time and that the more you know about the position, the less you know about the velocity, and vice versa. The theory explains that this inability to measure both velocity and position at the same time is not the result of the limitations of measuring devices but is inherent in the nature of quantum behavior. This restriction on measurement is fundamental and of philosophical and scientific importance. The effects of the uncertainty principle are observable only on a submicroscopic scale, as in the case of an electron whose momentum and position can not be simultaneously known.

The quantum mechanics of Schrödinger and Heisenberg was extended by the British physicist Paul Dirac, whose work in the late 1920s forms the basis of present-day research. Among other successes, Dirac predicted the existence of a particle that had the same characteristics as the electron but a positive charge. This antiparticle, the positron, was discovered in 1932.

The Copenhagen interpretation

The Copenhagen interpretation was developed by Neils Bohr as a means for explaining quantum phenomena. This theory marks an important break with classical physics, in which all events are potentially predictable. The Copenhagen interpretation emphasises that all quantum theory can predict is the probability of certain outcomes for particular experiments. Like the Heisenberg uncertainty principle, this theory explains that our inability to predict the exact behavior of matter is not due to the limitations of measuring equipment but is inherent within the nature of matter at an atomic and subatomic level. If, for example, a radioactive element is observed, it is possible to predict what percentage of the ele-

POLARIZATION

Light consists of a series of transverse waves, and the angle through which a light wave propagates is called its polarization. Light waves may be polarized vertically, horizontally, or at any angle in between and may also be polarized circularly. A polarizing filter permits only certain polarizations of light to pass through—a vertically orientated polarizer, for example, allows only vertically polarized waves to pass and blocks all other waves. If a horizontally orientated polarized filter is placed behind a vertically orientated polarizer, all waves are blocked (top). If, however, a vertically orientated polarizer is followed by a filter orientated at 45 degrees (center), 50 percent of the photons that pass through the first polarizer will then pass through the second polarizer, but they will now be polarized at 45 degrees. If the 45 degree polarizer is then placed between the vertical and horizontal polarizer, 25 percent of the photons are able to pass through the horizontal polarizer where none passed through before, but in this case, the waves will now be horizontally polarized. This peculiar phenomenon is explained by the quantum indeterminacy of the photon: the photon does not have a definite polarization until it is measured.

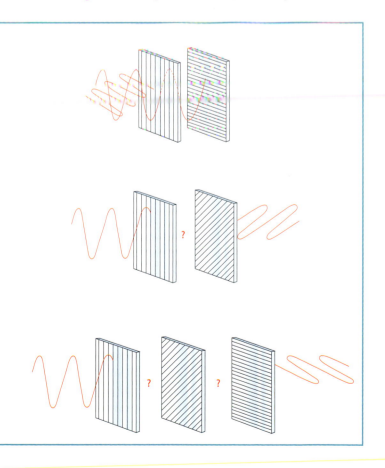

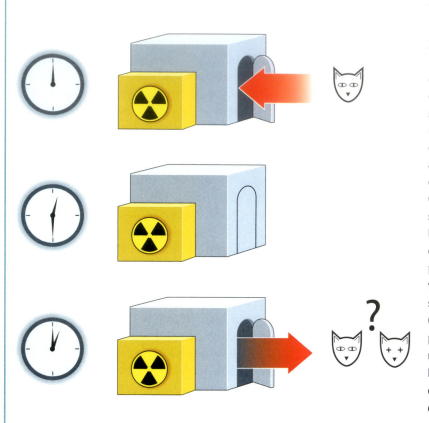

SCHRÖDINGER'S CAT

In 1935, the Austrian physicist Erwin Schrödinger published a paper that included a thought experiment devised to explain one of the problems of quantum mechanics. In quantum mechanics, the state of a particle is indeterminate until it is measured or observed and that this is not a limitation of our measuring devices but is a condition of matter at a quantum level. Schrödinger imagined a metal chamber inside of which is a cat and a vial of poison. Outside the chamber is a radiation detector and a small radioactive source. The radiation detector is linked to the vial of poison so that a single particle of radiation causes the vial to be broken, thus poisoning the cat. There is a 50 percent probability that within an hour, a nucleus in the radioactive source will decay and emit a particle of radiation. Conventional wisdom would say that after this time period, the cat is either alive or dead, but in quantum mechanics, radioactive decay has happened or not happened only when it has been observed. Until an observer looks in the box, the cat is neither alive nor dead but in an indeterminate state between the two.

ment will decay in a given time, but it is not possible to predict which nuclei will decay. The theory states that at the beginning of the observation, all of the nuclei are in exactly the same state and that there are no internal differences within individual nuclei that could be used to predict which of them would decay first. Many physicists found this theory difficult to accept, among them Einstein, and proposed theories of "hidden variable," suggesting that there were internal differences that could be used to predict the state of a particle. If this were the case, the determinacy of classical physics would remain. However, experimental evidence supports the Copenhagen interpretation, and it is therefore regarded by physicists as the best explanation for quantum phenomena.

The EPR paradox

In 1935, Einstein, working with the physicists Nathan Rosen and Boris Podolsky, identified some effects predicted by quantum mechanics that became known as the paradox of Einstein, Podolsky, Rosen, or EPR paradox. The EPR paradox was formed not to support quantum mechanics but to show why quantum mechanics must be incomplete. The EPR paradox states that one of the logical consequences of quantum mechanics is that two particles, such as two photons, can interact in such a way that they become entangled and that any subsequent measurement of the proper-

ties of one particle has an instantaneous effect on the properties of the other particle, even if one of the particles is allowed to travel to the other side of the Universe. It is not surprising that physicists found this theory difficult to accept, since it would imply some form of faster-than-light communication between the particles, regarded as impossible according to the theory of relativity. Einstein termed this phenomena "spooky action at a distance." In 1982, however, the French physicist Alain Aspect performed an experiment using the polarization of photons that proved that spooky action at a distance really does exist.

Further developments

Quantum mechanics was further developed by the British physicist Paul Dirac, U.S. physicists Richard Feynman and Julian Schwinger, and Japanese physicist Tomonaga Shinichiro to explain the interaction of light and matter. One theory, quantum electrodynamics (QED), led to another called quantum chromodynamics (QCD), which explains the interactions of certain properties of particles called quarks. This theory is so named because these particular properties are labeled with the names of colors.

SEE ALSO: ANTIMATTER • ATOMIC STRUCTURE • ELEMENTARY PARTICLE • PARTICLE ACCELERATOR

Quarrying

◄ Preparing charges for blasting at a quarry face. Holes are drilled, a detonator is placed in each, and a form of gunpowder used in quarrying called black powder is poured into them.

▶ An explosion in a stone quarry. The stone may then be ground to make crushed stone.

Quarrying is the removal of rock from Earth's crust for its subsequent use in construction, chemical, and other industries.

The three main types of rock are igneous, sedimentary, and metamorphic. Igneous rocks are formed under conditions of great heat and pressure; granite is a good example. Sedimentary rocks are mechanical agglomerations of particles; examples are sandstone and limestone. Metamorphic rocks are combinations of materials, mainly igneous but including others, that have subsequently been altered by temperature or stress.

There are two forms of quarrying: for dimension stone or for crushed stone. Dimension stone, such as granite or marble, is cut from the deposit in blocks. The product is suitable for both exterior and interior facing in building construction and for monuments and memorials. Sandstone is also produced as dimension stone and has been used in the construction of many cathedrals. Slate, a metamorphic rock, is a particular form of dimension material used for roofing, flooring, and cladding.

Crushed stone is mainly used in concrete manufacture and road construction. It is also used as railroad ballast, for drainage, and as a filter material in water treatment; and it is also bonded to form grinding wheels. Crushed limestone has many chemical and industrial applications, the main one being as a raw material for cement manufacture. It is also used as a fluxing stone in blast furnaces and for burning into lime.

◄ Charges being prepared for a quarry explosion. The detonator leads are then taken to a generator, and the charges are detonated from a safe distance.

In ancient times, quarrying was almost entirely of dimension stone. Peoples such as the Egyptians performed remarkable feats of quarrying, shaping, and transporting great blocks of stone using rudimentary tools and with few mechanical aids. In modern times, the tonnage of crushed stone far outweighs that of dimension stone because of the widespread use of concrete in building and civil engineering, the tremendous increase in road building since the introduction of the motor vehicle, and the industrial and chemical applications of crushed stone.

Once a workable deposit has been located, the first stage in quarrying is to remove the soil and weathered rock forming the overburden to expose the sound material. This part of the quarrying process is similar to the first stage of strip mining or opencast mining.

Crushed stone

The exposed rock is formed into steps or benches, these being advanced by drilling rows of holes for blasting. The holes are prepared by rotary or percussive drills (or machines combining both methods) driven by electricity, compressed air, or hydraulics. The diameter of the holes varies from 4 to 8 in. (10–20 cm), and they are charged with explosives and fired in groups to yield up to 20,000 tons (18,140 tonnes) in one blast.

The rock pile is moved by means of hydraulic excavators or wheel loaders into dumptrucks for transportation to the processing plant. The plant comprises a series of crushers, which can include gyratory, jaw, or impact machines, with ratios of feed size to crushed size ranging from 3:1 to 10:1. The material is then screened into the sizes required by the market. For special applications, it may be fine ground, or pulverized.

Dimension stone

Deposits for dimension-stone quarrying are chosen on the basis of the color and grain of the rock, particle size, and uniformity. Since the object is to get large blocks of sound stone, the use of explosives is avoided. Blocks must be removed carefully to preserve their quality and avoid cracking. Advantage is taken of natural joints in the rock, which allow the stone to be separated and removed more easily.

The first step is to make vertical cuts in the rock. A channeling machine is used for softer rocks, incorporating blades with chisel cutting edges. This machine cuts a channel several feet deep and about 2 in. (5 cm) wide. Automatic computer-controlled channelers may also be used. These channelers use a track system, resulting in greater levels of cutting accuracy. Channeling processes are most successful with rocks such as sandstone and limestone. For harder rocks, such as granite, the most common method is the wire saw, a continuous wire rope 0.2 in. (0.5 cm) in diameter that is fed with abrasives suspended in water as it runs.

If there is no convenient natural joint at the base of the block, it must be carefully separated from the bed. Horizontal holes are drilled and wedges used to break the rock loose. The blocks broken loose are often very large, so they are divided into smaller blocks on the spot, usually by a system called plug and feather. Holes are drilled, and two feathers (tapered lengths of iron, round on one side) are inserted into each hole.

▶ The Carrara marble quarry in Italy, said to have been the source of the stone Michelangelo used to sculpt many of his most famous statues.

A steel wedge is driven down between them. This process may be repeated several times before the combined force of several plugs and feathers causes the rock to split apart. The blocks are then taken to mills where they are finished by sawing, shaping, and polishing.

▶ Purbeck stone can be cut with a six-bladed, cross-cut saw. Water (which is mixed with abrasive to cut the stone) cools the blade.

SEE ALSO: CEMENT MANUFACTURE • CONCRETE • EXPLOSIVE • GEOLOGY • MINING TECHNIQUES • STONE CUTTING

Racing Car and Dragster

The early motor car was a fragile, temperamental machine; cars were built by people who were learning about them through hard experience. From the start, motor racing was a testing ground for engineering and technology, pushing engines and chassis, not to mention drivers, to the limit. The first competitions were endurance contests rather than races, but 1895 saw the start of motor racing as we know it. It was an instant success, and its popularity has never waned. In the early days town-to-town racing was the most common type, but even transcontinental races have been run, including a race from Paris to Peking.

At the beginning, races took place on public roads rather than on the specially designed circuits familiar to us today. The move away from racing on public roads to safe tracks where cars can run at high speeds was in response to a mounting number of horrific accidents. But the danger of motor racing remains part of its fascination. The worst accident in the history of motor racing happened in 1955 at the Le Mans sports car event, where 83 spectators were killed and the event was almost abandoned. In the United States, the famous Indianapolis 500 event claims, on average, one life every year.

▲ Racing cars are the ultimate in performance vehicles. Many changes have been made to the design of racing cars since the sport began, but all have to conform to strict rules laid down by motor racing's ruling body.

There are many different types of motor racing to be found around the world, each with its own governing body and set of rules.

Grand Prix racing

Grand Prix racing is the most glamorous of all the forms of motor racing, attracting teams from all over the world. It has its own world championship, and the sport's entourage moves around the world competing in many countries throughout the season. Grand Prix racing owes its existence to an American newspaper publisher who started the Gordon Bennett Cup in 1900. Six races were run between 1900 and 1906. In 1906, the French established the Grand Prix proper, and the Bennett Cup was abandoned.

Between World War I and World War II motor racing in Europe and the United States took on slightly different faces. In the United States, racing was pitched firmly toward entertainment, sometimes even racing on tracks made from wooden boards. In Europe, motor manufacturers competed with each other to produce awesome motor cars. In the early 1930s, Mercedes in Germany produced a 400-brake-horsepower car within the rules then being enforced, which limited the weight of the car to 1,650 lbs. (750 kg).

After World War II, a new set of rules was drawn up by all the motor-racing nations to make the sport international. The sport's first World Champion was an Italian, Giuseppe Farina, in 1950, and it was the first championship awarded on a points basis. The new rules saw the start of the evolution of today's familiar Grand Prix car shape. The early races used prewar cars, and superchargers were common, but regulation changes soon nullified their advantages.

The early 1950s saw cars becoming lower and more streamlined. Weight savings became an important area for engineering expertise to concentrate on. Rear-engine designs became common, eliminating the propeller shaft and enabling the driver to lay semisupine, reducing the frontal area and wind drag. The year 1962 saw the introduction of monocoque construction, which allowed further reduction in body weight to exploit the continually changing Grand Prix rules of the time.

Racing formulas

Each year the French Fédération Internationale de l'Automobile issues what is known throughout motor racing as the Yellow Book—its real title is the FIA *Year Book of Automobile Sport*. This document is over 400 pages long and contains all the rules and regulations that govern international motor sports. The constructional requirements of every car are defined, along with such things as safety and management standards for international racing circuits.

Formula 1 cars compete in the 17-race World Championship Grand Prix. The Yellow Book describes in great detail the specification for a Formula 1 car, but in general terms, the regulations state that the engine capacity must not exceed 3,000 cc (3 liters). Limits are drawn on the number of cylinders permitted—currently 10—and all engines must be of the four-stroke reciprocating type. Body weight of the car and driver must be above 1,320 lbs. (600 kg).

The dimensions of the cars are carefully defined, along with the location of fuel, oil, and electric lines, the rear overhang, wheel width, and so on. Teams must incorporate certain safety features into each car that competes. These safety features include such things as deformable structures to protect the fuel tank in a crash and rollover bars to protect the driver's head. Also, total fuel capacity is limited to reduce fire risks. All cars have an onboard fire extinguisher system. When it is activated by pulling on an external emergency handle, the engine is cut off and the battery disconnected.

In technical respects, some experts have suggested that there has been some stagnation in the design of Formula 1 cars as a result of the strict rules imposed by the FIA. Only teams with large research and development budgets can be expected to bring about major changes in design when proven components, particularly in the engine field, still have something to offer. The similarity between many Formula 1 cars does have one interesting by-product, though: since

▲ In wet weather tires with a pronounced tread are used. The tread channels away water and prevents the car from aquaplaning, which results in a dangerous loss of control at high speed.

▼ The Lotus 88 was a sensation when it appeared with its twin chassis, one carrying the driver, the other the bodywork. Unlike more conventional ground-effect cars, it developed its downward force through the secondary chassis without compressing the main suspension.

the cars are so closely matched, the result of a race depends to a great extent on the skill of the driver. It is significant, therefore, that in Grand Prix racing the World Championship is awarded to a driver, with a constructor's award for the team with the most overall points. In sports car racing, the championship goes to a car maker.

The international flavor of Formula 1 is not reflected in other variations in car racing. Many countries have their own specialized minor formulas, many of which also date back to the immediate post-World War II years. The United States saw the start of midget racing, with cars limited to a wheelbase of between 66 and 76 in. (167.5–193 cm), while in Britain a formula based on 500 cc motorcycle engines became popular because of their low cost and the close racing they provided. Many of the formulas have come and gone, while some have graduated from national to international status. The evolution of the Italian Formula Junior onto the international scene, together with its subsequent changes into Formula 3, is one example.

The great expense of racing even Formula 3 cars has caused a variety of national promotional single-seat racing formulas to spring up. The first of these was Formula Vee, introduced in 1961. Powered by a tuned Volkswagen Beetle engine, a Vee had many other standard elements in its design and gained popularity in Germany, the United States, and Brazil, where the formula was the training ground for the Formula 1 World Champion driver Emerson Fittipaldi.

In Europe, Britain has adopted Formula Ford, while France has its similar Formula Renault. These formulas are based on a mildly tuned Ford or Renault 4-cylinder, 1,600 cc engine. Narrow grooved racing tires are required, and aerodynamic aids are forbidden. From its

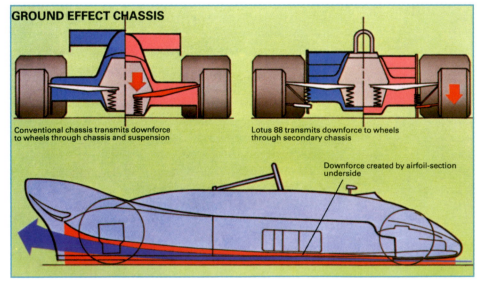

GROUND EFFECT CHASSIS

Conventional chassis transmits downforce to wheels through chassis and suspension

Lotus 88 transmits downforce to wheels through secondary chassis

Downforce created by airfoil-section underside

beginnings in Britain, Formula Ford has been exported to a number of other countries, including the United States, Australia, parts of Latin America, Scandinavia, and Austria.

These minor formulas have become training grounds for budding Formula 1 drivers. The cars are outwardly similar to Grand Prix cars but have a minimum of bodywork that can be damaged and are easy to work on. Racing and maintaining them is generally much cheaper. Formula Ford even offers some quite sophisticated features found on Formula 1 cars, such as easily altered gear ratios.

Nuts and bolts

Despite the strict regulations, Grand Prix cars continue to evolve. Mechanically, the start of the 1980s saw the reappearance of supercharging (to be more accurate, turbocharging), a practice that had fallen from favor some 30 years previously, when the regulations imposed a 1,500 cc capacity limit. However, safety concerns about the boost pressures that turbocharged engines produced eventually led to their being banned in 1989. Instead, 3,500 cc induction engines powered by unleaded fuel began to dominate the track. In 1995, the engine capacity was revised downward to its current limit of 3,000 cc.

Bodywork has seen more changes than engines, and most cars are now built of carbon fiber in a monocoque construction. In 1967, Ferrari introduced airfoil devices, a step that has been adopted by all racing teams, and it will almost certainly remain so. The principle behind these airfoils is exactly the opposite to that of aircraft wings; airfoils are designed to give reverse lift and to press the car against the ground as it moves along. The most effective place to mount them was found to be directly above the rear suspension. This discovery led to the easily identifiable style of the cars of the late 1960s with their spindly airfoils mounted high above the rear of the car to catch the maximum air flow. However, since 1969, their sizes and placement have been strictly limited by the FIA following a series of breakages leading to accidents. Similar restrictions apply to the height and size of the front-wing end plates.

Research in wind tunnels and hard experience on the track has shown teams where to place airfoils to get the maximum down force without infringing the regulations. The down force has to be balanced against the drag resulting from the airfoils. Throughout the 1970s, work progressed on the aerodynamics of Grand Prix car bodies, until today car bodies are designed so that the whole shape forces the car down onto the road—

▼ A racing team changes the wheels and fills the tank of a Ferrari in seconds during a pitstop. Races can be won or lost in the pits, so a large and highly skilled support team is a necessity.

some teams talk of ground-effects chassis. The early 1980s also saw so-called skirts appearing on cars. Although outlawed by 1983, their purpose was to create a partial vacuum, which drew the car toward the ground.

Tires and suspension

With engine and body design, tires and suspension are an important part of a racing car. The patch of tire that is in contact with the road is vital, because it transmits not only the power to provide acceleration but also the braking to slow the car when entering a corner and the grip that keeps it from sliding from the course. The coefficient of friction between the track surface and the tire contributes to the effectiveness of the tire.

Tire design is a sophisticated discipline. Many factors have to be taken into consideration when designing a tire for race use. Even the most effective combination of suspension and tires allows a car to drift when cornering, and the difference between the direction of travel of the car and the direction of travel of the tires is called the slip angle. For each tire design there is an optimum slip angle that yields the optimum performance from the tire.

Different tread patterns are used for differing ground conditions. Slick tires have a smooth surface with no tread as distinct from road tires. They are used in dry conditions, as they give maximum contact with the circuit's surface. If the surface becomes wet, slick tires are dangerous because they aquaplane at well below race speeds,

causing the driver to lose control. In 1998, rib-tread tires were made obligatory in place of smooth slicks, which were leading to dangerously high cornering speeds. Rib-tread tires have four longitudinal grooves on the rear rubber tire and three on the front to reduce the surface contact with the track. Another groove was added to the front tire in 1999 to reduce speeds still further. In wet weather, tires with treads are used so that the surface water can be channeled away.

The rubber compounds used for tires are designed to offer optimum grip allied with a toughness to withstand the stresses and wear of a Grand Prix. Compounds designed for use in the dry need to be able to withstand high operating temperatures and are consequently relatively hard. At the other end of the scale, wet tires use soft compounds because the water on the road cools the surface of the tire. The effect of using the wrong compound for the prevailing conditions can be dramatic. A hard compound cooled by water on the road loses its grip because the tire drops below its most efficient operating temperature. A soft compound run in dry conditions will rapidly overheat, and in extreme cases, the tread will melt. Intermediate tires have never been popular because they are too much of a compromise in racing conditions.

Suspension in racing cars inevitably has its own set of terms and difficulties, but without a well-designed suspension system, a racing car will not be successful. A suspension system moves about an imaginary point called the roll center,

▼ A top-fuel dragster wheeling off the line at Orange County International Raceway, California. This class of dragster can complete the strip in about 5.5 seconds.

◀ Dragsters use V-8 engines that have been heavily modified to achieve maximum power from the fuel. Top-fuel cars such as this one burn nitromethanol, which can produce up to 3,000 horsepower.

and the amount of roll is one of the critical factors in suspension design. A car with a low center of gravity will minimize changes in attitude from braking, accelerating, and cornering. Coupled with a suspension design that minimizes roll, wheel loadings will be kept at a constant level, allowing tires to work at something approaching their optimum performance.

Sports car racing

The sports car—or GT (gran turismo)—is usually a two seater designed for nimble handling rather than speed or power. It is theoretically a production car intended for private ownership and must be homologated—that is, a certain number must have been built. There are also special prototype classes.

Some builders of Grand Prix cars, such as Ferrari and Lotus, also make sports cars. Some of the most famous car races, such as the Le Mans 24 hours, are sports car events and are sometimes misleadingly called Grand Prix. In this case, the name means only that the race is an important international event, although in some cases, the speed and power of sports cars are not very different from their Formula 1 cousins.

Speedway racing

The United States has a number of unique kinds of motor racing. Some attribute the American fascination with these home-grown events as being a result of widespread car ownership in a country

without much rural public transport; there has always been a ready supply of old cars ripe for conversion to racing. Track racing based on the model of the Indianapolis Speedway is very popular, with a number of different championship classes being run.

Hot rod racing, for example, can be as much a hobby as a sport. The owners of cars usually do their own modifications and race preparation. They then compete with others against time or distance. The sport has had bad publicity because of its early links with illegal street racing but is now controlled by the National Hot Rod Association (NHRA). The cars may be ordinary street models modified for performance, or they may be modified to an extent that makes them unsuitable for street use. For example, a high-performance engine intended for high-speed use may be damaged by stop-and-go city driving, which involves a lot of engine idling.

Other popular kinds of speedway racing include dirt-car racing, run usually on one-mile amusement park tracks, and sprint-car racing—similar to dirt-car racing but using smaller cars and sometimes run on paved tracks. Midget-car racing is for still smaller cars, and stock-car racing for cars that are near to production specification.

Drag racing

Drag racing is an outgrowth of hot rod racing in which cars compete against the clock on a track called a drag strip, usually ¼ mile (393 m) long. The cars are specially built from scratch and are unsuitable for anything except the acceleration contest over the short distance. A dragster can accelerate from 0 to 100 mph in under one second.

Drag racing machines developed from stock car racing, that is, racing of modified production cars, and is said to have developed during the Prohibition era in the United States (1919–1933). Bootleggers of illegal spirits tuned up and modified the engines of their cars so they could outrun the police. Since World War II, drag racing, an outgrowth of racing of modified cars by amateurs, has become a very popular spectator sport. Top fuel cars can cover the quarter mile in 5.5 seconds, reaching a speed of 250 mph, and require two parachutes to help them stop.

The engine

American V-8 engines are popular for use in dragsters because of the high capacity, expressed in cubic inches, of their fuel combustion chambers. Ordinary automobile engines are built for durability and a certain minimum fuel consumption, factors that do not concern the drag racer, so the engines are completely disassembled and put back together with a great deal of balancing and polishing of the parts. The engine is heavily modified to achieve the maximum power. The cooling system—radiator, hoses, and water pump—is dispensed with, since the water in the engine's water jacket is sufficient for cooling during the quarter-mile run. The rebuilt engine incorporates a supercharger and a fuel-injection system; the fuel itself may be a nitromethanol mixture, which is highly combustible. The exhaust system consists of tuned pipes of exactly the right diameter to match the manifold on the engine for the right amount of back pressure. Mufflers are dispensed with, making drag strips very noisy places.

The chassis

For a certain class of drag racing, a slightly modified engine may be mounted in an ordinary car body, but a true dragster is a glamorous construction completely unsuitable for driving on the street. It may be built from scratch of welded steel tubing, with an aluminum skin covering it, and providing barely enough space for the driver. The tremendous accelerating power of a dragster tends to make the front end want to climb into the air, so it may be made as long as 22 ft. (6.7 m),

and the snout will be aerodynamically designed to keep it on the ground.

The classic slingshot dragster has now given way to the rail. The slingshot had the frame extending well beyond the rear axle, and the driver's seat was located there, like the stone in a slingshot. The rail configuration places the engine, with an airfoil, at the rear behind the driver and provides a long, extended front end covered with lightweight alloy paneling.

The rear axle halves themselves are often shortened to lessen the risk of snapping with the torque of acceleration. The wheels are made of magnesium alloy, combining light weight with high strength. Wrinkle-wall tires without any treads are used for maximum traction (the drag strip must be absolutely dry and clean). This type of tire is called a slick and is able to distort under acceleration without deflating and provides excellent surface contact.

To attain maximum grip the drivers often perform a burnout. First the slicks are driven through water to make them slippery, and then they are spun on dry ground by dropping the clutch. This procedure makes the tires hot and sticky and able to grip much better.

Classes

There are five classes of dragster: the street legal (essentially standard production vehicles) with engines in the region of 400 to 500 horsepower capable of 110 mph at the end of the strip; modified street (stripped out and lightened vehicles) with 600 to 700 horsepower engines attaining speeds of 130 to 135 mph; pro-stock (specially built vehicles with glass-fiber bodies) developing 700 to 800 horsepower and terminal speeds of 160 mph; and the two top rail type of vehicle classes—the pro-comp with methanol-burning 1,700 to 1,800 horsepower engines that can cover the strip in 6.3 seconds and, finally, the top fuel classes consisting of Funny Car and Pro Fuel Dragster with nitromethanol-burning engines, producing between 2,500 and 3,000 horsepower.

Jet and rocket cars are the latest development in the world of drag racing. With their flame shows and high power-to-weight ratio, rocket dragsters can now achieve elapsed times over a quarter mile of 3.5 seconds from a standing start. The popular fuel for rocket cars is hydrogen peroxide, and the jet cars are fueled by jet kerosene.

FACT FILE

- In the first Le Mans Grand Prix in 1906, the winner, by half an hour, was a 13 liter Renault, one of three identical Grand Prix Renaults costing $15,000 each. They had four massive side-valve cylinders, three-speed transmissions, and newly developed hydraulic shock absorbers.

- In 1965, the Indianapolis 500 was won for the first time in 49 years by a European car. It was a Lotus 38, which averaged 150.68 mph (242.49 km/h) for the 200 laps. The alcohol-burning engine was rearmounted, in contrast to the large front-engined U.S. roadsters with nitromethane engines that had dominated the race for many years.

- The 1921 French Grand Prix was a duel between U.S. Dusenbergs and French Ballots. The wheels of the big cars ripped up the circuit surface, loosening jagged flints, which were hurled through the air, smashing radiators. The Dusenberg won at an average 78 mph (125 km/h), just managing to finish with flint-pierced tires.

SEE ALSO: AUTOMOBILE • AUTOMOBILE SAFETY • BRAKING SYSTEM • CARBURETOR • CLUTCH • ENGINE COOLING SYSTEMS • FUEL INJECTION • INTERNAL COMBUSTION ENGINE • STEERING SYSTEM • SUPERCHARGER AND TURBOCHARGER • TIRE

Radar

Radar systems measure positions, speeds, and surface characteristics of objects from the radio waves they reflect. The word *radar* is an acronym derived from *radio detection and ranging*, which refers to the earliest and most basic applications of radar systems: spotting aircraft and measuring their distances from the ground station of the radar system.

History

The reflection of radio waves was discovered by the German physicist Heinrich Hertz in the late 1880s. Realizing that radio and light waves are both forms of electromagnetic radiation, he set about demonstrating the properties that they have in common. Of particular relevance to radar was his demonstration that electrical conductors, such as metals, reflect radio waves.

The application of radio for detecting aircraft was developed in the 1930s, when the existence of long-range aerial bombers started to be recognized as a military threat. The British inventor Sir Robert Watson-Watt became involved in the development of a radio-frequency long-range detection system almost by accident: when asked to comment on the possibility of developing a "death ray"—an antiaircraft weapon in the form of powerful radio waves—Watson-Watt pointed out that, while such a weapon would be impracticable, it would be quite possible to use radio waves to detect an approaching aircraft long before it could be seen by eye.

▲ This police officer in Santa Monica, California, uses a radar "gun" to check the speeds of passing vehicles. Drivers who exceed the speed limit are liable to be penalized.

◄ The discus-shaped pod mounted on this EC2 Hawkeye aircraft protects and streamlines a radar antenna. When airborne, the radar can scan over a much broader horizon than when on the ground. Thus, airborne radar is useful in detecting low-flying aircraft for early-warning defense systems.

Out of this suggestion arose Watson-Watt's invention of a radar system in 1935. Four years later, by the outbreak of World War II, the British military was operating the Chain Home early-warning radar system as part of its defense against hostile aircraft. By that time, most of the other major military powers had also developed radar for military use, but the Chain Home was the most advanced system operational in 1939.

Radar continues to play an important role in early-warning systems, and it has acquired several civilian applications in recent decades. Possibly the most important of these applications is in air-traffic control, where radar systems locate and identify aircraft. Air-traffic controllers use this information to coordinate aircraft movements within the airspace under their supervision.

The development of Doppler radar techniques, which measure speed of motion relative to a radar antenna, have extended the applications of radar yet further. Doppler radars can produce real-time maps of rainfall that help in weather forecasting and in storm-warning systems; they can also be used as fixed or portable roadside speed-checking devices for law enforcement. Fender-mounted microwave Doppler radars also help motorists park in tight spaces by emitting a series of audible tones whose frequency increases as the distance decreases between the fender and a reflecting object, such as a wall.

Basic principles

The phenomenon of acoustic echoes is familiar: sound waves reflect off buildings and cliffs, and the time taken for the echo to arrive back at its source depends on the distance traveled by the sound, which is twice the distance between the source and reflecting object. Sonar devices use pulses of sound to measure distances between submarine objects, the range of an object being half the time interval divided by the speed of sound in water—around 0.94 miles (1.5 km) per second in seawater that contains 3.5 percent salt.

Radar uses exactly the same principle as sonar, but with radio waves instead of sound waves. Radio waves travel at the speed of light—around 186,000 miles (300,000 km) per second—which is around 200,000 times the speed of sound in water. Radio waves are also more easy to focus into narrow beams, and when focused into such beams, they lose intensity much less rapidly with distance than does a wave that spreads out in all directions. Hence, more focused beams travel farther before becoming too weak to detect.

Another advantage of more focused beams is that they are more effective in identifying the angular position of the reflecting objects relative to the radar antenna. The angular position is found by relating the time when the reflected pulse is received to the angular sweep rate of the radar.

Pulsed radar

Radar systems can use either continuous radio waves, similar to those used in radio and television broadcasting, or they can use pulsed signals, which consist of regular short bursts of radio-frequency radiation. In practice, pulsed radar has a number of advantages over continuous-wave radar and therefore is more widely used.

In pulsed radar, a radio transmitter connected to a directional antenna—one that concentrates radiation in a beam—emits a stream of short pulses of radio waves at frequencies between 400 MHz and 40 GHz. Each pulse is normally a few millionths of a second long but may be even shorter, and the pulses are separated by a time interval much longer than the time taken for a pulse to reach an object of interest and return.

Any reflecting object in the path of the transmitted beam sends some of the pulse back toward the antenna, where a radio receiver detects incoming pulses. After each outgoing pulse, the receiver may detect numerous reflected pulses, each corresponding to an object within the "view" of the radar at that time. A microprocessor then calculates the range of each object from the time displacement of its reflected pulse relative to the outgoing pulse. Those ranges, combined with the angular position of the radar at the time of the outgoing pulse, provide the data needed to plot the positions of objects on a screen.

Occasionally, separate antennas emit outgoing pulses and detect reflected pulses; this arrangement is called bistatic radar. More usual is the monostatic arrangement, where a single antenna both transmits and receives. Since outgoing pulses are many orders of magnitude stronger than reflected pulses, the receiver circuit must remain isolated from the antenna during the brief period of the transmitted pulse. If it were not, the transmission pulse would overload the receiver. The device that switches the antenna between connections to the transmission and reception circuits is called the transmit-receive (TR) cell.

PLAN-POSITION RADAR

Search, surveillance, and air-traffic-control radars are all forms of plan-position radar—radar systems that give two-dimensional plots of the positions of reflecting objects relative to a ground station that houses the radar antenna. The basic principle is that the time taken for a radar echo to return to the antenna depends on the range of the reflecting object (near right). When the radar antenna rotates (far right), the system combines range and angular position to produce a plan display of all the reflectors within a given range.

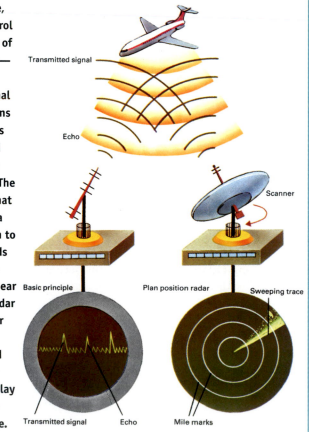

Transmitted signal

Echo

Scanner

Basic principle

Plan position radar

Sweeping trace

Transmitted signal   Echo

Mile marks

Transmitters

The transmitter of a pulse radar must be capable of producing short pulses of radio energy of high intensity but at substantial intervals of time. The length and timing of pulses is called the duty cycle of the transmitter.

A typical transmitter might produce pulses 4 microseconds long, spaced at intervals of 4 milliseconds. With this duty cycle, the transmitter operates for one-thousandth of the total operating time of the radar. Accordingly, the mean power of the transmitter is only one-thousandth of the power generated during the pulse, so a transmitter that produces one-megawatt pulses has an mean power output of only one kilowatt.

The two most important types of transmitting tubes used in radar are the cavity magnetron and the klystron. The cavity magnetron is a tuned circuit that resonates at the transmission frequency, whereas the klystron is an amplifying circuit that takes an input signal at microwave frequency and amplifies it to the power required for the radar. Other transmitters include the traveling-wave tube (TWT) and solid-state transmitters.

Range and wavelength

Radar waves, like light waves, travel in straight lines when in the vacuum of free space. In Earth's atmosphere, however, the decrease in atmospheric density with height causes a small amount of downward refraction, or bending. As such, radar can "see" marginally beyond the horizon, although the increase in scope caused by atmospheric bending is so small that it can be ignored when estimating the capability of a radar system.

In effect, the range of a single search radar is limited by the curvature of Earth—a serious disadvantage when sea level or low-flying objects are the targets for detection. Raising the radar by any amount extends the horizon, which is why ground-based radar stations are usually located on hilltops, and naval radars are mounted on the tops of ships' masts. A much greater increase in horizon is achieved by mounting the antenna in an aircraft, an approach known as an airborne warning and control system, or AWACS. An alternative approach is to feed the inputs from several widely spaced antennas into a single system. The signals from individual radars are communicated to a control station by radio or satellite links.

All objects are capable of reflecting radio waves to some extent, and the ability of an object to reflect radio is expressed as its scattering coefficient. The scattering coefficient of an object depends on its shape and size, the material of which it is made, and the wavelength used. Large objects such as ships and aircraft reflect well at

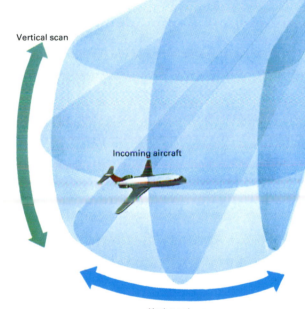

Vertical scan

Incoming aircraft

Horizontal scan

Ground station

◀ A phased-array antenna such as this rotates to scan in azimuth; it scans in elevation by altering the size of the phase shift between the individual elements of the antenna.

▲ Radars that can scan in azimuth and elevation are used to locate objects in three dimensions. An example of their use is in the landing approach radars used by controllers at all major airports.

wavelengths up to 35 ft. (10 m)—the first British early-warning radars used wavelengths between 35 and 50 ft. (10 and 15 m), for example. Smaller objects escape detection at such great wavelengths, and most modern radars use wavelengths in the range 1 to 10 in. (2.5–25 cm). These wavelengths correspond to microwave frequencies, whereas the longest radar wavelengths correspond to high-frequency (HF) radio frequencies.

A typical modern long-range surveillance radar for early-warning or air-traffic-control (ATC) purposes might use a klystron to produce a wavelength of 10 in. (25 cm) with a peak power of 2 MW and a mean power of 2 kW. The associated antenna might be 39 ft. (12 m) wide and 16 ft. (5 m) high and rotate at 10 rpm. Such a system would be able to detect high-level aircraft at ranges as great as 300 miles (483 km).

Scanning modes

In the most common operational mode for search or surveillance radars, a single-beam antenna scans around a vertical axis. The angle from a fixed point—usually true north—is called the azimuth, and the antenna beam is no more than one or two degrees wide in azimuth. In the fan-beam arrangement, the beam extends vertically from the horizon to perhaps 15 or 20 degrees elevation. Reflections from such beams provide range and bearing information only.

To obtain three-dimensional positional information, reflections from different parts of the elevation must be distinguished in some way. In one technique, the fan beam is replaced by a number of pencil beams, each with an elevation range no greater than one or two degrees. This stack of beams is scanned simultaneously in azimuth; the reflected pulses indicate the angular positions of reflectors within small ranges of azimuth and elevation, and the timings of those pulses reveal the ranges of objects, as before.

In other systems, elevation information is obtained by scanning a narrow pencil through a range of elevation angles at a rapid rate while scanning the azimuth at a much slower rate. In this way, a single beam analyzes the sky in narrow cone-shaped volumes. In such systems, the relatively slow azimuthal scan is usually done by physical rotation of the antenna. The elevational scan is done by varying the phase relationship between the signals to a phased array.

A phased array consists of a number of bar-shaped antennas, each fed by different signal generators. Interference determines the angle of the beam without the need for physically moving the antenna. When the signals are all exactly in step, they produce a narrow beam that extends along an axis perpendicular to the array; when the phase shifts of the outputs increase in equal steps from one side of the array to the other, interference effects produce a narrow beam at an angle from the perpendicular, and that angle increases with the size of the phase shift between elements.

In search radars with a rotating beamed antenna, the direction of a target is obtained from the direction of maximum received signal. When greater angular precision is required, two directional beams can be arranged so as to overlap partially. In the overlapping area, the positions of objects can be measured with great accuracy from the ratio of echo strengths in the two antennas.

Tracking mode

Some radars are required to follow a single object closely rather than to detect all the objects in a broad space. Examples of applications of such radars include missile-tracking systems and the guidance systems of antiaircraft weaponry. Such radars are called tracking radars, and they employ antenna beams that are narrow cones or are parallel. Once the radar has found a target, the scanning system follows automatic control that keeps the echo intensity at a maximum; the system is then said to be locked on to the target.

PULSE RADAR OPERATION

Most radar systems use a single antenna to send out beams of intense pulses of radio-frequency radiation and to detect the weak echoes reflected by objects in the beam. A timing circuit controls the magnetron that produces the outgoing pulses, and a TR (transmit-receive) cell switches the antenna between the magnetron circuit and the detection and analysis circuit.

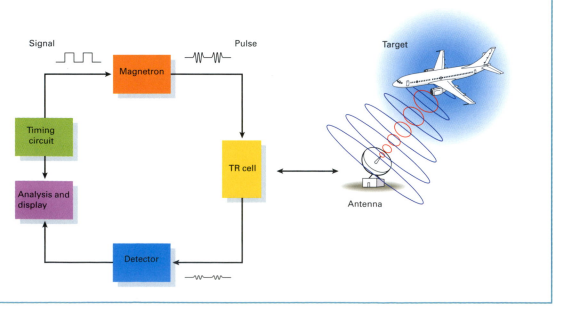

Secondary radar

The form of radar thus far described, which relies on the passive reflection of radio waves, is also called primary radar. This term distinguishes simple radar systems from a more complex form, called secondary radar, or secondary surveillance radar (SSR). In secondary radar systems, the target—usually an aircraft—carries a small device that both detects and transmits radar signals. This device is called a transponder.

When the transponder detects a pulse from a ground radar, it responds by transmitting a pulse to ground at a slightly different wavelength. Using techniques from radio technology, the transmitted pulse is modulated to convey such information as an identity code, which might be the call-sign of the aircraft, and altitude. Equipment at the ground station decodes this information and presents it alongside the "blip" that represents the plan position of the aircraft, which is measured by the usual ranging and direction-finding functions of the radar.

The information provided by secondary radar systems is of great value in air-traffic control, and it is now mandatory for certain categories of aircraft to carry the appropriate transponders when flying in controlled airspace. Secondary radar also forms the basis of a military identification system known as IFF (identification, friend or foe).

Doppler radar

Not only do passive radar echoes consist of positional information, they can also be analyzed to calculate the relative velocity of the reflecting object along the direction of the beam. This object is achieved using the Doppler effect, whereby the frequency of the reflected radar signal shifts according to the speed of the reflector.

The acoustic Doppler effect is responsible for such phenomena as the change in pitch of the sound from a locomotive's horn that occurs as the locomotive approaches, passes, and then recedes from a stationary observer. While the locomotive is approaching, the sound waves from the horn are compressed—their wavelength is less than it would be if the locomotive were stationary. The shorter wavelength corresponds to a higher frequency and higher pitch of sound. Similarly, sound waves from the receding locomotive are elongated, and the pitch is lower than the natural pitch of the horn. In fact, the observer hears the true pitch only at the instant when the locomotive passes, when the velocity along the line between the track and the observer is zero.

In the context of radar, the frequency shift of reflected pulses can be analyzed to measure the speed of approaching aircraft or missiles, for

◄ This antenna is typical of those that provide radar signals for air-traffic control. It produces a fan-shaped beam that spreads over 15 to 20 degrees in the vertical plane but is narrow in the azimuth. The antenna rotates to scan the whole horizon.

example, provided the target is moving along the line between it and the radar antenna. The frequency shift is zero for stationary objects and in the extremely unlikely event of an object following a circular trajectory centered on the antenna.

The Doppler effect is used in many ways. In search and surveillance radar, for example, echoes from stationary objects can be eliminated from the display, so buildings, trees, and hills are rendered invisible, thus making traces from moving targets, such as aircraft, much easier to see. Aircraft can use radar to measure ground speed from the frequency difference between echoes from the ground below and objects ahead. Other systems that use the Doppler effect include weather radars, which detect the movement of raindrops and hail stones; speed radars for law enforcement; and missile-guidance systems.

Displays

Radar displays tend to be based on cathode-ray tubes, which form visual displays in glowing phosphors. In the earliest radar systems, the cathode-ray tube would be used as an oscilloscope: the beam would traverse the screen from left to right at a steady rate, with each sweep of the screen corresponding to one cycle of the radar. The start of the sweep would be synchronized with the moment of emission of the transmitter pulse, and any echoes would be displayed as blips—brief vertical deflections of the scanning beam. The position of each blip in such a display is a measure of the time taken for the outgoing pulse to be reflected and return as an echo; this time is an indication of the range of the reflecting target. The angular position of targets could be determined by adjusting the antenna direction until the magnitude of the blip reached its maximum.

In virtually all modern systems, the cathode ray is adjusted so that its intensity is slight in the absence of echoes but grows stronger when an echo is received. The beginning of the trace coincides with the center of a circular display on the screen, and a radial line rotates in synchronism with the scanning antenna. In this way, the screen shows a circular map, centered on the antenna, of the positions of reflecting objects. This map is called a plan-position indicator, or PPI, and it is usually calibrated to show the distances of objects.

Some displays indicate information beyond the simple plan position of reflecting objects. Secondary radar systems show the information emitted by the onboard transducers of aircraft, for example, while Doppler radar for storm tracking shows the different Doppler shifts of echoes as false colors in the plan-position indicator.

Applications

Some important applications of radar, such as early-warning defense systems and the long-range aspects of air-traffic control, have already been mentioned. Both defense and ATC also make use of medium-range (100–150 miles, or 160–240 km) search radars, the former for the control of fighter aircraft and antiaircraft missiles, the latter for the airfield approach.

Search radar is used on ships both for defense purposes and for navigation in poor visibility. Its use by merchant ships for the latter purpose is now extensive. Shipborne search radars are also used to provide marine coverage radar defense networks. Shipborne tracking radars are primarily of value in such operations as the control and guidance of antiaircraft weapons.

Radar has many uses in aircraft. General-purpose applications include weather radars, navigation radars, and radar altimeters, which measure the height above ground from the delay of the echo reflected off the ground. Airborne military applications include systems for locating and tracking enemy aircraft and systems for reconnaissance. A mode called moving-target indication (MTI) produces displays and printouts in which only those objects whose positions change between sweeps are apparent. This system is useful in monitoring troop movements.

Portable radar packs, such as the French Rasura (DR-PT-2A), are useful for battlefield surveillance. Equipment such as this can detect a vehicle at distances as great as 6 miles (10 km), a standing person at up to 4.4 miles (7 km), and a crawling figure at up to 1.3 miles (2 km).

Radar has applications in surveying and prospecting, particularly in terrain where access is difficult. A device called a tellurometer uses microwave-frequency radar to measure distances, and ground-penetrating radar (GPR) can be used to detect buried objects. One application uses GPR at around 1 GHz to detect land mines for their subsequent removal or destruction.

Meteorological applications include the use of Doppler radar to detect and monitor the progress of tropical storms that might intensify to hurricane strength or pass through populated areas. Tracking radar is used to follow atmospheric sounding balloons as they drift in the upper atmosphere, thus revealing the strength and direction of upper atmospherics.

Safety

The radiation used in radar is of similar wavelengths to that used in microwave ovens and has the potential to increase the temperature of living tissues. However, the signal intensity necessary to produce harmful effects is much greater than that used by all but the most powerful radars, such as those used to detect intercontinental missiles at long ranges. Even then, the intensity falls to safe levels within a short distance of the antenna.

▼ A typical plan-position indicator for showing radar-reflecting objects around a search radar. The azimuth values are marked around the circumference of the screen, and a high-persistence screen ensures that the image remains visible from one sweep to the next, which may be an interval of a few seconds.

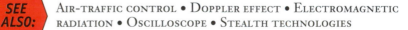

SEE ALSO: AIR-TRAFFIC CONTROL • DOPPLER EFFECT • ELECTROMAGNETIC RADIATION • OSCILLOSCOPE • STEALTH TECHNOLOGIES

Radiation Belt

▲ Auroras are a visible indication that highly energetic particles are bombarding Earth from the Sun. The solar wind is a stream of protons and electrons traveling at very high speed that strike the Van Allen belts, causing magnetic storms that create turbulence among the particles of the belts. Some of these particles spiral downward near the poles, where they interact with molecules in the upper atmosphere. As the electrons in the molecules change energy levels, light is emitted, which is manifested as the colored curtains of light of the aurora.

Radiation belts have been found circling all the planets in the Solar System that have a strong magnetic field, namely Jupiter, Saturn, Uranus, Neptune, and Earth. Earth has two belts, known as the Van Allen radiation belts, which are doughnut-shaped regions within Earth's magnetic field in which charged atomic particles are trapped. They were discovered by the American physicist James Van Allen while he was analyzing observations made by America's first satellite, *Explorer 1*, which was launched on January 31, 1958. A Geiger counter, which formed part of the satellite's 18 lb. (8 kg) instrument load, registered the anomalously high radiation in the belts. However, the existence of the Van Allen belts was not totally surprising—they had in fact been predicted.

Earth's magnetic field, or magnetosphere, extends outward into space, like the field of a bar magnet. Earth has magnetic poles, too, which resemble the north and south poles of a magnet. The charged particles in the Van Allen belts—mostly protons and electrons—are acted on by electromagnetic forces that cause them to spiral around the lines of the magnetic field and to oscillate back and forth between Earth's magnetic poles.

At high altitudes, the magnetic field is fairly constant and there are few gas molecules, so collisions that could deflect the particles are rare. Consequently, it is not easy for particles within the inner belt to escape by collision, so they stay within the belt for an average of 10 years. Particles in the outer belt can cycle more rapidly, leaving or entering during disturbances known as magnetic storms.

Most particles at high altitudes can travel distances many times the diameter of Earth before they are deflected, and then only by the natural curve of the geomagnetic field. At lower altitudes, the field is more complicated, but it closely approximates that of a bar magnet. As well as spiraling back and forth between the poles along magnetic field lines, particles also drift slowly in longitude. Electrons, being negatively charged, drift eastward, and protons (positively charged) drift in the opposite direction. This drifting ensures that once particles have entered the belts, they spread out to envelope Earth.

There is no actual gap separating the two Van Allen radiation belts, but they are distinguishable by the types of radiation and by the energies of particles within them. The inner belt is comprised mostly of protons and electrons. It stretches from 620 miles (1,000 km) to 3,100 miles (5,000 km) above the equator and has a mean radius of 1.6 times the radius of Earth. Protons are the most energetic particles within this belt, with energies up to hundreds of millions of electron volts.

The source of these high-energy protons is thought to be neutron decay—a mechanism triggered when cosmic rays collide with molecules of gas. Such collisions produce albedo neutrons, some of which are reflected back into the inner belt. Neutrons have a half life of 12 minutes before they decay into protons and electrons.

The outer Van Allen belt is comprised mostly of electrons. There is no distinction between inner- and outer-belt electrons, but protons in the outer belt are less energetic than those in the inner belt. Furthermore, as distance from Earth decreases, proton energies in the outer belt increase. These factors help to distinguish the outer belt as a region extending from 9,300 miles (15,000 km) to 15,500 miles (25,000 km) above the equator, and it has a mean radius of 3.5 times the radius of Earth.

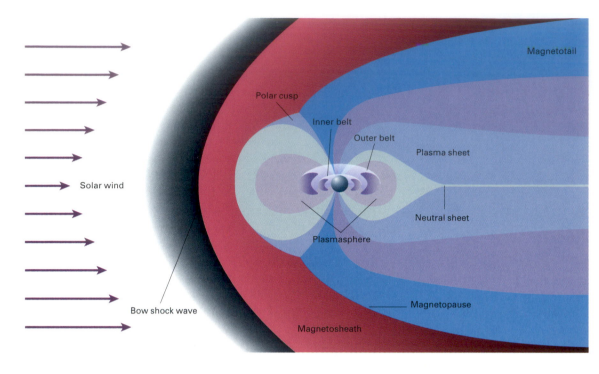

Solar wind

Bow shock wave

Magnetosheath

Polar cusp

Inner belt

Outer belt

Plasmasphere

Magnetotail

Plasma sheet

Neutral sheet

Magnetopause

◄ The effect of Earth's magnetic field on the solar wind. As the wind hits the field, it modifies it, creating a cavity called the magnetosphere, which shelters Earth from the particles in the solar wind. There are two boundaries, the bow shock wave and the magnetopause, enclosing deflected particles from the solar wind in an area called the magnetosheath. Some of these particles reach Earth by being channeled down the polar cusps. The magnetotail contains fewer solar particles, most of which migrate to the plasma sheet. The neutral sheet is where the north and south magnetic fields cancel each other out.

▼ Jupiter is another planet that experiences auroras at its poles. Unlike Earth's, its aurora is affected by the electric currents produced by its satellites, which can be seen as the bright points of light to the left and center of the picture.

The particles that make up the Van Allen belts slowly but continuously leak out of the polar ends of their magnetic constraint. The supply of charged particles is replenished by particles from the solar wind, which consists mainly of protons and electrons that stream away from the Sun at about a million mph (1.6 million km/h). The wind is essentially the outer atmosphere, or corona, of the Sun expanding continuously into space.

Another source of charged particles for the Van Allen belts is cosmic rays. Cosmic rays are extremely fast charged atomic nuclei that originate in deep space. When cosmic rays strike Earth, they smash apart atoms in the upper atmosphere and so create plentiful charged particles for the Van Allen belts. The source of cosmic rays is somewhat of a mystery, although astronomers suspect that active galactic nuclei, quasars, or gamma-ray bursts outside our own galaxy may be responsible.

Van Allen radiation is intense, so satellites cannot be orbited within it for fear that the delicate electronic equipment will be damaged. It is also hazardous for astronauts, who must wear protective outer suits and not spend time in the region.

Auroras

At Earth's magnetic poles, the Van Allen belts curve downward, as the particles follow the magnetic field lines. Particles within the belts attain their lowest altitudes over the poles, where they occasionally collide with and excite atoms in the upper atmosphere of Earth. An electron orbiting an excited atom must give up its excess energy, and it can do so only by emitting a photon (a quantum of light). This de-excitation radiation

constitutes beautiful auroral displays or the spectacular light shows in the night skies of regions of Earth close to the poles. The Aurora Borealis (or northern lights) and Aurora Australis (the Southern Hemisphere equivalent) appear as curtains of colored light draped across the night sky. Northern lights have twice been seen as far south as Mexico. Auroras usually occur following intense magnetic storms, which are the result of powerful solar eruptions that change the speed and composition of the solar wind. The color varies with the intensity of the magnetic activity, from green or white curtains in calm conditions to bright red when the magnetosphere is undergoing maximum turbulence.

SEE ALSO: EARTH • ELECTROMAGNETIC RADIATION • MAGNETISM

Radio

Radio is the name given to the system of transmission and reception of information by the propagation of electromagnetic radiation as radio waves through space. It is the most significant contemporary technique for the transmission of information over distances.

After amplification, a signal source is used to modulate a carrier wave, and after further amplification, it is fed to an antenna for transmission. At the receiver, the radio wave is selected (to the exclusion of all other radio waves), demodulated, amplified, and fed to the loudspeaker, which reproduces the original sound.

Modulation

If some means were not available for distinguishing between the desired radio signal and all other signals being broadcast, the result would be very poor reception. Furthermore, the situation would deteriorate with the number of transmitters in a given area, especially if the desired signal was from a less powerful or more distant transmitter.

To overcome this problem, modulation is used. First, each transmission is provided with a "signature tone" called the carrier frequency. Each transmitter has its own signature tone so that any transmission can be selected. Then the signal is in some way superimposed on this carrier wave before transmission—this process is modulation. The receiver is "tuned into" this frequency and, with suitable electronic circuitry, segregates the carrier wave from the signal (demodulation), amplifies the latter, and feeds it to the speaker.

In transmission, as with reception, a number of different techniques are possible. With one particular type of transmitter or receiver, the circuit design can have even greater variety. The description below refers only to the basic types, the major classifications being on the type of modulation employed.

▲ This yachtsman uses a very-high-frequency (VHF) radio to communicate with the mainland and with other vessels.

AM radio transmitters

The first requirement of an amplitude-modulated (AM) transmitter is a stable carrier frequency. If it is not stable, the reception at the receiver will be inconsistent in quality and likely to fade and distort. Stability is provided by a crystal oscillator. Piezoelectric crystals are used, of which the quartz crystal has by far the best characteristics. The design of quartz oscillators for these applications is similar to those used in quartz clocks, where stability is of the utmost importance.

The voltage output from the crystal oscillator is a sine wave; this output is amplified to a high power level by several amplifiers in series. Such amplifiers require special design because of the high frequencies involved, from 30 kHz in the low frequency (LF) band to upwards of 30 MHz in the very high frequency (VHF) band. They are known as radio frequency (RF) amplifiers. The greatly amplified sine wave then passes to a modulated amplifier.

The signal to be transmitted is first amplified using an LF amplifier and then passes to the modulating amplifier. The output from this amplifier alters the amplitude of the high-power carrier sine wave in the modulated amplifier according to the instantaneous magnitude of the signal—this process is amplitude modulation. The AM signal then passes through a matching network and on to the antenna for transmission.

The type of circuit described above produces a double-sideband (DSB) AM transmission, so-called from the way in which the signal and carrier wave are combined—essentially by multiplication. In general, the multiplication of one sine wave (frequency f_1) by another (frequency f_2) produces a waveform containing two frequencies $(f_1 + f_2)$ and $(f_1 - f_2)$. Where the signal contains a range of frequencies, as in speech, the resulting AM signal contains the original carrier

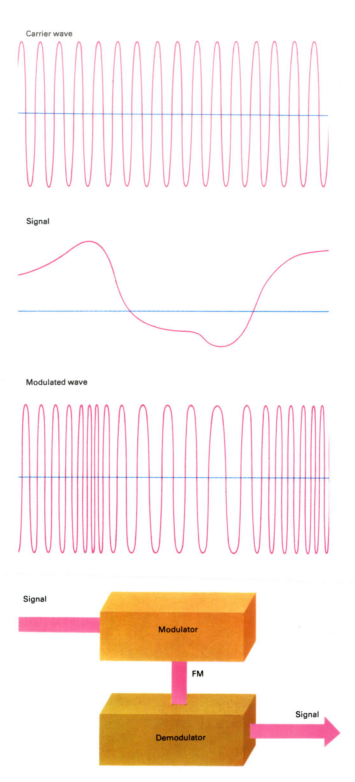

Carrier wave

Signal

Modulated wave

Signal

Modulator

FM

Demodulator

Signal

▲ The principles of frequency modulation. The carrier wave alters its frequency in proportion to the changes in amplitude of the signal to produce the modulated wave. The demodulator reverses the process and reproduces the original signal.

frequency, f_c, with two sidebands about this frequency. If, for example, the signal has frequencies up to 4 kHz (typical speech) and the carrier frequency is 100 kHz, then the total frequency band width of the AM signal is 8 kHz about the 100 kHz mark—that is, from 96 kHz to 104 kHz. The frequencies on either side of the 100 kHz mark are known as the sidebands.

There is a certain redundancy in this situation, because the information about the original signal is contained separately in both sidebands. Also, the transmission bandwidth is twice what is really necessary. Where the radio spectrum is crowded, as it generally is between LF and VHF, there results an extravagant waste of band space.

Single-sideband (SSB) transmission is therefore used in some situations by filtering out one of the sidebands. Furthermore, using two such circuits with one common carrier frequency, two independent sidebands (representing two independent signals) can be superimposed about the carrier frequency for transmission. Such systems are used, for example, in remote-control models—providing two separate control signals in one transmission—and for stereo transmissions.

AM receivers

The receiver must be able to receive any program from the broadcasting spectrum, that is, to select a particular carrier frequency and its sidebands and exclude everything else.

Before disentangling signal from carrier, it is usually necessary to amplify the antenna signals, a task that requires an RF amplifier. Next, the signal is demodulated by the detector circuit and the resulting audio signal amplified using an LF amplifier. Frequency selection is carried out in the preamplification stage before demodulation and is achieved with a resonant circuit whose frequency is adjustable by means of a variable capacitor.

Because of the density of broadcasting, especially in the lower-frequency part of the spectrum, the selectivity of the tuning circuit is important when considering high-fidelity reproduction. In some systems based on the above scheme, two or more resonant circuits are coupled together through amplifier stages. They are individually tuned with variable capacitors, but these capacitors are "ganged" together with a common control knob for ease of tuning.

Another extensively used method is to take the frequencies in the region required (a rough selection) and transfer them to another part of the frequency spectrum called the intermediate frequency (IF). This end is achieved using the heterodyne principle in which two sine waves are mixed to produce beats, and this type of receiver is known as a supersonic heterodyne (superhet). The superhet principle is that it is better to change the carrier frequency to suit a fixed-tuned circuit instead of tuning the circuit to the carrier frequency, because a tuned circuit can be designed to have the best possible characteristics. The filtered signal from this stage passes to an IF amplifier and from here on to the detector.

Distortion, noise, and FM

The reason for turning a simple radio principle into a complex arrangement of LF, IF, and RF amplifiers, tuned circuits, and detectors is to make sure that at every stage the signal or carrier or both are being handled in the best possible way. For example, it is virtually impossible to design an amplifier that will handle low-frequency (audio) and high-frequency (radio) signals equally well. It must be designed to do one or the other.

The factors that an engineer looks for in an electric circuit and in the final sounds from the speaker are distortion and noise. Distortion implies unfaithful reproduction and is mainly caused by nonlinearities in the amplifier. For example, if a 10-volt signal is amplified to 20 volts, but a 20-volt signal is amplified to 35 volts, then the gain is not the same for all input signals, and distortion results.

Noise is any unwanted signal that is received. It could be interference from an electric machine

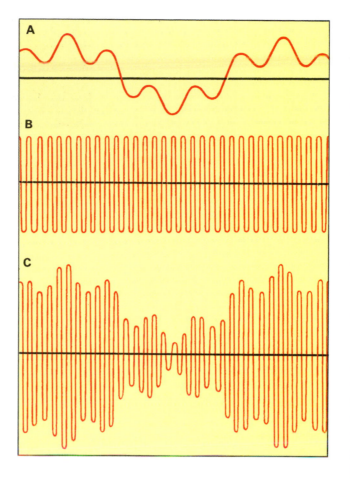

▲ An AM signal is formed by combining the wave of the signal to be transmitted (A), which is an irregular mixture of different frequencies, with the carrier wave generated by the transmitter (B), which is a sine wave of much higher frequency at constant amplitude, so that the amplitude of the carrier is modified by that of the signal (C).

or closely packed broadcasting stations straying into the fields of reception. AM systems do not cope with noise as well as frequency modulation (FM) systems.

Frequency modulation

In FM, the carrier wave is made to change in frequency around a central frequency. The change in frequency is made proportional to the amplitude of the signal to be encoded. For example, if the frequency changes by 1 kHz for every 1 volt of input signal amplitude, then an amplitude of 5 volts produces a change in frequency of 5 kHz. If the input signal to be encoded is a 2 kHz sinusoidal wave form with a peak amplitude of ±10 volts, then the frequency fluctuations are ±10 kHz about the carrier frequency. With a carrier frequency of 1 MHz (1 MHz = 1,000 kHz), fluctuations from 1.01 MHz to 0.99 MHz and back again 2,000 times a second would be required.

To achieve this effect in practice, some means is required to change the frequency of an oscillator according to the amplitude of the signal. In high-fidelity FM broadcasting, the circuit can be extremely complicated to provide the required quality of reproduction. However, there are several ways of achieving an approximate and cheap equivalent. A simple oscillator, for example, can be constructed using an inductor-capacitor (LC) circuit in the feedback path of an amplifier. The oscillator frequency is determined by the values of inductance and capacitance. By varying either the inductance or the capacitance, the oscillator frequency can be changed.

The one major disadvantage of FM is that it requires a much larger frequency bandwidth to transmit a given signal than the equivalent DSB AM method. In the VHF and ultrahigh frequency (UHF) broadcasting bands, however, there is much more room, and FM is used extensively. The complete radio frequency spectrum from LF to UHF can accommodate over 50,000 AM channels or 5,000 FM channels even without duplication. Because the broadcasts can be limited to a specific region or country, those same channels can be used elsewhere without too much interference (depending on the power of the transmitter).

Digital radio

One of the future directions of radio is in digital audio broadcasting (DAB), which involves the digitizing of radio signal in much the same way that compact discs contain digital recordings of analog signals. This process requires radio transmitters that convert analog signals into digital signals and receivers that are able to produce the reverse effect. Some radio stations are already broadcasting DAB, and many more are under development, all of which promise to provide sound quality similar to that of a compact disc.

Antennas and matching networks

When a stone is thrown into a pond, the wave ripples spread out in concentric rings. A similar process occurs when an alternating current travels along a conductor, except that the ripples are electromagnetic in nature. The antenna is the conductor in the case of radio broadcasting, and the alternating current is the AM or FM signal from the last amplifier stage in the transmitter.

Using a simple straight antenna of wire, the radio waves produced would, if they could be seen, appear like ever-expanding doughnuts. Such an antenna is omnidirectional. By careful design of the antenna, radio waves can be directed or beamed, and at microwave frequencies, antennas begin to look like the reflectors used in a flashlight.

To maximize the power that can be transmitted by an antenna system, an antenna-matching network is required. The principle of such a net-

▶ Tagging icebergs with automatic radio beacons that transmit their location via satellite has proved an ideal way of keeping track of these potentially hazardous islands whose direction of drift is largely determined by wind motion.

work can be explained as follows. If a battery has an internal resistance of, say, 8 ohms, then the maximum power that can be dissipated in an external circuit to which it is connected will occur when that circuit has a resistance of 8 ohms. If the resistance is more or less than this value, less power will be dissipated. Thus, to obtain the best power transfer from battery to circuit, the resistances must be equalized, or matched. Similar reasoning can be applied to alternating currents and voltages, but here it is the impedance that must be matched in some way.

The antenna will have a certain impedance to a power source such as an RF amplifier, and this impedance must be matched to the output impedance of the amplifier (which will be different) by using a matching network. The better the power transfer at any point in the system, the better the quality of the final signal. Matching is thus an important technique wherever stages are interconnected, whether they be amplifier to amplifier or amplifier to antenna. The result is usually a significant improvement in the signal-to-noise ratio.

The receiver antenna operates in reverse fashion to the transmitting type, which has voltages and currents induced in it according to the instantaneous magnitude of the passing radio wave. It too has a characteristic impedance and must be matched to the receiver input circuitry for maximum power transfer and signal-to-noise ratio.

FACT FILE

- *In World War II, radio receivers were distributed for use in remote areas and were wired up to special oil lamps. An array of metal fins above the lamp burners would produce a sufficient electric charge as they heated and cooled to power the simple receiver for the duration of the crucial news broadcasts.*

- *The radio emissions of quasi-stellar radio sources (quasars) are so powerful that they can be picked up by small radio telescopes at a distance of billions of light years. Small "radio nuclei" appear to jet radiating plasma toward giant clouds of radiation at up to ten times the speed of light. The clouds, hundreds of thousands of light years across, beam the emissions picked up on Earth.*

SEE ALSO: ANTENNA • CELLULAR TELEPHONE • ELECTROMAGNETIC RADIATION • RADAR • RADIO ASTRONOMY • RADIO CONTROL • SOUND • TRANSMISSION, BROADCASTING • WAVE MOTION

Radioactivity

Radioactivity is a property of certain kinds of elements whose atomic nuclei are unstable. In time—typically thousands of years—each such nucleus achieves stability by a process of internal change called radioactive decay, which involves a release of energy in a form known as radiation. The energy is very large by comparison with that released by chemical reactions involving the same amount of material, and the mechanism by which it is released is totally different.

Radioactivity was discovered in 1896 by the French chemist Antoine Henri Becquerel during his studies of fluorescence. He found that an unexposed photographic plate wrapped in black paper was affected as if by visible or ultraviolet light (or by X rays, newly discovered by the German physicist Wilhelm Röntgen) when the package was placed in contact with compounds of the heavy element uranium. He deduced correctly that some form of radiation must be coming from the uranium and penetrating the paper to reach and affect the photographic emulsion. Careful study by Becquerel and other scientists, including Marie and Pierre Curie, Frédéric Joliot, Frederick Soddy, Ernest Rutherford, James Chadwick, and Hans Geiger, revealed that a number of heavy chemical elements, many of them previously undetected because of their rarity, appeared to be internally unstable and gave off penetrating radiations. In the process, they themselves changed into different elements following intricate but well-defined paths to eventual stability. This phenomenon, entirely unlike anything previously encountered, was given the name radioactivity, and the process of change was called radioactive decay.

The nuclear atom

In the atomic nucleus, there are two sorts of particles, protons and neutrons. The protons each carry a single positive charge, and because they can bind to the atom an equal number of negatively charged orbiting electrons, their number governs all the atom's chemical properties. The number of protons is called the atomic number and is symbolized by the letter Z. For naturally

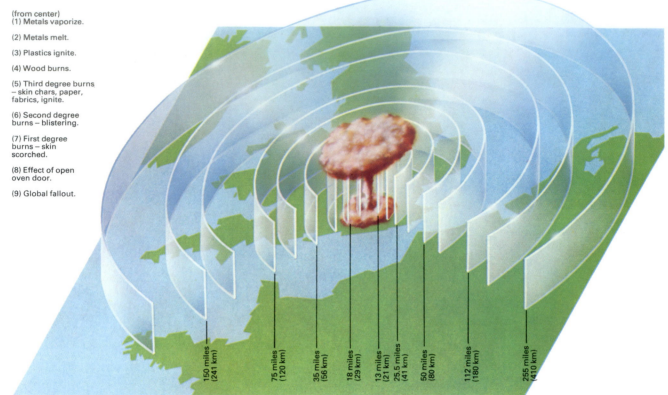

HEAT/RANGE EFFECTS FOR 100 MT BLAST

(from center)
(1) Metals vaporize.

(2) Metals melt.

(3) Plastics ignite.

(4) Wood burns.

(5) Third degree burns
– skin chars, paper,
fabrics, ignite.

(6) Second degree
burns – blistering.

(7) First degree
burns – skin
scorched.

(8) Effect of open
oven door.

(9) Global fallout.

150 miles (241 km)   75 miles (120 km)   35 miles (56 km)   18 miles (29 km)   13 miles (21 km)   25.5 miles (41 km)   50 miles (80 km)   112 miles (180 km)   255 miles (410 km)

occurring elements, Z ranges from 1 for hydrogen (including its isotopes deuterium and tritium) to 92 for uranium and, for identification purposes, can be regarded as an alternative to the element's name. The neutrons are electrically neutral and therefore have no effect at all on the chemical properties of the atom. The number of neutrons ranges from zero in ordinary hydrogen to 146 in uranium, which is the heaviest natural isotope.

The sum total of protons and neutrons in a nucleus is called its mass number (designated A and, written after the element name, is used to identify a particular isotope: carbon-14, for example, is the carbon isotope with 6 protons and 8 neutrons. Only certain combinations of Z and A give nuclei that are stable: if there are too many or too few neutrons, the nucleus will sooner or later undergo radioactive decay that will, in one or more steps, bring it to stability. The degree of instability shows up in the energy emitted in the process and rate of decay. The latter is measured in terms of half-life, or halving time, which is the time taken for half the number of atoms initially present to have undergone decay. Halving times range from fractions of a second to millions of years. When a radioactive nucleus (the parent isotope) decays into another element, this product is known as a daughter isotope. This isotope may in turn be unstable, and so further decay will result. There are several different ways in which radioactive decay can take place.

Alpha decay

In a nucleus that is too heavy to be stable, a compact group called an alpha particle, consisting of two protons and two neutrons, is ejected, leaving the nucleus four units lighter in A and two units lower in Z—in other words, two steps down in the periodic table. Structurally, an alpha particle is identical to a helium-4 nucleus. Alpha decay is common among the heaviest natural elements (uranium, polonium, and radium, for example) but does not lead directly to stable nuclei. First, intermediate isotopes are produced, which undergo further decay.

Alpha particles have energies of up to five million electron volts (MeV), a common unit of energy when dealing with particles, but they are so bulky that they pass through only an inch or so of air and can be stopped by a sheet of paper or the outer layers of the human skin. For that very reason, however, they can cause serious internal damage when emitted by alpha-active materials that have been inadvertently absorbed by the body as airborne dust or through contaminated wounds. The natural alpha emitters, such as radium, are of limited practical use now that a wide variety of artificial radioisotopes are freely available. However, uranium and its artificial by-product, plutonium (another alpha emitter), are also both fissile—capable of breaking down into two lighter particles. This quality can be exploited as a source of nuclear energy since the

▲ The devastating effect of a 100-megaton bomb dropped on London. Apart from the initial explosion, nuclear bombs produce radioactive fallout that may be carried by air currents far from the site of the explosion.

process of decay produces heat, which is then used to power gas turbines and so produce electricity. Controversy over the safety of these power stations and the methods for storing nuclear waste have, however, curtailed the use of nuclear energy in many countries.

Beta decay

In a nucleus with too many neutrons, one neutron changes to a proton plus an electron, the latter being ejected from the nucleus. An electron emitted in this way is called a beta particle. The nucleus is left with an additional positive charge and is therefore one unit higher in Z and one step up in the periodic table. Beta particles have maximum energies ranging from 0.02 to 5.3 MeV and penetrate up to several feet of air and a few inches of tissue, metal, or plastic (which provides adequate shielding). However, these particles can cause severe surface burns or serious internal harm, especially if emitted inside the body for long periods.

Beta decay is the commonest mode of radioactive decay, both among artificial isotopes and among the radioactive products of natural alpha decay. A few of the artificial radioisotopes made in particle accelerators or separated from the fission products formed in nuclear reactors have too few neutrons rather than too many. They decay by emitting positrons (positively charged electrons), which interact almost immediately with ordinary electrons to produce "annihilation radiation" of 0.51 MeV energy with the qualities of gamma rays. Isotopes that emit positrons (for example, technetium-147) have applications in medical diagnosis.

Gamma ray emission

Gamma ray emission occurs whenever alpha or beta decay has not carried away enough energy to give complete stability to the nucleus. Many natural and artificial alpha and beta active isotopes are gamma ray emitters. Gamma rays are a form of electromagnetic radiation like X rays, having energies between 0.15 and 2.5 MeV. They are reduced in intensity by passing through matter to an extent that depends on their own energy and on the physical density of the absorbing matter. Gamma rays are not stopped in the way that alpha or beta particles are, nor are any materials opaque to them as to light. From 2 to 10 in. (5–25 cm) of lead or up to 9 ft. (2.7 m) of concrete may be needed to provide adequate shielding against high-energy sources of gamma radiation. Excessive external radiation can cause serious internal damage to the body but cannot induce radioactivity in it or anything else.

Other modes of radioactive decay include internal conversion, where a reorganization within the nucleus results in the emission of X rays, and electron capture, where a nucleus with too many protons captures an electron from an inner orbit of the same atom, converting a proton to a neutron, with the emission of X rays and a drop of one place in the periodic table. The nuclei of the alpha emitters uranium-235 and uranium-238 very occasionally decay by spontaneous nuclear fission, producing any pair of a range of possible fission product nuclei and free neutrons. The artificial radioisotope californium-252 decays exclusively by spontaneous fission and provides a useful source of neutrons. A few fission product isotopes, notably iodine-122, decay by delayed neutron emission soon after they are formed and play an important role in the control of nuclear reactors.

The modes of decay, the halving times, and the energies of emission (maximum energies in the case of alpha and beta particles) are together uniquely characteristic of the particular isotopes involved: they can be used in the identification and measurement of the emitters, and hence of their precursors, by the technique known as activation analysis.

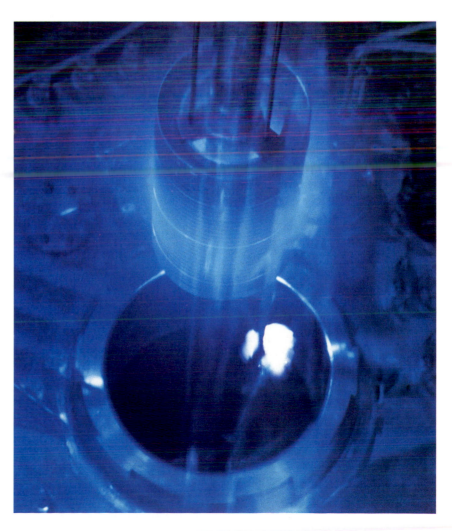

▼ The removal of a fuel element in a nuclear reactor submerged under water. The blue glow is caused by Cerenkov radiation and is caused by energetic charged particles from the radioactive fuel traveling faster through water than light can. This phenomenon occurs when the refractive index of the medium is high.

Rates of decay

The rates of decay of different radioactive nuclides vary widely, though all nuclides decay exponentially. The change in the fraction of the parent nuclides present is proportional to the change in time and may be expressed as follows:

$$\Delta N/N \propto \Delta t$$

where ΔN is the number of nuclides likely to decay and N is the number of nuclides present at the beginning of the time period Δt. Each radioactive nuclide also has a decay constant represented by the Greek letter λ (lambda), which can then be used to form the equation

$$\Delta N/N = -\lambda \Delta t$$

This equation can be rearranged as follows to obtain a value for the number of nuclides of a particular radioactive element or isotope that will decay over a given period of time:

$$\Delta N = -\lambda \Delta t \times N$$

Radium-226, for example, has a value for λ of around 10^{-11} per sec., which means that in one second only 1 in every 10^{11} nuclei of radium will decay. Therefore, over a short time period it is extremely unlikely that a particular radium-226 nuclide will decay, but when large numbers of nuclides are present, a measurable proportion will decay. If, for example, we have a sample of 10^{15} atoms of radium and a time period of 10 seconds, then the number of nuclides that will have decayed over this period is as follows:

$$\Delta N = -10^{-11} \times 10 \times 10^{15} = -10^5$$

The minus sign indicates that 10^5, or 100,000, nuclides have decayed.

Radioactive-decay series

When a radioactive parent nuclide decays, it does not always decay into a stable daughter nuclide. Sometimes the daughter nuclide decays into another nuclide, which in turn may decay into another, thus forming a long decay series with each decay having a different half-life forming a different element or isotope. Four decay series exist, three of which are found naturally and one of which results from the artificial production of an element heavier than radium called neptunium (Np). The decay series for uranium-238, for example, (with a half-life of 4.5×10^9 years) begins with a decay into thorium-234 by alpha emission. Thorium-234 has a half-life of only 24 days and

◄ The effects of the first two nuclear bombs used in war were devastating. These bombs—dropped on the Japanese cities of Hiroshima and Nagasaki— instantly killed hundreds of thousands of people; many also died later from the effects of radiation.

decays by beta emission into protactinium-234, which in turn decays by beta emission to form uranium-234. The next four decays all occur by alpha emission through thorium-230, radium-226, and radon-222 to polonium-218. After this point, the polonium nuclide either decays by beta emission into astatine-218 or by alpha emission into lead-214. Astatine-214 in turn has two pathways, and so the decay series from this point becomes more complex. The ultimate outcome, however, is that all the nuclides end up as lead-206, beyond which no further decay occurs.

Practical applications of radioactivity

Apart from the use of radioactivity to produce nuclear energy, radioactive isotopes are used as tracers in both medicine and industry. In medicine, for example, the radioisotope iodine-131 is commonly used to assess the activity of the thyroid gland. Alternatively, radioisotopes may be inserted directly into a malignant tumor so that the radiation destroys the tumor cells. In science, radioactivity has been used by geologists for the absolute dating of rocks and archaeological remains. Carbon dating, for example, uses the decay of carbon-14, which has a half-life of around 5,700 years, to assess the age of organic remains up to around 50,000 years old.

SEE ALSO: ATOMIC STRUCTURE • NUCLEAR EMERGENCY • NUCLEAR REACTOR • NUCLEAR WASTE DISPOSAL • NUCLEAR WEAPON • RADIOISOTOPIC DATING • RADIOLOGY • RADIOTHERAPY

Radio Astronomy

Astronomical objects produce not only the visible light that we usually associate with the stars and other celestial bodies but also all the other wavelengths of an electromagnetic radiation, from short gamma rays to radio waves. Of these, only optical and radio waves can reach Earth's surface without being blocked by the atmosphere. Therefore, there are two wavelength "windows" for astronomical observations; optical telescopes use the first and radio telescopes use the second.

The energy received from space as radio waves is extremely small, the total amount collected by all radio telescopes since the beginning of radio astronomy being much less than the energy needed to light a flashlight bulb for a millionth of a second. To prevent interference from broadcasting stations, certain radio frequencies have been allocated by international agreement for the exclusive use of radio astronomy.

History

Extraterrestrial radio waves were first discovered accidentally in 1932 when a U.S. radio engineer, Karl Jansky, was investigating radiation from thunderstorms. He found a source of interference—static—that was at a fixed position relative to the stars and so appeared to move as Earth rotates. The source of the radiation was near the constellation of Sagittarius, where the center of our galaxy (the Milky Way) lies, and further work by another U.S. radio engineer, Grote Reber, showed that the whole of the Milky Way emits radiation at wavelengths of a few meters. Reber published contour maps to display the intensity of radiation from different parts of the sky (similar to ordinary maps but with peaks of intensity instead of height), and such maps are still used to present radio astronomy results.

Hydrogen, by far the most common element in interstellar space, can exist in three forms: HI, neutral unbonded atoms, HII, ionized atoms or free protons, and H_2, diatomic hydrogen molecules. When news of Reber's research reached the Netherlands it inspired the Dutch astronomer Hendrik van de Hulst to realize that HI would emit radiation at just one wavelength, 8 in. (21 cm). If this HI line is observed to be at a slightly different wavelength, it indicates that the hydrogen cloud emitting the radiation is moving toward or away from Earth, because the wavelength is changed by the Doppler effect, the same effect that, when applied to sound waves, causes the pitch of a rapidly moving whistle to fall as it passes the listener. The change in wavelength gives directly the velocity of the hydrogen cloud, and so HI spectrometry is a very valuable branch of radio astronomy, quite distinct from the continuum (all-frequency) type of radiation first investigated by Jansky and Reber. Both branches of radio astronomy, however, have advanced only through continual improvement in the radio telescopes used as detectors.

Basically, any radio telescope consists of three parts. First, there is the antenna, which actually receives the radio waves and converts them into an electric output; second, an amplifier increases the very weak signal from the antenna to a large enough power to drive the third part, the output device, which displays the result or stores it on magnetic tape for later analysis.

Antenna

The antenna of a radio telescope can take many forms, the simplest being just a large number of simple dipole antennas (like a television antenna) spread over an area of ground and wired together. The most familiar type, however, is the "big dish," in which the radio waves are reflected to the focus of a concave metal bowl and are there detected by one simple dipole. The two largest fully steerable dishes in the world are very similar in size—the 328 ft. (100 m) in diameter dish at Effelsberg in Germany and the recently completed Robert C. Byrd Green Bank Telescope (GBT) in Virginia, which is 328 ft. (100 m) by 361 ft. (110 m) across and 485 ft. (148 m) tall. This telescope is now the most sophisticated steerable radio dish in the world. The largest fixed dish is 1,000 ft. (300 m) in diameter and 167 ft. (50 m)

▲ In New Mexico, 27 dish antennas make up the Very Large Array (VLA) radio telescope. The ability to easily move the dishes to new positions enables astronomers to obtain detailed information on distant objects in various parts of the sky.

deep and is built in a depression in the ground at Arecibo (Puerto Rico). This enormous radio dish, covered with almost 40,000 perforated, adjustable aluminum panels, permits detection of extremely faint radio signals from space. Sensitive receivers are employed that are bathed in liquid helium to maintain a very low temperature, which reduces background noise caused by electrons, thus enhancing clarity of reception.

Very large arrays

There are two reasons for making an antenna with as large a collecting area as possible, the first being that a large antenna collects more of the power from the source, enabling it to detect fainter astronomical objects. The second reason is that the resolving power (the ability to detect small detail) of any kind of telescope depends on the wavelength of the radiation divided by the diameter of the telescope. Radio waves are so much longer than light waves that a radio telescope that could resolve as much detail as a large optical telescope would need to be several miles in diameter. Such a dish would be impossible to build in practice, but the resolving power of a large dish, though not its collecting area, can be synthesized by combining electrically the outputs from a number of smaller antennas. This technique, known as interferometry, enables signals received at slightly different times by different receivers to be combined into a single image. Some engineers believe that single telescopes are

nearing a technological limit so that, in the future, arrays of antennas using interferometry will provide the increasing levels of detection required by radio astronomers.

Many such arrays are already in use, and one of the best known examples is the Very Large Array (VLA) at Socorro, New Mexico, which can synthesize an aperture 16 miles (27 km) across. All 27 of the VLA's 75 ft. (25 m) diameter dishes are arranged on a Y-shaped track that enables astronomers to easily adjust the distance between the receivers. The receivers are connected by cables that deliver the electric output of each antenna to a central processing facility. A larger array using fewer dishes, known as the multi-element radio link interferometer network (MERLIN), straddles the west Midlands of Britain covering a distance of 135 miles (217 km). A plan to build sixty-four 39 ft. (12 m) dishes spanning an area of more than six miles in Chile's Atacama Desert is currently being developed by the National Radio Astronomy Observatory and the European Southern Observatory.

Still larger, intercontinental arrays of radio telescopes are used intermittently to synthesize Earth-size dishes. The technique here is called very long baseline interferometry (VLBI) and the radio signals from each telescope are recorded on magnetic tapes and later flown to a central processing facility where they are combined electronically to give the interference pattern of the source. One such system, the Very Large Baseline Array, connects ten radio dishes spanning from the Virgin Islands to Hawaii—a distance of 53,300 miles (86,000 km). The largest array, however, is the orbiting VLBI, which extends out into space and includes satellite radio dishes as well as Earth-based dishes. Future developments include a satellite called ARISE (advanced radio interferometry between space and Earth) being designed by NASA's Jet Propulsion Laboratory. To reduce costs, this satellite will use an inflatable antenna (25 m) across.

Amplifiers

Radio telescopes often work at the highest possible frequency (shortest wavelength), because it gives the best resolving power for a particular size antenna, and the progress of radio astronomy has depended on the development of electronic amplifiers to work efficiently at these very high frequencies (up to several GHz, or one billion cycles per second). A number of specialized types of amplifiers have been developed (some of which use a maser, the radio equivalent of a laser), and one of these amplifiers is generally placed at the focus of the antenna so as to preamplify the very weak signal before it passes down a cable to the main amplifier, which may be several hundred meters away. The preamplifier also converts the signal to a lower frequency, because such a signal is less attenuated by the cable and also so that it can be amplified by a conventional transistor amplifier at the other end.

Output devices

The output device may simply be a chart recorder in which the deflection of the pen shows the strength of radiation from different parts of the source as the telescope scans over it. An Earth-rotation-synthesis telescope, on the other hand, requires continuous observation for twelve hours before a map can be made of the source, and so the signals must be recorded as they come in. At the end of twelve hours, the recorded signals are processed to produce a map that can then be drawn by a contour-map plotter.

In the case of a radio telescope that is observing the neutral hydrogen line at 8 in. (21 cm), the output is split up into different frequencies by an electronic circuit known as a spectrometer, and the output at each frequency, corresponding to HI clouds at different velocities, can be displayed using either of the above methods. Alternatively, for just one position in the sky, a graph of the radio power at different frequencies will distinguish between HI clouds that lie at different distances along the same line of sight, each having a slightly different velocity.

▼ The Arecibo dish in Puerto Rico consists of a 1,000 ft. (300 m) hollow in the hills strung with reflecting wires; the antenna (seen as a triangular shadow) hangs above the center of the dish in the cage, which is supported by wires strung from the towers. The dish is constructed using almost 40,000 perforated aluminum panels.

Active galaxies and black holes

High-resolution arrays have allowed astronomers to make detailed pictures of some of the most enigmatic objects in the Universe: the so-called active galaxies. Ever since the early days of radio astronomy, it has been known that some galaxies are pouring vast amounts of energy out of a tiny region in their cores. These objects go by many names—quasars, QSOs, Seyfert galaxies, BL Lac objects, N galaxies, and blazars—but astronomers now think that the same process is at work in all of them.

According to this view, the power source at the heart of the galaxy is a black hole, a region of space where gravity is so strong that not even light can escape. The hole is likely to have been created by the crashing together of stars and gas soon after the galaxy was formed.

Although the hole itself cannot be seen, its effects on its surroundings are dramatic. Gas and stars falling toward the hole are swept into a swirling disk around it before being dragged inward like water going down a drain. Some of the gas is then blasted out again in the form of two opposing jets, which shoot far out beyond the galaxy. Radio astronomers now have many fine images of these gas jets, but theorists are still developing theories to explain them.

Recycled pulsars

One field of radio astronomy for which big dishes are essential is the study of pulsars. Pulsars are neutron stars, which are the remnants of stars that ended their lives in supernova explosions. These highly magnetic objects, just a few miles across, rotate rapidly and emit a beam of radio waves that seems to pulse as it passes over Earth, much like the beam from a distant lighthouse. Over a period of a few million years they radiate away their rotational energy and fade out.

Pulsars have also been discovered in globular clusters. These clusters contain only ancient stars, and any pulsars formed there should have long since disappeared. The explanation seems to be that these may be recycled pulsars arising from very old neutron stars created by supernova activity early in the life of the cluster. These recycled pulsars have then been captured into orbits around ordinary stars and spun back to life.

Dozens of recycled pulsars are now known, mainly in globular clusters. In 1991, a British-Australian team announced the discovery of 11 superfast pulsars in one cluster, named 47 Tucanae, all of them with pulse rates of less than six milliseconds. Since then, a further 11 pulsars have been found here. Why this cluster should be so favored remains a mystery.

In the summer of 1991, a team of radio astronomers from Manchester University in Britain announced that they had discovered a planet circling a pulsar. By carefully timing the pulses, they found that the star was being pulled back and forth by an unseen companion about 10 times the mass of Earth. The discovery made the headlines because it appeared to be the first definite news of a planet beyond the solar system.

Astronomers around the world rushed to observe other pulsars. Early in 1992, an American team announced that they had observed a pulsar called PSR 1257+12 with two planets in orbit around it. It suddenly seemed that pulsar planets might be commonplace.

Within days, the astronomical community was thrown into confusion. Professor Andrew Lyne, whose Manchester group had discovered the first planet, told a meeting of the American Astronomical Society that he had made a mistake. The planet was nothing more than an error in the program used to analyze the data. When the error was corrected, the planet disappeared.

The astronomers who discovered the second planets hastily checked to see that they had not also fallen into this trap, but they had not. It appears that the two companions to PSR 1257+12 really were the first planets to be found outside our Solar System.

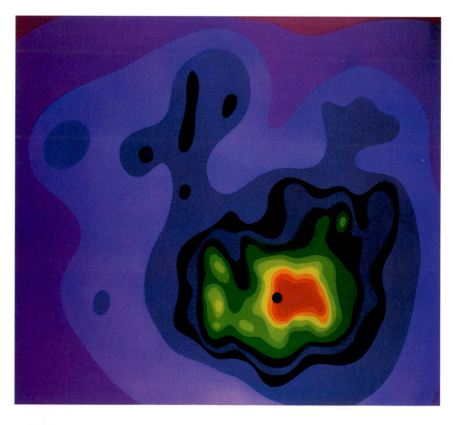

▼ This image of the Vela supernova remnant was produced using radio astronomy. The intensity of the radio emissions is color coded, ranging from red (most intense) to purple (least intense). The black dot shows the collapsed core of the original star, which exploded 11,000 years ago.

SEE ALSO: ANTENNA • ASTRONOMY • ASTROPHYSICS • ELECTROMAGNETIC RADIATION • TELESCOPE, OPTICAL • TELESCOPE, SPACE

Radio Control

Radio control (RC) is an offshoot of military and space-age electronics. It has benefited from the technology of missiles, space rockets, satellites, and space probes, for which high-quality miniature electric motors, rechargeable batteries, and remote guidance systems have been developed. This technology has also been used to control experimental pilotless aircraft, a recent example of which is the Helios solar-powered airplane. More conventional radio-controlled aircraft find many practical applications, such as overflying electricity power plant cooling towers to measure temperatures and humidity and to carry cameras for survey work. Aircraft such as these are also used by military organizations for reconnaissance and spying missions. A further use for radio control is in robots employed by the military for bomb disposal.

New uses are being found every day for radio-controlled application—not all for peaceful purposes. In the film and TV business, radio-controlled models of aircraft, trains, trucks, and other vehicles are used to represent full-size machines. Similarly, RC is used by scale-model hobbyists to simulate the movements of a large number of vehicles. Radio-controlled models and toys are now the most common application of RC.

Radio-controlled models

Radio control relies on the conversion of mechanical signals into radio messages, which are reconverted by the receiver into mechanical signals that effect the controller's intentions. It uses repeated patterns of radio signals (called frames) comprising pulses and pauses. Each frame of signal contains the pulsed information for each radio channel (function) and an off period, known as a synchronization pause, to reset each frame at the receiver. By sending out these frames of information at a high rate (typically, 50 per second), a smooth control movement that increases uniformly with signal strength is achieved. The system can be compared with the working of a movie projector, which sends out a series of still picture frames at a speed sufficient to give the appearance on a screen of a continuous movement. Like a movie, radio frames are of equal duration, but the contents vary with succeeding frames.

Information to be transmitted is generated when the controller moves the control sticks, levers, or switches on the control box (the transmitter). As each control is moved, the corresponding information pulse in the frame increases or decreases proportionally in successive frames.

The control movements are translated into output pulses by an encoder and a master clock, which times the frame rate continuously. From the encoder, the output pulses are passed to a modulator, where they are converted to precisely shaped pulses suitable for transmission.

Radio frequencies are strictly allocated by radio-transmission authorities, and several modelers use the same frequency. Interference between frequencies and between equipment on the same frequency is prevented by ensuring that signals are accurately processed before transmission and by restricting signal strength. Low-power transmission—of about one watt—limits the range of the signal so that models as close as 2 miles (3 km) apart can be controlled without interference.

The receiver

Transmitting a stable signal of constant strength is important, but the receiver has a more difficult task. The distance between the transmission point and the receiver is constantly varying, and the strength of the signal is affected by the position of the transmitter antenna and the climatic conditions. The receiver must, therefore, be able to accept signals of widely different strengths and to reject any spurious signals. Effectively, the receiver decodes the received signals so that each element arriving at a control mechanism is a replica of what was transmitted.

Signals alone do not move the controls of a model; the final link in the chain is performed by a servo, which moves the controls. The variable pulses are amplified and compared with an internally produced pulse. Depending on whether the pulses are longer or shorter than the reference pulse, the servo moves in a direction to equalize the incoming and reference pulses. When the discrepancy is corrected, the movement comes to rest. In practice, the servo movement is constantly changing and varies according to the position of the control movement on the transmitter. The servo is powered by a small electric motor that moves the control surface.

Radio-control equipment varies according to application, mainly in the number of its control functions. A two-channel system is sufficient for controlling the steering and motor speed on a model car but would not be capable of coping with the complexity of a radio-controlled helicopter. Radio sets can have from two to eight functions. A detailed model with a built-in engine self-starter, retracting undercarriage, flaps, functional navigational lights, and the usual functions of rudder, elevator, throttle, and aileron control would require an eight-channel radio to operate all these controls remotely.

The number of electronic components used in RC equipment is being reduced as the use of miniature electronics increases. Some equipment features variable control movement rates, auto-

▼ In radio control, mechanical signals are first converted into radio messages. These are reconverted in the model into mechanical signals that carry out the controller's intentions. By sending out frames of information (repeated patterns of radio signals made up of pulses and pauses), the controller can achieve movement that increases smoothly and uniformly with signal strength. The control movements are translated into output pulses by an encoder from which they are passed to a modulator, where they are converted to pulses suitable for transmission.

matic roll for aircraft, mixing of different channels, servo-output direction reversing, and digital clocks for timing the operation of the model.

The sport

Scale models are only a small part of the radio-controlled model aircraft hobby. Clubs offer flying field facilities, insurance cover, and social and instructional talks. Many modelers are content to fly sports models. To some, however, the greatest excitement comes from competition. Competitions help to improve the design of models and equipment; precise flying is necessary, and the accuracy of radio equipment essential. Pylon racing, with four models flying a short triangular course at speeds well over 100 mph (160 km/h), calls for excellent equipment, accuracy of flying, and a powerful engine.

Developments

Engine performances have greatly improved as a result of the requirements of competitors in RC aerobatics and racing. Electric power has become more popular as electric motor and rechargeable battery efficiencies have improved. Electric power is also clean and relatively quiet. The typical internal combustion engine is noisy and dirty. Commonly a two-stroke, its lubricating oil is discharged mostly through the exhaust and onto the model. Nevertheless, internal combustion engines add realism and are unlikely to be completely replaced by electric power.

Construction techniques have also progressed through the striving of scale and sailplane competition modelers, leading to lighter, stronger structures and overall efficiency. Construction techniques follow the full-size practice, using glass-reinforced plastic (GRP) fuselages and veneered, expanded plastic-cored wings. Generally, the techniques include traditional materials—balsa wood and plywood. Many enthusiasts build models of their own designs; others need only a plan.

Helicopters, boats, and cars

The rotor and control mechanisms of a model helicopter or autogyro are faithful reproductions of the full-scale machines. Flying a model helicopter is particularly difficult, because the controller can easily become disoriented, and as a result, an expensive model may be damaged.

A less risky hobby is the construction and racing of radio-controlled model boats. Internal combustion engines for

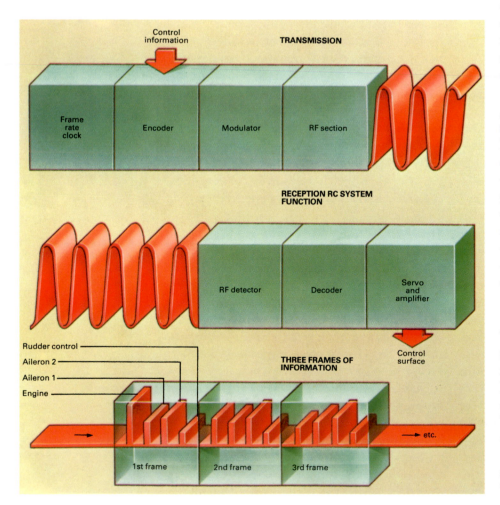

boats are similar to those used in radio-controlled model aircraft. The engines are converted to be water cooled and to take a flywheel and flexible connection for the propeller shafts. Electric power is also increasing in popularity with boating enthusiasts. Modern batteries can be recharged rapidly, and a boat can be ready for a further run after only 15 minutes. Racing and navigational competitions are the best supported events, but there are some international contests for large warships, liners, and freighters.

Yachts, sailing boats, and sailing ships appeal to the modeler with a desire for less frantic action while retaining a high degree of skill. Rigging of the models is the same as for full-sized boats, as are the methods of control. Radio-controlled servomotors function as winches to pull in or let out the sheets. Single-design classes, in which every competitor is sailing the same type of yacht, are popular. In these classes, the skills of construction and sailing decide the winner.

Radio-controlled cars are now popular among model-racing enthusiasts. Today the hobby has the fastest growth rate of all the radio-controlled model classes. Nearly all the larger cars are designed for racing. Most exciting are the one-eighth scale Grand Prix and GT types, powered by high-performance 3.5 cc (cm^3) internal combustion engines. During a race, engine speeds of 30,000 rpm can be reached.

Car design uses standards similar to those of the genuine Grand Prix racing cars, as they use tuned chassis, tuned exhaust pipes on the engines,

independent suspension for the wheels, and a selection of racing tires to suit track conditions. A tuned car, use of the right fuel (nitro-methane is added to improve performance of the standard methanol oil mix), and high degrees of driving skills and concentration are needed.

The smaller one-twentieth-scale electric-powered cars have been successful because they can be operated and raced indoors, such as in school gyms, without mess or noise. Kits for these cars are available in many styles, and a minimum of work is necessary to install two-channel control equipment and to get the car running.

Off-road vehicle racing is also increasingly popular. The design and construction of these models enables them to drive over rough surfaces, leap ditches, and climb hills. Time trials are held over testing courses, and the scope for simple, fun operation is much greater than with conventional models. Solo motorcycles, however, seem to have particular problems for RC modelers—there is little room for the RC equipment, and there are problems with stability. Japanese designers have overcome these problems, and internal combustion engine- and electric-powered two-wheelers are commercially available in kit form. Steering is managed by leaning the model rider, and thus the bike, into the corner, and most of the RC equipment is housed in the model driver.

▲ Radio-controlled helicopters provide an exciting alternative to model airplanes and cars for enthusiasts.

| **SEE ALSO:** | ANTENNA • ELECTRIC MOTOR • MISSILE • RADIO • SATELLITE, artificial • SERVOMECHANISM • SPACE PROBE |

Radioisotopic Dating

Various techniques are available for radioisotopic dating, a method for dating rocks and archeological remains, but they all rely on the decay of radioactive isotopes and the measurement of the proportion of these isotopes in a given sample. Prior to the discovery of radioactivity in 1896 by the French scientist Antoine Henri Becquerel, geologists used a relative method to estimate the order in which rocks occurred. That is, lower rock strata were known to be older than the layers of rock above them but the absolute age of a particular rock sample was not known. Nor was it possible to order rock strata from different locations accurately. After 1896, it became clear that the regular decay of radioisotopes could be used to estimate the age of rocks, and with the invention of the mass spectrometer, around 1950, geologists were able to estimate the absolute date of rocks with reasonable accuracy.

Carbon dating

In 1947, a method for using the decay of carbon-14 for dating samples up to 50,000 years old was devised by a team of scientists headed by the American chemist Willard F. Libbey. Like many elements, carbon exists in different forms called isotopes in which the nuclei of the atoms contain the same number of protons but different numbers of neutrons. The three isotopes of carbon, for example, are carbon-12, -13, and -14, all of which possess six protons but six, seven, and eight

neutrons, respectively. In addition, carbon-14 is radioactive and decays by beta radiation into nitrogen. After a period of approximately 5,730 years, the number of carbon-14 atoms in a given sample will have reduced by 50 percent—this number is the radioisotope's half-life.

The percentage of carbon-14 is maintained at a fairly constant level in the atmosphere by the effect of cosmic rays. If one of these rays collides with an atom, it causes the atom to release an energetic neutron. This neutron may then collide with an atom of nitrogen-14, causing it to split into carbon-14 and a hydrogen atom. In this way, the decay of carbon-14 and the production of new carbon-14 are kept in a state of equilibrium. Plant life obtains carbon in the form of carbon dioxide from its surroundings for the purpose of photosynthesis. Animals in turn obtain their nutrition from plant life, which contains the carbon used in photosynthesis. Because plants and animals take in carbon-14 at a constant rate, the amount of this isotope that decays in an organism is in equilibrium with the amount of carbon-14 obtained from the environment, and so the average ratio of carbon-14 to the much more abundant carbon-12 remains constant. When an organism dies, however, it ceases to take in carbon-14, and thus, as this isotope decays, the ratio of carbon-14 to carbon-12 reduces. For a given sample, this ratio may be obtained using mass spectrometry. The age of the sample may then be calculated using the following equation:

$$t = [\ln(N_f/N_0)/(-0.693)] \times t_{1/2}$$

where N_f/N_0 is the fraction of carbon-14 remaining in the sample (obtained by mass spectrometry), and $t_{1/2}$ is the half-life of carbon-14.

Other techniques

For dating geological samples older than 50,000 years, similar techniques using radioactive isotopes with longer half-lives may be used; Uranium-238, for example, has a half-life of 4.5 billion years and eventually, after passing through several different stages of decay, becomes lead. Uranium-238 is called a parent isotope, and the isotopes it decays into, such as uranium-234, are called daughter isotopes. The ratios of parent to daughter isotopes may be used to date rock samples. Other radioisotopes suitable for dating include rubidium–strontium and potassium–argon.

SEE ALSO: Archaelogical technologies • Atomic structure • Carbon • Geology • Mass spectrometry • Paleontology • Radioactivity • Uranium

Radiology

Radiology is a branch of medicine that uses a variety of techniques to obtain images of the body's internal organs and tissues. These techniques combine the technical skills of the pharmacist, biochemist, and physicist with the medical expertise of the physician. Originally, radiology was restricted to the uses of X rays, but many other methods, such as ultrasound and magnetic resonance imaging, have been developed that enable doctors to diagnose a wide range of diseases.

One technique involves introducing nuclear sources into the body, and the radioactivity produced can then be detected to form images that indicate whether organs and tissues are functioning properly. Gamma radiation (high-frequency photons), for example, can pass through several centimeters of human tissue. Thus, a trace of gamma rays from a source taken into the body will shine through the body, and the escaping radiation can be detected by a camera sensitive to gamma radiation outside the body.

The gamma camera is used to look into the body and map out the sites where a gamma-emitting radionuclide (radioactive material) has been deposited. This simple mapping procedure is the keystone to diagnosis by nuclear medicine. Its major advantage is that most of the gamma radiation escapes from the body. The radiation dose to the patient is often much lower than that from a conventional chest X ray.

One problem with the use of X rays is the limited amount of information they provide. For example, X rays of a patient's left and right kidneys might both appear normal even though one is, in fact, performing normally whereas the other is grossly abnormal. This additional physiological, functional information can, however, be obtained by a nuclear medicine imaging technique that uses radioactively labeled chemicals. The radiopharmaceutical's specific chemical characteristics determine the way it moves through and is taken up by the body, and its radionuclide label enables it to be seen inside the body by a suitable camera.

To test whether a kidney is functioning, for example, a pharmaceutical is used that can be filtered out of the blood by the kidneys. This pharmaceutical is coupled to a radionuclide whose radiation is readily detectable. If and only if the kidney is working will it filter out the chemical, which will then show up as a hot spot on a radionuclide scan. In the same way, since the repair of bone involves the uptake of phosphate, a phosphate-labeled pharmaceutical can be used to show up the site of new bone formation or repair.

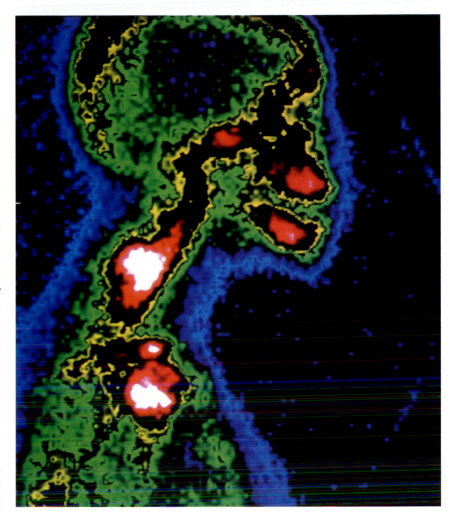

▲ A false-color scintigram (gamma-camera scan) of a human skull and upper chest region. The brighter areas on the neck and shoulder indicate the presence of cancerous growths within the bones of the skeleton.

In a static scan, an image of the radiopharmaceutical distribution is obtained at a particular point in time. A dynamic study, on the other hand, involves the collection of a time sequence of consecutive images (usually beginning at the time of administration). The images can be viewed one after the other, rather like a strip of movie film. The shape of the image will indicate where the radiopharmaceutical is situated, and the brightness of the image indicates the rate at which the radiopharmaceutical is being assimilated by the body.

Bone scan

The most common static scan—and indeed the most common investigation carried out in a nuclear medicine department—is the bone scan. In a normal scan, the manufacture of bone can be seen to be occurring throughout the skeleton and particularly in the hips, spine, and shoulders. However, the bone scan can show up a particular problem, such as an ill-fitting artificial hip. The artificial hip causes increased wear on the surrounding bone and leads to a local increase in the

rate of bone remodeling. The increase in remodeling is revealed as a telltale hot spot on a nuclear scan since it leads to an increase in the uptake of the radiopharmaceutical.

Lung and kidney tests

Another example of a static scan involves injecting very small spheres of human albumin labeled with technetium. The size of the spheres is chosen so that they will be carried in the bloodstream as far as the capillaries (the smallest-diameter blood vessels) in the lung, where absorption of oxygen takes place. The spheres are, however, too large to pass through the capillaries and lodge there in the lung.

In a normal image, the uniform deposition of radioactive spheres indicates that the blood supply to the lungs is intact. If, however, there is no radioactivity present in, say, the middle zone of the right lung, the test indicates that there is no blood supply to this region. Such a clearly defined defect results from a pulmonary embolism (in which a large blood clot blocks one of the arteries supplying blood to the lung). If the patient is treated with anticoagulants, the clot may be broken up and the blood supply restored. Thus, the lung scan can be used first to help make the diagnosis and then to monitor treatment.

A dynamic study is typified by the renogram—the investigation of kidney function. The kidney is a collection of about a million tiny filter units, called nephrons. They remove waste products and foreign materials from the bloodstream, concentrate them, and pass them to the bladder in urine. In order to test the filtering function, a chemical, such as hippuric acid labeled with radioactive iodine, is injected into the bloodstream. A series of images is collected at 20-second intervals starting at the time of injection, and the gamma camera is connected to a computer that stores the images. For each image in the series, the computer calculates the amount of radioactivity present within the kidney and displays the result in the form of curves known as activity time curves.

The curve rises initially, corresponding to the extraction of the radiopharmaceutical from the blood, before output into the urine takes place. Then the curve reaches its peak (as the rate of extraction is balanced by the rate of outflow into urine). Finally, the curve falls, corresponding to a phase in which the radiopharmaceutical is excreted from the kidney. Any variation from this pattern—such as when the kidney is not filtering material from the blood or when the filter-

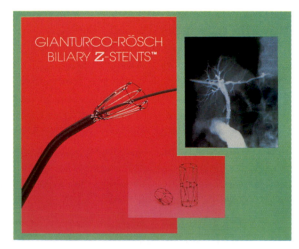

ing function is intact but the kidney is not excreting the material into the urine—produces its own distinctive curve.

Blood flow and senility

The blood flow to the brain can be investigated by studying the time of appearance and the amount of radioactivity present in various regions following the cerebral injection of radio-labeled red blood cells. A small sample (2 to 3 ml) of the patient's blood is withdrawn and put into a centrifuge to separate out the red cells. They are labeled with technetium and reinjected into the patient. The gamma camera, again linked to a computer, is positioned to look down vertically on the top of the patient's skull. From this angle, a series of images is obtained at 0.3-second intervals, and activity time curves are generated. After some mathematical processing, it is possible to calculate the rise of blood flow through the brain's arteries.

The total blood flow can be used as a measure of the severity of senility (senile dementia), and variations in the pattern of flow can show up narrowing or blockage of an individual artery or its branches. Another method of presenting the data is to make a plot of the arrival time of the radioactivity at each point in the brain. A later appearance time is indicative of a narrowed or blocked artery. The rest can be used to assess the success of an arterial operation to circumvent a cerebral blockage—comparing results before and after surgery.

Nuclear cardiology is a technique that offers the cardiologist a much less invasive method of obtaining data than the standard technique, which is called contrast angiography. Angiography involves inserting a hollow tube (catheter) into an artery at the thigh and passing it along until it reaches the heart. A radio-opaque dye is then injected into the heart via the catheter and a series of X-ray images obtained. This technique involves a small risk of serious complications, requires hospitalization, and is traumatic.

Radionuclide tests cannot always supply all the data that can be obtained by conventional angiography, but they do still have a wide range of applications. The most widely used radionuclide tests give information on heart-chamber-wall motion. They are particularly useful for indicating damage to the heart muscle following a heart attack (myocardial infarction), poor blood supply to the heart muscle (perfusion defects), and abnormalities of blood flow between the chambers of the heart (cardiac shunts).

Nuclear cardiology is mainly concerned with the health and functioning of the left ventricle and the arteries that supply it, since it is this chamber of the heart that is most prone to damage and disease. A nuclear angiogram can be performed by passing a pulse of labeled material through the heart (the first-pass technique). With this method, a gamma camera is arranged to record images of the passage of the radionuclide through the heart at the rate of between 25 and 100 exposures per second.

The gamma camera is positioned so that it records activity in both chambers of the heart. From the gamma camera image, it is then possible to calculate the time taken for the blood to travel from one side of the heart to the other. It is also possible to feed into a computer information from successive beats of the heart. The computer can then be instructed to combine the images to produce an accurate representative cardiac cycle.

The representative cycle images can be displayed in the form of a moving pattern on a television screen to help doctors analyze heart-wall motion. The pattern of movement can be used to identify a patient with an aneurysm—a segment of heart muscle that has died and hardened following a heart attack. The dead fibrous segment is weak and may bulge out into the ventricular wall of the heart, which will then move out of sequence with the rest of the ventricle.

Another method of performing a nuclear angiogram is to introduce a radioactive label into the body so that it becomes uniformly distributed throughout the bloodstream (the equilibrium-gated method). Again, the gamma camera information is fed into a computer, which then builds up a typical representative cycle.

It is also possible to conduct nuclear imaging tests after the patient has exercised on a bicycle ergometer or treadmill so that the patient's heart rate is raised to a predetermined level. The purpose is to unmask abnormalities of wall motion that are not present when at rest.

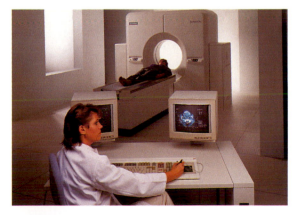

◄ Computer tomography (CT) scanners provide X-ray images of thin slices of the body to provide doctors with three-dimensional views of internal organs.

SEE ALSO: BODY SCANNER • CANCER TREATMENT • ELECTROMAGNETIC RADIATION • LUNG • RADIOACTIVITY • RADIOTHERAPY • X-RAY IMAGING

Radiotherapy

A patient undergoing cobalt therapy—one of the methods used in the treatment of cancer. The radiation from cobalt destroys the invading cancer cells and some healthy ones.

The negative effect of radiation on body tissue is well documented, but medicine has learned to use this destructive ability to its advantage. Both malignant and nonmalignant tissue can be destroyed—strictly, the cells are stopped from multiplying—by irradiating it.

Radiotherapy has a history dating back almost to the early work on radioactive isotopes by the scientists Marie and Pierre Curie (Polish and French, respectively) in the closing years of the 19th century. At this time, radioactive isotopes were used to treat malignant tumors. Radiotherapy and chemotherapy are the principal tools used today in medical oncology, the study and treatment of tumors. Sometimes radiotherapy is called radiation oncology.

Cancer and radiotherapy

Cancer is no longer necessarily a terminal illness; three major treatment methods often lead to a cure: surgery, chemotherapy, and radiotherapy. While not every patient is curable, doctors involved with radiotherapy claim that almost all patients receiving the treatment show some improvement in their symptoms.

While radiotherapy undoubtedly is a very useful weapon in the armory against cancer, the nature of radiation means that treatment has to be carefully considered before commencement. During treatment, radiation needs careful monitoring so that the therapeutic effects are not counteracted by its harmful effects.

Most cancers are localized in nature (particularly if the condition has been recognized at an early stage), and therefore, radiation sources are generally designed to be highly directional. However, in a condition such as leukemia, the entire body needs to be irradiated. Small doses are normally given in total body irradiation (TBI), but in extreme cases, high-dose TBI is used. If unsuccessful, bone marrow transplants are the only recourse.

Radiation sources

Radiotherapy uses a range of radiation sources, from X-ray machines to sealed needles and tubes containing isotopes. Low-power superficial therapy units are in the 60 to 140 kV range. These units, as the name suggests, are useful for treating tumors lying on or near the surface of the skin—there is rapid falloff of radiation with increasing depth. Alongside the therapeutic X rays, so-called soft X rays, which cause skin reactions, are produced, so superficial therapy units are usually equipped with aluminum filters to remove these unwanted components.

To achieve greater tissue penetration, ortho-voltage therapy units are used, operating at between 250 and 500 kV. Again, soft X rays are filtered out, but the higher-energy hard X rays produced by the equipment penetrate a number of centimeters into the skin. The maximum dose occurs at the surface of the skin, but excessive doses to healthy skin can be avoided while still treating tumors effectively.

For tumors sited more than a few centimeters below the skin, X-ray sources producing up to 1 MV must be used. The practical limit of conventional X-ray machines is around 300 kV, so betatrons, linear accelerators, and Van der Graaf generators are the usual high-energy radiation sources. All three devices produce X rays associated with electron beams, and thus, this radiation is labeled particulate rather than electromagnetic, as produced by X-ray machines.

Aside from the ability to penetrate to greater depths than lower-energy rays, the greatest concentration of energy becomes concentrated away from the surface of the skin, saving unwanted radiation effects. In fact, the higher the X-ray energy, the further below the skin surface the area of maximum energy is located.

In order to give patients more radiation without inducing unacceptable side effects, the radiation must be fractionated that is, given in small, frequent doses. Traditionally, this practice has meant receiving one dose of radiation a day, five days a week for about six weeks. Recent research has shown, however, that radiotherapy is more effective if patients receive two or three smaller doses of radiation a day, seven days a week. This method, called hyperfractionation, also makes it possible to reduce the period over which radiotherapy is given.

Radioactive isotopes may produce alpha, beta, or gamma radiation and particulate or electromagnetic radiation and are used by inserting needles directly into tumors and cavities (interstitial treatment) or in applicators, which are inserted into body cavities (intracavity treatment). In the early days of radiotherapy, radium-226 (Ra-226) isotopes were used. More recently, though, the naturally occurring Ra-226 isotope has been replaced by cesium-137 (Cs-137), a reactor by-product. Iridium-192 (Ir-192) has also found favor in interstitial treatment.

Isotopes with short half-lives—those that decay to stable nonradioactive products very quickly—such as gold-128 (Au-128) and iodine-125 (I-125) are available as encased metal seeds. These seeds can be permanently implanted in malignant tissue with no long-term adverse effects to healthy tissue.

Cobalt-60 (Co-60) has a particular application in radiotherapy. The Co-60 teletherapy (distant therapy) machine was developed in 1952 and consists of a spherical shield encasing the isotope. Co-60 teletherapy is used to treat tumors located beneath the skin and does not cause serious skin damage if used carefully.

Radiation and the body

Radiation interacts with body tissue in a variety of ways. The energy carried by radiation is passed on to tissues and causes ionization, a number of biological effects, and the production of heat. The exact form of the biological effects depends on the type of radiation employed and its energy as well as the nature of the tissue itself.

The amount of radiation that a particular tissue can safely absorb—its dose limit—varies greatly, so any course of therapy has to be very carefully planned if lasting damage is not to result. The most radiosensitive tissue is in the eye, where even a small dose of radiation may cause cataracts. At the other extreme, the smooth muscle in the uterus and cervix is extremely resistant to radiation and can safely be given 50 times the dose that causes damage to the eye.

Negative radiation effects may become apparent only some time after treatment, so patients need effective monitoring for many years after treatment. Tumors, both benign and malignant, can be formed by treatment, as well as being destroyed by that same radiation. Children are most at risk from these effects and are also open to a number of other effects that are not apparent in adults. For example, it is common for patients who have not attained physical maturity to have impaired tissue and organ development.

Positioning the patient

The dangers inherent in using radiation treatment mean that the radiation must be carefully localized. During treatment, the therapist will aim to make the patient stay in one position. One of the most important considerations is that skin problems do not occur.

One way of minimizing these effects is to irradiate the tumor from more than one direction. However, the mobility of skin in relation to internal organs (caused by the patient's changing position) may lead to the same area of skin receiv-

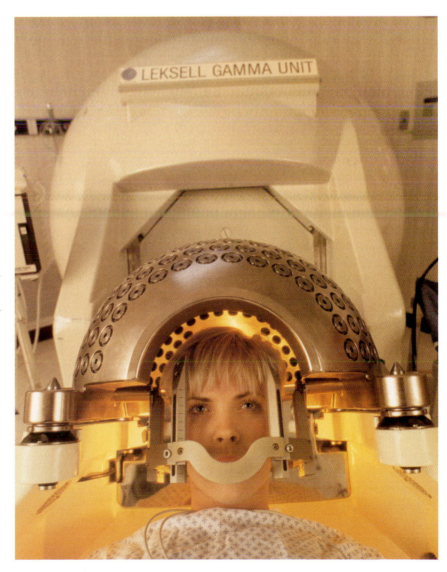

▼ The Gamma Knife Radiosurgery helmet is used for treating brain tumors and other disorders. The helmet has 201 holes in it so that the cobalt radiation sources can be focused exactly on the tumor without damaging other areas of brain tissue. As it is noninvasive and does not require anesthetic, the procedure can take less than an hour and the patient can resume their normal lifestyle within 24 hours of treatment.

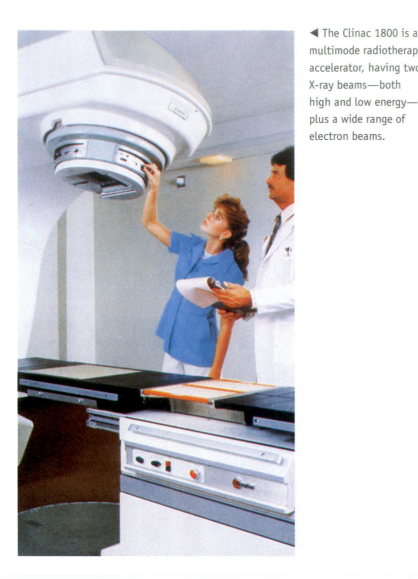

◀ The Clinac 1800 is a multimode radiotherapy accelerator, having two X-ray beams—both high and low energy—plus a wide range of electron beams.

ing a dose of radiation from both directions. Conversely, if guide marks are made on the skin, and the patient then changes position, the wrong internal area may be irradiated. In some cases, the sheer mass of an internal organ may cause displacement as a patient changes position.

Positioning of the patient is so important that special couches are used to keep the patient both immobile and comfortable. Polaroid photographs are often used to record patient positioning and irradiated areas on a day-to-day basis, and precise alignment of patient and radiation beam is achieved using lasers that produce beams that cross at the intended point of maximum concentration of radiation.

Conformational therapy

In the past, the shape of the radiation beam was determined by the shape of the aperture of the cobalt machine or linear accelerator. Now, however, a device called a multileaf collimator makes it possible to shape the radiation beam so that it matches more closely the shape of the tumor. Such collimators contribute to another technique called conformational therapy, which

has also been successfully used in conjunction with linear accelerators.

Before beginning conformational therapy, the patient has a series of computer tomography (CT) scans to determine the three-dimensional shape and size of the tumor. During the therapy, a moving arc of radiation is directed at the tumor, and its speed is calculated to deliver the correct dose to each part of the tumor from different angles, according to its thickness. The collimator, the linear accelerator, and the machine that moves the beam are all under computer control.

Nuclear medicine also uses beta radiation, a short-range killer of cells. It comprises a stream of electrons that are rapidly absorbed in tissue. Because the electrons give up their energy over such a short distance, they deliver a high radiation dose that kills the tissues through which they pass.

However, this cell-killing ability can also be exploited for safe and nontraumatic therapy. If the radionuclide is aimed so that its lethal effects are restricted to the site of a tumor, the beta radiation will destroy the cancer cells without damaging the normal healthy surrounding cells. For example, if radioactive iodine is administered, the body will tend to concentrate it in the thyroid gland just as it concentrates normal iodine. Thus—like a magic bullet—the radionuclide finds its way to this small target where it kills cancer cells. In this way, radioactive iodine can be used for the treatment of cancer of the thyroid gland, which is located in the throat.

Monoclonal antibodies that "seek and destroy" tumor cells are also being developed for use in radiotherapy. In principle, an antibody that binds to a specific tumor protein should be able to seek out rogue cells wherever they have spread in the body. The antibodies can be linked to poisons or to mildly radioactive chemicals that show up on a body scan and indicate where the cancer has spread. In addition, it is possible to combine the antibodies with highly radioactive particles in the hope that they will kill the cells that they bind to. In practice, however, it is difficult to find antigens that are specific only to tumor cells. Antigens are also treated by the body as foreign substances, and many are therefore eliminated by the immune system. Monoclonal antibodies are currently used for the treatment of breast cancer and some kinds of lymphomas. Researchers hope that more antigens may be found to treat other forms of cancer.

SEE ALSO: BODY SCANNER • CANCER TREATMENT • ELECTROMAGNETIC RADIATION • ELECTRONICS IN MEDICINE • RADIOACTIVITY • RADIOLOGY • SKIN • X-RAY IMAGING

Railroad System

The essential feature of a railroad system is the track that guides and supports the trains and that must be strong enough to take the traffic loads. Many railroad systems use the standard gauge (track width between the inner edges of the rails) of 4 ft. 8½ in. (1.435 m), although both wider and narrower gauges are in use.

Even with standard gauge systems, the maximum size for the rolling stock—known as the loading gauge—varies considerably. For example, in Britain, a legacy of tunnels and bridges from the earliest days of railroad development restricts the height of rolling stock to 12 ft. 8 in. (3.86 m) and the width to 9 ft. 3 in. (2.82 m). By contrast, in the United States, the maximum height increases to 15 ft. 6 in. (4.72 m) and the width to 10 ft. 9 in. (3.28 m), allowing the use of much larger rolling stock.

▲ Railroads are complex structures that rely on highly automated and computerized systems to keep services rolling efficiently and with maximum safety to passengers and staff.

A number of different forms of track construction are used depending on the service conditions, with rail weights of over 150 lbs. per yard being used where heavy axle loads have to be carried. The rails are carried on cross ties at a normal rate of 2,112 per mile in Britain and 3,250 per mile in the United States. Ties may be made of creosote-impregnated wood (common in the United States) or reinforced concrete (common in Europe), with the rail being fixed in place by spikes or base plates and spring clips. This technique enables the rail to transmit the pressure, perhaps as much as 20 tons per sq. in. (308 MN/m^2), from the small area of contact with the wheel to the ground below the track formation, where it is reduced through the sole plate and the tie to about 400 psi (2.8 MN/m^2). The track is laid on a solid bed of ballast, and in soft ground, thick polyethylene sheets are generally placed under the ballast to prevent pumping of slurry under the weight of trains.

U.S. rail is supplied in lengths of around 50 ft. (15 m), 98ft. (30m) in Europe. It is normally welded into continuous lengths of 600 ft. (180 m) or more before laying. The laid track is then welded on site into continuous track with pressure-relief points at intervals of several miles. Use of continuous welded rails makes for a steadier and less noisy ride, reduces maintenance requirements, and gives increased track life. Sometimes the rail is hardened to reduce wear and tear still further, particularly if heavy cars are to be used or on sharp curves.

Following the Hatfield disaster in Britain in 2000, in which gauge-corner cracking was blamed for a rail breaking and throwing a high-speed train off the tracks on a sharp curve, contributory factors such as rail characteristics, the inspection regimes for metal fatigue, and rail grinding and maintenance activities are subject to regular review.

Steel rails may last 15 or 20 years in use, but to prolong the undisturbed life of track still further, some countries are putting down paved concrete track (PACT), which is laid by a slip paver in a similar way to highway construction in reinforced concrete. The foundations, if new, are similar to those for such a highway. If on the other hand, existing railroad formation is to be used, the old ballast is sealed with a bitumen emulsion before applying the concrete, which carries the track fastenings glued in with cement grout or epoxy resin. The track is made resilient and wheel noise reduced by using rubber-bonded cork packings.

Signaling

The second important factor contributing to safe rail travel is the signaling system. Originally railroads relied on the time interval to ensure the safety of a succession of trains, but defects rapidly manifested themselves and a space interval, known as the block system, was adopted. In this system, signals prevent a train from entering a particular stretch of track before the train ahead has left it. A more recent advance on that system is the "moving block," in which computerized detection systems control the signals in such a way as to maintain a set distance between trains, rather than simply ensuring that just one train is present in a set distance of track. The block length is determined not by a fixed distance but by the relative speeds and distance between successive trains. In a standard moving-block system, track devices transmit continuous coded signals to receivers on the train, giving information on the status of trains ahead. A receiving device on the train compares this data with its own location and speed, calculates the safe stopping distance, and continuously calculates the maximum speed for maintenance of that gap. The moving-block system was mainly devised for urban rapid-transit or light-rail systems, where maximum train speeds are fairly low. In such cases its flexibility enables the throughput of a larger number of trains in a set time, a necessity on high-use urban lines.

Semaphore signals became universally adopted on running lines, and the interlocking of switches and signals (usually accomplished mechanically by tappets) to prevent conflicting movements being signaled was required by the Railways Act of 1889. Lock-and-block signaling, which ensured a safe sequence of movements by electric checks, was introduced on the London, Chatham, and Dover Railway in 1875.

Track circuiting, by which the presence of a train is detected by an electric current passing from one rail to another through the wheels and axles, dates from 1870, when William Robinson applied it in the United States. In Britain, the Great Eastern Railway introduced power operation of switches and signals at Spitalfields goods yard in 1899, and three years later, track-circuit operation of powered signals was in effect on 30 miles (48 km) of the London and South Western Railway main line.

Day-color-light signals, controlled automatically by the trains through track circuits, were installed on the Liverpool Overhead Railway in 1920, and four-aspect day color lights (red, yellow, double yellow, and green) were provided on Southern Railway routes from 1926 onward. They enable drivers of high-speed trains to have a warning two block sections ahead of a possible need to stop. With track circuiting, it became usual to show the presence of vehicles on a track diagram in the signal cabin, allowing routes to be controlled remotely by means of electric relays. Today, panel operation of considerable stretches of railroad is commonplace. In modern panel installations, the trains are not only shown on the track diagram as they move from one section to another, but the train identification number appears electronically in each section. Computer-assisted train description, automatic train reporting, and operation of platform indicators are now usual. The latest development in signaling is the use of solid-state technology for interlocking. Duplicate or triplicate systems are used for cross checking in order to achieve the required safety levels.

Whether points are operated manually or by an electric switch motor, they have to be prevented from moving while a train is passing over them, and facing switches have to be locked and proved to be locked or "detected" before the relevant signal can permit a train movement. The blades of the switches have to be closed accurately (0.16 in., or 0.4 cm, is the maximum tolerance) so as to avert any possibility of a wheel flange splitting the point and leading to a derailment.

Other signaling developments of recent years include completely automatic operation of simple switch layouts. On the underground system in London, a plastic roll operates junctions according to the timetable by means of coded punched

▼ A computerized railroad signaling system. The presence of a train on a section of track is detected electrically. Switches, operated by remote control, are moved as necessary by trackside electric motors. Signals are controlled automatically by the trains through track circuits, so drivers have a warning two blocks ahead of a possible need to slow down or stop.

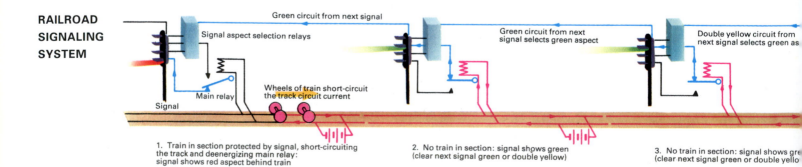

RAILROAD SIGNALING SYSTEM

Green circuit from next signal

Signal aspect selection relays

Green circuit from next signal selects green aspect

Double yellow circuit from next signal selects green as

Main relay

Signal

Wheels of train short-circuit the track circuit current

1. Train in section protected by signal, short-circuiting the track and deenergizing main relay: signal shows red aspect behind train

2. No train in section: signal shows green (clear next signal green or double yellow)

3. No train in section: signal shows gre (clear next signal green or double yello

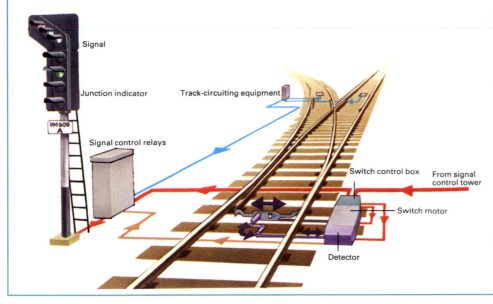

Signal

Junction indicator

Track-circuiting equipment

Signal control relays

Switch control box

From signal control tower

Switch motor

Detector

A RAILROAD SIGNAL

When the signaler has set up a train route, the switch-control box checks the position of the switches and changes them if necessary. The detector checks that the switches are properly in position. Before the signal will clear, the signal-control relays check that the detector is in position, lock it, and clear to the appropriate aspect, depending on the track circuits of the route that has been set up by the operator on the control center console. As the train passes over the switch, the signal is set to red behind it.

holes, and on the Victoria Line, trains are operated automatically once the driver has pressed two buttons to indicate that the train is to start. The driver also acts as the guard, controlling the opening of the doors, closed-circuit television giving a view along the train. The trains are controlled (for acceleration and braking) by coded impulses transmitted through the running rails to induction coils mounted on the front of the train. The absence of code impulses cuts off the current by command spots in which a frequency of 100 Hz corresponds to one mile per hour (1.6 km/h), and 15 kHz shuts off the current. Brake applications are so controlled that trains stop smoothly and with great accuracy at the desired place on platforms. Occupation of the track circuit ahead by a train automatically stops the following train, which cannot receive a code.

Systems with even greater degrees of automatic control, such as the Docklands Light Railway in London, have no driver at all, simply a conductor whose job is to open and shut the doors, check tickets, and return the train to computer control after a station stop. The computer performs all the normal driver functions, receiving instructions as coded signals sent via the track

from a master control system. A manual override is provided in case of emergencies or computer failure, enabling the train "captain" to take over control of the train's movement.

Automatic warning systems give the driver a visual and audible warning of passing a distant signal at caution in the cab. In the simplest system, the driver is able to cancel the alert and decide on appropriate action, but this system has been blamed for a number of rail disasters, including the 1999 Ladbroke Grove train crash in London. In more sophisticated systems, if the driver does not acknowledge the warning, the brakes are applied automatically. The basic system, in use since the 1920s, accomplishes this action by magnetic induction between a magnetic unit placed in the track and actuated according to the signal aspect and a unit on the train.

A further refinement, known as automatic train protection, has been developed since World War II. In this system, a display in the driver's cab gives information on signal status ahead of the train and up to ten instructions on speed to be maintained approaching them. The display receives information in the form of coded impulses passed through the rails or track-

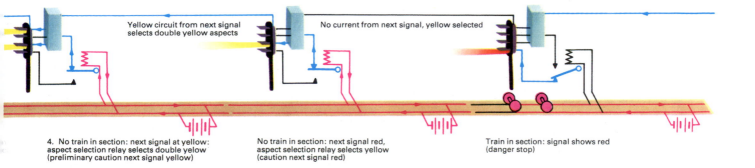

Yellow circuit from next signal selects double yellow aspects

No current from next signal, yellow selected

4. No train in section: next signal at yellow: aspect selection relay selects double yellow (preliminary caution next signal yellow)

No train in section: next signal red, aspect selection relay selects yellow (caution next signal red)

Train in section: signal shows red (danger stop)

◀ The centralized traffic control center at Victoria Station, London, from which all train movements, color-aspect signals, and switches are controlled. Today, panel operation of very great stretches of railroad is quite usual—most of the 1,500 miles (2,400 km) of track in the region south of London is controlled by only 13 such stations.

mounted cable loops, which are picked up by inductive coils on the train. If the driver fails to respond to an instruction, the brakes are automatically applied and power to the train reduced. Locomotives are also controlled by a device known as the "dead man's handle," which the driver has to keep depressed at all times. In the event that the driver is incapacitated, the lever will be released, causing the brakes of the train to be applied automatically.

Train control

In Britain, train control began in 1909 on the Midland Railway to expedite the movement of coal trains and to see that guards and engineers were relieved at the end of their shift and not called upon to work excessive overtime. Comprehensive train-control systems depending on complete diagrams of the track layout and records of the position of engines, crews, and rolling stock were subsequently developed. Refinements of control include advance traffic information (ATI), in which information is passed from yard to yard by telex, giving types of freight car, car number, route code, particulars of the load, destination, and consignee. Modern applications use computerized freight information and traffic-control systems like TOPS (total operations processing system), which was developed by the Southern Pacific company in the United States and is now frequently used on most railroads.

Although a great deal of rail traffic is handled by block trains from point of origin to destination, much of the originating tonnage is less than a train load. As a result, freight cars must be sorted at switchyards, or shunting depots, on their journey. This type of system requires the speed of calculation and the information storage and classification capacity of a modern computer, which has to be linked to points dealing with or generating traffic throughout the system. The computer input covers details of loading or unloading of freight cars and their movements in trains, the composition of trains and their departures from and arrivals at yards, and the whereabouts of locomotives. The computer output includes information on the balance of locomotives at depots and yards, with particulars of when maintenance examinations are due, the numbers of empty and loaded freight cars with aggregate weight and brake force and whether their movement is on time, the location of empty cars and a forecast of those that will become available, and the numbers of trains at any location, with collective train weights and individual details of the component cars. In the United States, photoelectric scanners are used to identify individual cars as they come into the yards so that the use of privately owned stock can be monitored.

A closer check on what is happening throughout the system is thus provided, with the position of consignments in transit, delays in movement, delays in unloading freight cars by customers, and the capacity of the system to handle future traffic among the information readily available. The computer has a built-in self check on wrong input information. In the 1980s, the United States and Canada developed the Advanced Train-Control Systems project to integrate the latest developments in microelectronics and communications. In this system, trains would continuously automatically relay to a control center their exact location and speed. A scanner mounted on the front of the train would read this information from trackside transponders, each with its own individual code.

The Burlington Northern Railroad has gone even further and has tested the use of an on-train computer receiving signals from global-positioning satellites. This system would allow for extremely precise location of trains.

Freight handling

The so-called merry-go-round system enables coal for power plants to be loaded into hopper cars at a coal mine without the train being stopped, and at the power station, the train is hauled around a loop at 0.5 mph, a trigger device automatically unloading the hopper cars without the train being stopped. The arrangements also provide for automatic weighing of the loads. Other bulk loads can be dealt with in the same way. In the United States, there are trains that have more than 100 cars and are pulled by several large diesel locomotives, which transport loads of up to 10,000 tons (9,000 tonnes).

Bulk powders, including cement, can be loaded and discharged pneumatically, using either freight cars or containers. Iron ore is carried in 100-ton (90-tonne) gross cars (72 tons, 65 tonnes of payload) whose coupling gear is designed to swivel so that the cars can turn through 360 degrees for discharge without uncoupling from their train. Special vans take palletized loads of miscellaneous merchandise or such products as fertilizer, the van doors being designed so that all parts of the interior can be reached by a forklift vehicle without difficulty.

In Europe, special container services use easily stackable steel containers in international standard sizes, 8 ft. (2.4 m) wide by 8 ft. high and 10, 20, 30, and 40 ft. (3.1, 6.1, 9.2, and 12.2 m) long. These containers are carried to their destinations on flat cars. Piggyback freight cars are used to carry road trailers.

Another European development has been the swap body, which is a cheaper and more lightweight container system that is directly transferrable to the back of a standard trailer truck.

Such trailer-type containers cannot be stacked and are not suitable for transfer to shipping but have proved acceptable for rail-to-road transfers.

Automobiles are handled by double-tier freight cars in Europe, with the higher loading gauge in the United States allowing three tiers. The car industry is a big user of "company" trains, which are operated for a single customer so that the railroad becomes an extension of the factory transportation system. Company trains frequently consist of cars owned by the trader, with the oil industry being another major industry that frequently uses such single-product, single-owner train transportation systems.

Cryogenic (very low temperature) products are also transported by rail in high-capacity insulated freight cars. Such products include liquid oxygen and liquid nitrogen, which are taken from a central plant to strategically placed railheads where the liquefied gas is transferred to road tankers for the journey to its ultimate destination.

Passenger services

Passenger services have suffered badly from the competition of the automobile for short journeys and air transport over longer distances so that in some regions passenger transport in the United States has been effectively limited to commuter services. Efficient rail systems are recognized as being an important part of a modern transportation system, however, and government assistance has been provided in many countries for the rationalization and development of passenger services. In particular, attention has been concentrated on the development of high-speed services between major population centers. Where cities are relatively close together, as in much of Europe and Japan, such high-speed systems can offer journey times that are comparable with those of air transport. One of the first examples was the Japanese Shinkansen line (known as the bullet

◄ The control center for the Kowloon Bay depot, headquarters of the Hong Kong mass transit system, which is highly automated throughout.

◀ The driver's cab in a TGV. Because of the high speeds the TGV travels, particular attention had to be paid to its design and to the way essential information can be presented to the driver: signals are displayed in the cab, while contact between signal controller and driver is maintained by radio.

train), which opened in 1964 with a Tokyo-to-Osaka service. Journey time is just over three hours for the 322 mile (515 km) trip, corresponding to an average speed of 100 mph (160 km/h), with trains running at 15-minute intervals throughout the day. To achieve this high speed, a completely new track system had to be laid with very gradual curves and to a high standard of construction, with no other traffic being allowed to travel on the same line to simplify the system.

A more recent development is the French TGV (Train à Grande Vitesse) system, which started operation between Paris and Lyon in 1981. It involved a completely new track, in this case, designed to allow operation at speeds of up to 186 mph (300 km/h) to give a two-hour journey time for the 317-miles (507 km) distance.

The construction of completely new railroad lines for high-speed operation is very expensive, and considerable effort has been applied to the development of rolling stock that can operate at high speeds on existing rail networks. In Britain, diesel-powered high-speed trains (HSTs) run at 125 mph (200 km/h) on major routes, sharing the track with slower passenger and freight services. When high-speed trains are run on conventional track systems, passenger comfort can suffer owing to the high centrifugal acceleration experienced on curves. This effect can be minimized by tilting the carriages, and such systems were examined in a number of countries; for example, that was the principle of Britain's Advanced Passenger Train (APT). Unfortunately it tended to cause "seasickness" among passengers, and the tilting system was not sufficiently advanced, so occasionally the train stuck at a tilt or tilted the wrong way, exacerbating the effect it was intended to reduce.

However, a new generation of tilting trains is now being developed, and it is said that these will have eliminated the teething problems found with the APT. Tilting trains have been run successfully in a number of European countries, particularly those used in Italy.

Future developments

Train developments of the future might follow the design of the Aerotrain, developed in France in the 1970s. It is an air-cushioned vehicle that uses a "cushion" of low-pressure air to keep the vehicle afloat on a guide track with a vertical central guide beam that keeps the train in place.

Magnetic levitation, or maglev, has also been developed in Germany and Japan. The German system uses magnetic attraction—the vehicle's deep skirts contain powerful electromagnets that are attracted to the ferromagnetic guide rails at the outside of the track. The Japanese version uses high-powered, helium-cooled superconductor magnets and coils, similarly polarized, in the guideway, thus working on magnetic repulsion.

However, these systems have one major failing—they are incompatible with the rest of the United States or European train network and so are likely to remain curiosities. Safety, efficiency, speed, and passenger comfort are likely to remain preoccupations for future train systems.

SEE ALSO: FREIGHT HANDLING • LOCOMOTIVE AND POWER CAR • MASS TRANSIT AND SUBWAY • MONORAIL SYSTEM • RAILROAD YARD

Railroad Yard

Freight traffic on today's railroad systems falls into two main classes: bulk, consisting of large quantities of a single commodity such as coal, grain, or oil and general mixed goods. Often bulk loads are carried on regular runs—such as between a coal mine and a power plant, with permanently coupled trains operating on a merry-go-round principle. Attempts have been made to extend this method of operation to general freight traffic with scheduled trains running between traffic centers. These trains are of fixed length, and if there is insufficient freight, some of the cars remain empty, thus avoiding the need to reform the train for each trip.

However, this approach is suitable only for a limited number of heavily used routes, and other arrangements are needed where a large quantity of general freight traffic has to be moved between a number of different locations. For the most efficient use to be made of the railroad tracks and locomotives, freight traffic has to be made up into large trains, usually by assembling the trains in a railroad yard, marshaling yard, or switchyard. They are also known as classification yards because they are used to classify (or sort) the incoming cars according to their destination.

In their simplest form, switchyards consist of a series of sidings, or classification tracks, with the freight cars being moved between them in cuts, or groups, by a shunter, or switcher (a small locomotive) until the required order is achieved.

As railroads became more complicated in their system layouts in the 19th century, the scope and volume of sorting necessarily became greater, and means of reducing the time and labor involved were sought. In one early system, groups of sidings were laid out on the slope of a hill with gravity providing the motive power. The steepest gradient was 1 in 60 (one foot of elevation in 60 feet of siding). Chain drags were used for braking the cars. A shunter uncoupled the cars in cuts for the various destinations, and each cut was turned into the appropriate siding. Some yards relied on whistles to advise the signaler what track was required.

In the late 19th century, the hump yard was introduced to provide gravity where there was no natural slope of the land. In this yard the trains were pushed up an artificial mound with a gradient of perhaps 1 in 80 and the cuts were humped down a somewhat steeper gradient on the other side. The separate cuts would roll down the selected siding in the fan, or balloon, of sidings, which would end in a slight upward slope to assist in the stopping of the cars. The main means of

▲ This railroad yard, viewed from the CN Tower in Toronto, Canada, shows the circular turntable used to rotate the trains so that they can be stored in the surrounding sheds.

stopping the cars, however, were railway employees called shunters who had to run alongside the cars and apply the brakes at the right time.

Such yards appeared all over North America and England. In Germany, small hump yards appeared, some having only three sidings on which to do the sorting. Much ingenuity was devoted to the means of stopping the cars; a German firm, Fröhlich, came up with a hydraulically operated retarder that clasped the wheel of the car as it went past.

Automation

An entirely new concept came when Whitemoor yard near Cambridge, England, opened in 1929. When trains arrived in one of ten reception sidings, a shunter examined the car labels and prepared a cut card showing how the train should be sorted into sidings that was sent to the control tower by pneumatic tube; there the switches for the 40 sorted sidings were preset in accordance with the cut card; information for several trains could be stored in a simple pin-and-drum device.

The hump was approached by a grade of 1 in 80. On the far side was a short stretch of 1 in 18 to accelerate the cars followed by 210 ft. (64 m) at 1 in 60 where the tracks divided into four, each equipped with a Fröhlich retarder. Then the four tracks spread out to four balloons of ten tracks each, comprising 285 ft. (87 m) of level track followed by 699 ft. (213 m) falling at 1 in 200, with the remaining 1,140 ft. (348 m) level. The switches were moved in sequence by track circuits actuated by the cars, but the operators had to estimate the effects on car speed of the retarders on the basis of whether the retarders were lubricated by grease or oil.

Pushed by an 0-8-0 small-wheeled shunting locomotive at 1½ to 2 mph (2½ to 3 km/h), a train of 70 cars could be sorted in seven minutes. A yard had a throughput of about 4,000 cars a day. Apart from the sorting sidings, there were an engine road, a brake van road, a cripple road for cars needing repair, and a transfer road to three sidings serving a tranship shed, where small shipments not filling entire cars could be sorted.

Electronic yards

Automation and rapid handling remain the main feature of modern switchyards, with extensive use being made of electronic controls and computer systems. A typical switchyard today has three main working areas: the receiving yard, the classification yard, and the dispatch yard—together with such facilities as car repair and locomotive servicing. Incoming trains are directed to the receiving yard, where the locomotives that have hauled the trains to the switchyard are uncoupled and moved on to the service area. In the most automated yards, electronic sensors mounted by the side of the tracks read coded information from identification plates carried on the cars. This information is stored in the central control computer and used to control the subsequent car-sorting operation.

From the receiving yards the trains are shunted to the hump by a locomotive at the rear of the train. In some modern systems the shunting locomotives are driverless, operating by remote control. Individual cars or groups of cars for different destinations are uncoupled from the train either automatically or manually and allowed to pass over the hump and roll down

toward the classification yard under the action of gravity. A large yard may have 40 or more tracks.

The computer also calculates the amount of braking that is applied to the car by the retarder system. The level of braking required depends on such factors as the number of cars already in the siding (this information is stored in the computer and updated as more cars are moved in), the character of the route to the siding, and the weight and rolling resistance of each car. This last factor varies greatly and is measured by trackside equipment as the cars pass through the system. Accurate setting of the rolling speed is needed to ensure that the cars will roll right into position against the other cars on the classification track but without hitting them too hard and possibly damaging them or their contents.

Groups of about 40 cars are built up on the classification tracks and coupled up for transfer to the departure yard. Here the individual groups are made up into complete trains, which may contain well over 100 cars. Assembly of the trains from groups of cars is also controlled by the central computer, which can then produce a printout detailing the makeup of the train and the destination of each car.

▼ This railroad yard uses automation to ease the process of switching freight cars. The overall process is monitored from the control tower and the hump cabin. When a freight car reaches the hump, it is detached from the cars connected to it and allowed to roll down the hill. Retarders slow its process, and points direct it to the correct siding, where it is coupled to other cars.

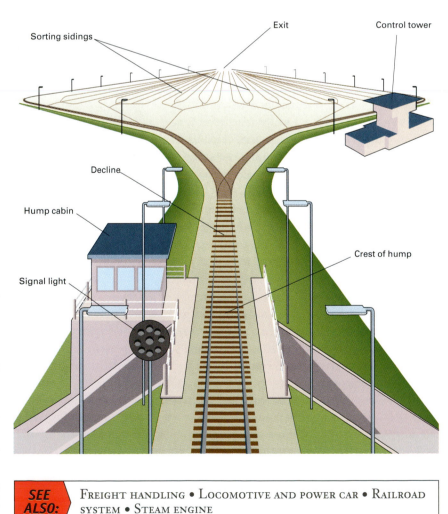

Sorting sidings · Exit · Control tower · Decline · Hump cabin · Crest of hump · Signal light

SEE ALSO: Freight handling • Locomotive and power car • Railroad system • Steam engine

Rain and Rainfall

Rain is the precipitation of water vapor from the atmosphere. Other forms of precipitation include snow, drizzle, and hail, but they all involve the condensation of water molecules onto tiny airborne particulates. The size of a raindrop varies between 0.2 mm and 6 mm in diameter, as larger droplets become unstable and break up into smaller drops. The size of the drop also affects the speed at which it falls, bigger droplets falling at a faster rate than drizzle.

Water droplets form around very small particles of salt, dust, or chemicals released into the atmosphere by industry, motor vehicles, or natural processes. These particles are known as condensation nuclei. When the temperature of the atmosphere drops below the dew point (the temperature at which air holds as much water vapor as it can), the water vapor begins to condense on the nuclei.

Formation of rain clouds

A large part of Earth's surface in the intertropical zone is covered by oceans that have warm surface water. This warm water evaporates from the sea surface and pumps a great deal of water vapor into Earth's atmosphere. The trade winds that pass over the area pick up more and more water vapor in the course of their journey. When air has water vapor added to it, it becomes less dense, so it will tend to rise toward the cooler surroundings of the atmosphere above the ocean surface.

The atmosphere itself is most dense at Earth's surface but becomes less dense as it goes higher. As the warm air rises, it faces lessening pressure from the air around it and expands. This expansion outward and upward uses up energy that is paid for in heat, so the moist air cools still further. When the air has cooled so much that it can no longer hold water vapor, the water condenses into tiny droplets that become visible as clouds.

Some of the clouds formed in tropical zones will be carried to other parts of the atmosphere by Earth's system of winds, but others will boil up to great heights in the tropic zone. As this warm, moist air rises, some cloud droplets will amalgamate with others as they keep colliding, and eventually large drops of water will form that are heavy enough to fall as rain through the rising air. This circulation provides the heavy annual rainfall of the tropic region.

As the warm, moist air of the tropics rises and is dispersed poleward, the pressure at sea level decreases, and drier air from cooler regions is drawn in to replace it. This basic pattern of air circulation, coupled with the twist given to air currents by Earth's rotation, has established the weather patterns that dominate the various areas of the atmosphere. The distribution of land surface and its effect on rainfall makes some areas very arid and others very moist, but the basic pattern is for warm, moist air to be carried toward the pole in southwesterly air currents in the Northern Hemisphere and for northwesterly winds to bring colder, drier air back toward the equator. This situation is reversed in the Southern Hemisphere.

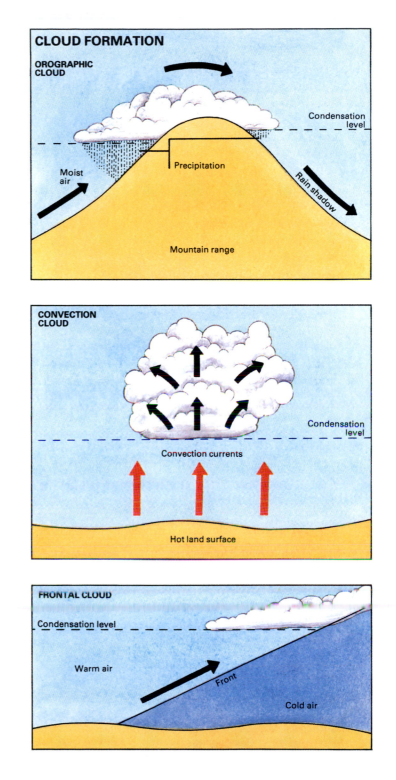

▲ Clouds can form by air rising over a barrier, such as a mountain (top), or by convection as warm currents rise from a hot land surface (middle). The bottom diagram shows clouds forming at the meeting of two air masses.

The basic result is that regions close to the tropics experience warm, dry conditions, and the polar areas have cold, dry conditions. Between these zones, the middle latitudes experience variations between dry, high-pressure systems (anti-cyclones) and moist, low-pressure systems (cyclones). Because a cyclone is, by definition, an area of low air pressure, it is squeezed out of existence by air spiraling into it from all sides. Some of this air will be the cold, dry air moving toward the tropics from the poles, and this air will tend to undercut the rising, warm, moist air traveling poleward.

As the moist air is pushed higher, the water droplets in the clouds turn to ice or snow in the colder regions of the upper atmosphere. These frozen drops have enough weight to fall to Earth, frequently thawing and changing back to rain as they return through the warmer, lower regions. So cyclonic conditions bring belts of rain or snow, and in some places (where air has to pass over long, high mountain ranges, for instance), their development is caused by the shape of the land surface. In other places, cyclones are the result of uneven divergence of the air flowing poleward from the tropics.

Climatic regions

There are five main climatic divisions of the globe, varying from the megathermal climate of the equatorial regions to the ice cap of the polar areas. The temperature and topography of each

▲ Working through a heavy cloudburst. Some of the clouds formed in tropical zones will be carried to other parts by the atmosphere and by the winds. Others will boil up at great heights and break periodically into heavy rainfall.

affects the quantity of annual rainfall. The megathermal area is where clouds boil up to great heights to give heavy rainfall, but it also contains drier savanna regions where it fringes the second, or xerophilous, areas: the desert and steppe regions, where rainfall is negligible. The desert climates occur around 30 degrees north or south of the equator, where very large cells of high, dry pressure are found, and the steppe regions are to be found in the center of large land masses that have already absorbed most of the available rainfall before it reaches the interior. Then there are the mesothermal climates of the temperate, rainy zone, where the low-pressure systems of the mid-latitudes bring much of the rainfall. Mesothermal regions vary from the heavy, year-round rainfall that can be experienced on the west coast of a continental mass, which receives a succession of cyclones, to the genial Mediterranean-type climates, which experience hot, dry summers as the high-pressure system of the desert regions shifts poleward and mild, rainy winters when it shifts back toward the other hemisphere.

The microthermal climate is limited to the Northern Hemisphere alone, as there is an insufficient land mass in the south bordering the Antarctic Circle. The microthermal climate experiences slight rainfall because winter in those latitudes usually brings anticyclones, and in summer, the high mountains of North America or the land masses of Europe and Asia prevent moist air from reaching them.

FACT FILE

- In August 1975, London experienced its heaviest rainstorm in recorded history when 6.7 in. (17 cm) of rain fell in 2½ hours, bursting sewers and washing away objects as large as cars and trucks.

- The torrential rain that fell on Calama, Chile, in February 1972 was, according to reports, the first for 400 years. It was shortly followed by catastrophic flooding and deadly landslides.

- A chronicle of prodigious events published in Basel, Switzerland, in 1557 described and illustrated showers of toads, fish, and crosses. Modern oddity showers, well documented, have included maggots, spiders, and frogs. Colored rain has been caused by sand and dust in the atmosphere.

SEE ALSO: CLIMATOLOGY • FLOOD CONTROL • HURRICANE AND TORNADO • METEOROLOGY • RAINBOW • THUNDERSTORM

Rainbow

The rainbow's arch of seven bands of color is a common sight whenever there is a conjunction of sunshine and rain. The color sequence is violet, indigo, blue, green, yellow, orange, and red, and it never varies although colors can seem more or less brilliant depending upon the brightness of each rainbow. In cases where two rainbows appear, one above the other, the colors in the upper, or secondary, bow are fainter and appear in the opposite order to the lower, or primary, bow.

History of rainbow physics

One of the earliest descriptions of a rainbow was made around 200 C.E. by the Greek philosopher Alexander of Aphrodisias, who noticed the dark band of sky around the outer edge of the rainbow. This phenomenon is now referred to as Alexander's dark band. The first known attempt to explain the causes of a rainbow was given by another Greek philosopher, Aristotle, who correctly theorized that rainbows are caused by light reflected at a fixed angle. It was many hundreds of years, however, before any further developments were made in the understanding of the rainbow. The next major step was made in 1344 by a German monk, Theoderic of Freiburg, who proposed that each raindrop produced its own rainbow. Theoderic's ideas were rediscovered more than 300 years later, in 1656, by the French mathematician and philosopher René Descartes.

Descartes and Theoderic both used spherical water-filled flasks to simulate the refraction and reflection of light in a raindrop. Using this simulation, they were able to observe that the primary bow is formed when light reflects once within a raindrop, while the secondary bow is formed after two internal reflections. They also discovered that most of the light entering a raindrop is emitted after the first internal reflection, explaining why the secondary bow is fainter.

The arrangement of the colors is the result of the refraction of sunlight through raindrops. Light is a form of electromagnetic radiation and is not white as it seems but a compound of all colors (with an infinite range of gradations between each color). When light is passed through a pair of angled transparent surfaces (such as the walls of a glass prism or two of the boundaries of a raindrop), it can be made to bend—just as a bullet might ricochet off a slanting surface. As bullets of different weights might ricochet at different angles, the different light frequencies are bent at different angles and separated out. This process of bending light is called refraction. Both

▲ Double rainbows occur where raindrops are very large. The colors in the upper, or secondary, rainbow are in reverse order to those of the primary rainbow.

Theoderic and Descartes noticed that when looking through their simulation of a raindrop, different colors of light appeared at slightly different angles. They were then able to hypothesize that the different colors of the rainbow are made by different raindrops.

The fact that the arc we see is caused by the refraction of sunlight at an exact angle accounts for the difficulty of reaching the rainbow's end. For the angle to be perfect, the Sun must be behind the observer, and the bow itself will be in front. Because the sunlight is refracted through drops of rain, if the observer advances on the rainbow, it will advance ahead by being refracted through different raindrops. The angle of refraction can never change.

The angle between the observer, the primary rainbow, and the Sun—and therefore the angle between the rainbow, the observer, and the

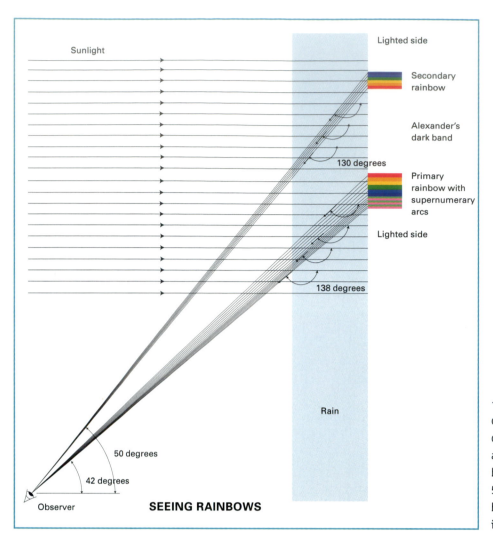

SEEING RAINBOWS

Sunlight

Lighted side

Secondary rainbow

Alexander's dark band

130 degrees

Primary rainbow with supernumerary arcs

Lighted side

138 degrees

Rain

50 degrees

42 degrees

Observer

for example, are extra bands of color that occasionally appear near the inner band of the primary rainbow. These bands can be explained by interference and occur where the size of the raindrop is very small. Interference occurs where waves of the same frequency combine to form areas of differing intensity. If two wave peaks occur together, the overall intensity increases, and the interference is said to be constructive. If, however, a peak and a trough combine, the two cancel each other out, and the interference is said to be destructive. Interference in supernumerary arcs occurs as a result of differences in the path lengths of light, and path lengths change more slowly with small droplets, thus increasing the possibility of there being enough interference over a broad enough angle to produce a visible band of color.

◄ When light is reflected within a raindrop, the different wavelengths are concentrated at certain definite angles. This fact explains why primary and secondary rainbows occur only at angles between the sun and the observer of 42 and 50 degrees, respectively. Little light is emitted between these two angles, and so a dark region is formed called Alexander's dark band.

ground—is always 42 degrees, while the angle for the secondary rainbow is 50 degrees. The reason that light does not just scatter widely from a raindrop but forms the intense regions of color at these precise angles is because of the way light reflects within a drop of water. Light does not pass out of a raindrop with an even distribution but is concentrated at the angles that produce the primary and secondary bows. In addition, although some light is emitted at angles greater than 50 degrees and less than 42 degrees, very little light is emitted between these two angles, thus explaining the dark region between the two bows known as Alexander's dark band.

The brightness of the rainbow depends upon the size of raindrop through which the sunlight is bent—the larger the drops, the more brilliant the colors will seem. Most bows are a faint sheen of color, but when light reaches an observer through very large drops, the bow may be very clear and, in this instance, may also be accompanied by a secondary bow.

Although most of the factors creating a rainbow can be explained using simple geometry, some of the more unusual phenomena require more complex explanations. Supernumerary arcs,

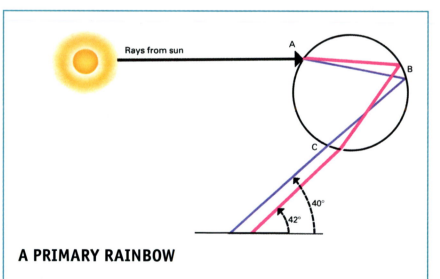

Rays from sun

A

B

C

40°

42°

A PRIMARY RAINBOW

A primary rainbow is formed when light entering a raindrop is refracted and undergoes a single internal reflection before being emitted from the raindrop. It is the process of refraction that causes the light to split into its constituent colors—red, orange, yellow, green, blue, indigo, and violet. Secondary rainbows are formed after two internal reflections.

SEE ALSO: COLORIMETRY • ELECTROMAGNETIC RADIATION • LIGHT AND OPTICS • PRISM • RAIN AND RAINFALL • SPECTROSCOPY

Razor

Razor blades have come a long way since the aptly named "cutthroat" of the 19th century. The British company Wilkinson Sword first introduced the safety razor in 1898—a big step in shaving technology because it enabled the user to shave simply and safely. The revolutionary razor had a guarded blade and hollow-ground blades that could be resharpened—quite different from razors that were simply thrown away when they threatened to snag on a whisker.

The male beard consists of two types of hair. The very fine lanugo hair shafts have diameters in the region of 0.0004 in. (0.01 mm), whereas the coarser hairs are around 0.004 in. (0.1 mm) in diameter and have a hard, scaly outer layer (the cuticle) surrounding a pigmented cortex in the center of which is the medulla. The lanugo hairs have no medulla.

The beard areas of adult males have between 6,000 and 25,000 of the coarse hair fibers, which grow at a rate of something like 0.016 in. (0.4 mm) in a 24-hour period—though this varies from beard to beard and from area to area within each beard. Most beards grow faster in summer than in winter, and although the growth rate is slightly faster just after shaving, over a 24-hour period, the rate of growth is the same whether or not one shaves. Despite popular myth, shaving does not coarsen beard growth or permanently accelerate it.

Hair fibers rarely emerge from the skin surface at a conveniently choppable 90 degrees. Most come out at an angle between 30 and 60 degrees, and in some areas, the hair fibers emerge from deep pits in the skin. Most hair shafts are associated with sebaceous glands, which cover the fibers with an oily secretion. The film of oil should be removed before shaving to allow the water to penetrate and soften the hair and make the work of the razor blade that much easier.

Shaving geometry

The shaving angle—the difference between a close shave and a bloody shave—is determined by the set of the guard bar and the top cap and the protrusion of the blade between them. If the shaving angle is too low or the protrusion too high, there is likely to be some blood shed. Too high a shaving angle and the roots are torn. Too low a protrusion and the so-called five o'clock shadow might be obvious much earlier.

Controlled shaving "geometry"—what razor manufacturers and shavers alike seek most—means a close, smooth shave. The best shaving

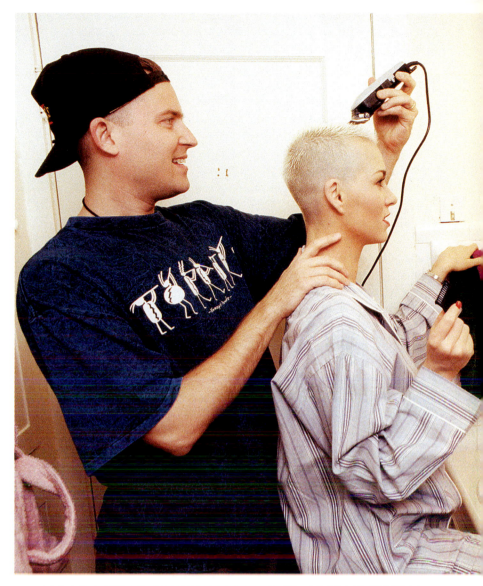

▲ Electric hair clippers are provided with a number of different attachments or blades that allow the hair to be cut to a variety of different lengths. The hair can be cut extremely close to the skin, making clippers a much safer way of shaving the head than a wet razor.

angle is achieved by precisely locating the extreme tip of the blade between the top cap and guard bar and keeping it rigidly in position during the shave. The tolerances are acute, and with a dismantleable razor, wear can eventually reduce the level of shaving efficiency; thus, the bonded razor—in which the top cap, guard bar and blade are fixed together to form one unit—has become a popular alternative. The entire blade of this unit can be thrown away and replaced by another geometrically precise shaving unit.

The blade

The guard bar has an important role beside keeping the blade in position—it tensions the skin slightly before the blade passes over it, thus helping to make the facial hairs stand up slightly to ensure a smoother shave.

The modern blade undergoes a sophisticated stream of processes before it is judged to be shave-worthy. It has to be extremely sharp along its entire length—and sharp means having a cutting edge no more than 0.000002 in. (0.00005 mm) in radius. This microfine edge has to be maintained through 12 days of shaving—130,000 hairs—before being thrown away.

The blade itself is made from a strip of stainless steel only 0.004 in. (0.1 mm) thick—about the same diameter as a hair. The strip is first hardened by heat treatment and then sharpened into a faceted edge. The ground edge is then stropped (sharpened) on ox-hide leathers to produce a fine-quality tip with a gothic arch cross section.

One of the most significant improvements in shaving technology was the introduction of PTFE (polytetrafluoroethylene) coating onto the edge of razor blades. This is the substance that makes nonstick pots and pans nonstick. The same slippery qualities help the blade slide through a hair without tugging and also reduce the cutting load by five or six times. The PTFE layer is quite thick, but during the first few strokes of a shave, a large proportion of the coating peels back,

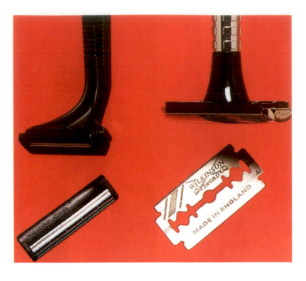

▶ The safety razor, introduced by the British company Wilkinson Sword in 1898, revolutionized the practice of shaving.

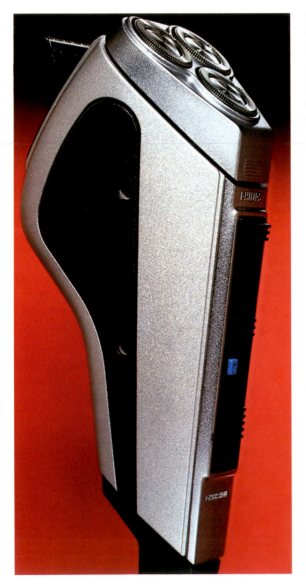

◀ Electric shavers, although convenient, do not give quite so close a shave as a wet razor, but this rotary razor is designed to catch hairs growing in all directions.

unnoticed by the shaver, to leave just the right amount on the blade.

Though made from stainless steel, the blade can still be attacked by corrosion. To overcome this problem, an extremely thin layer—less than 0.000001 in. (0.000025 mm) of corrosion-resistant chromium is applied to the blade. The blade is further improved by adding an equally thin layer of a special ceramic material between the chromium and PTFE. To achieve the required thinness of the coatings, a sputtering technique is used.

Electric shaver

A popular alternative to the wet razor is the electric shaver. These cutting devices come in two basic types—the foil razor and the rotary razor. Foil razors have a moving cutter covered with a perforated foil that protects the skin while allowing the hairs to pass through the perforations to the blades. They are available in single foil with one cutter or double or triple foils with two or three cutters. Rotary razors have two or three circular heads, each covering spinning blades. The circular heads act like the perforated foil on a foil razor, allowing the hairs to pass through to the revolving blades while protecting the skin from damage.

Hair clippers

Clippers used to cut head hair are powered either with vibrating electromagnets or are motor driven. The vibrating type are commonly used for home cutting and have fixed blades, but attachments can be added to provide different cutting lengths. Motor-driven clippers are used professionally and have detachable blades of different length rather than attachments.

SEE ALSO: ELECTRIC MOTOR • ELECTROMAGNETISM • HAIR TREATMENT • POLYTETRAFLUOROETHYLENE (TEFLON)

Rectifier

Alternating current is easier to distribute than direct current, owing to the ease with which the associated voltage may be altered by use of transformers. For many applications, however, power supplies giving a constant, direct current (DC) output are essential.

Rectification is the process whereby an alternating current (AC) input is converted into a DC output. Alternating current continually reverses its direction of flow, rising to a maximum value in one direction, dropping to zero, and then rising to a maximum in the opposite direction. To convert such an oscillating system into a unidirectional current, a device is required that allows current to flow in only one direction—such a device is known as a diode.

If an alternating current supply is applied to a diode, the current will be conducted only during alternate half cycles, giving a pulsating but unidirectional output current—a process termed half-wave rectification. Improved efficiency results if both halves of the alternating input cycle are used, a goal achievable by either using a center-tap transformer with two diodes connecting the ends of the secondary coil to the center tap, or by using a bridge of four diodes. This process is called full-wave rectification.

One of the simplest forms of diode is the two-electrode discharge tube. The conduction electrons are produced by heating one electrode,

the cathode, and are attracted toward the second electrode, the anode, only when it is at a positive potential with respect to the cathode. Connecting both to an AC supply will lead to conduction every other half-cycle, giving half-wave rectification, but by including a second anode, full-wave rectification is possible.

Discharge tubes may be evacuated (vacuum type) or filled with mercury vapor (mercury-arc type) or an inert gas at low pressure (hot-cathode gas rectifier). With the hot-cathode gas type, the gas filling is ionized during conduction to produce additional conduction electrons. The gas-filled device has a higher efficiency than the evacuated discharge tube and is used for the supply of large DC currents.

Another important thermionic device is the mercury-arc rectifier. Electron emission occurs from a hot spot produced by generating a spark at the surface of the cathode, a pool of metallic mercury. These electrons are attracted to anodes within the valves when these are made positive by the alternating supply.

The output of a rectifier can be controlled by the application of a small, secondary electric sig-

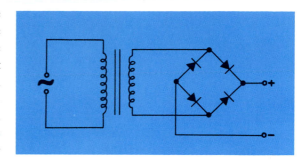

▲ Full-wave rectification is often achieved using four diodes in a bridge arrangement as shown. Achieving full-wave rectification with only two diodes is possible if there is a center tap on the transformer secondary coil.

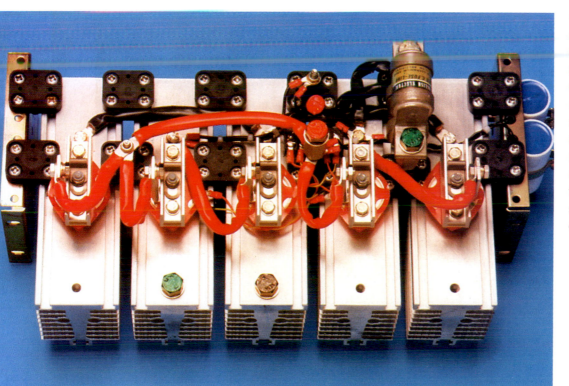

◄ The type of rectifier and the nature of the associated smoothing and stabilization depend entirely on the intended application of the resulting supply of power. This air-cooled AC controller is most commonly used to control heating elements, induction motors, and small resistance-welding equipment.

nal, which is applied to a third electrode, or grid, within the valve; such a device is called a thyratron.

Solid-state rectifiers

Solid-state rectifiers can be subdivided into metal rectifiers and semiconductor devices.

The required asymmetric conduction of a metal rectifier occurs between a metal and a coating applied to it. The two principal commercial types are the copper oxide rectifier and the selenium rectifier. The layer between the metal and its coating allows current to be conducted readily in one direction but provides a high resistance to current flow in the opposite direction.

The copper oxide device has an oxide coating on a copper disk, while the selenium rectifier consists of a layer of selenium overlaid, typically, with a layer of lead. Both devices are produced as disks that are mounted in series to give the required handling capacity. They are cheap, easily produced, robust, and maintenance free. The copper oxide rectifier is used principally in low-power devices, and the selenium rectifier in medium-to-high-voltage applications.

Semiconductors are extensively used in rectifier applications. A semiconductor material has an electric conductivity between that of a conductor, such as a metal, and an insulator, such as rubber. Silicon or germanium can be rendered electrically conducting by the addition of controlled amounts of specific impurity elements. Suitable choice of additive produces positively charged p-type and negatively charged n-type semiconductors. In an n-type semiconductor, for instance, the current carriers are negative electrons. The semiconductor diode consists of a p–n junction, and the boundary between these exhibits asymmetric conduction. A p–n junction rectifier exhibits high efficiency. When a control of the output is required, it can be achieved using the thyristor, which is a p–n–p–n sandwich.

Smoothing and stabilization

A simple rectified output consists of a series of half sine waves, and although classed as DC, it is not smooth. This variation in amplitude is termed ripple and, while being of little consequence in certain applications, produces unacceptable hum

▲ An electronic conductor can be powered by batteries, or it can get the direct current it needs from an alternating current via a rectifier.

in audio and amplifying circuits, for example.

The rectified output must be smoothed for such applications by use of a filter circuit. A capacitor is charged by the unsmoothed output and discharges only slowly until recharged to peak value by the next current wave, resulting in a direct current with a reduced amount of ripple. Further improvement is obtained by use of an inductor, or choke, which is a wire coil wound onto a metal core. An inductor allows a direct current to pass through relatively unhindered but virtually eliminates the remaining alternating current ripple component.

In addition, a further capacitor is frequently used to absorb any remaining ripple, yielding a practically pure DC output.

Variations in the alternating input result in fluctuations in the rectified output. When a constant output is required, some means of stabilizing the output voltage, or current, must be provided. This end is achieved by passing the rectified output through a device whose conduction properties are essentially independent of the input.

Rectifier applications

Situations in which rectification is applicable are all applications in which DC electric power is required from an AC supply. These are innumerable but include electric traction, electrolysis, battery charging, industrial processes such as anodizing, metal refining, and gas production, and radio, television, and amplifier applications.

In general terms, mercury-arc rectifiers are used for very high power applications, that is, several hundreds of kilowatts. For applications in the range 10 to 100 kW, the hot-cathode, mercury-vapor rectifier is often used. It is also suitable in the range from 1 to 10 kW, but in this low range, the metal rectifiers are often more economically attractive.

For small-power installations, such as home radio receivers, the semiconductor diodes and (to a decreasing extent) the vacuum diode are the principal rectifying elements.

 SEE ALSO: CAPACITOR • DIODE • DISCHARGE TUBE • ELECTROLYSIS • ELECTRONICS • SINE WAVE • THYRISTOR

Recycling

It is possible to recover and reuse a large proportion of the waste material produced by modern society. Whether or not a particular material will be recycled depends on a number of different factors, including the economics of the recovery process and the effect on the environment of dumping the material in question. One of the most important aspects of recycling is the treatment of household refuse to extract and reuse materials such as paper, metals, plastics, and glass. No less important but much lower profile is the routine recovery of such materials as solvents and catalysts by the chemicals industry.

Recycling is set to play an increasing role in the management of waste as landfill space becomes scarce. Nearly 61 million tons (54 million tonnes) of waste was recycled in the United States in 1997. Although this figure represents only 28 percent of the total waste collected, it is double that of the mid-1980s. The aim is to reach 35 percent by 2005. The benefits of recycling will include less energy spent on incineration along with reduction of pollutants, saving of landfill space, and greater value of the materials salvaged.

Paper

By far the greatest proportion (almost 40 percent) of household waste is paper, which is one of the most important sources of pulp for paper production. Unfortunately, the cost of recycling paper is relatively high, mainly because the necessary collecting, sorting, and transportation is expensive, as reflected in the fact that the proportion of paper recycled in the United States in 1997 was only 41 percent of the total collected for disposal.

In the recycling process, the wastepaper is pulped mechanically in the presence of water to give a pulp suspension that is then treated with an alkali to remove unwanted material. Finally the pulp is washed and bleached to remove the ink, giving a product that can be used to make book paper. The deinking of wastepaper is often a rather uneconomical process—as much as 25 percent of the paper input can be lost—and this, together with the fact that the quality of pulp from wastepaper is inferior to that derived directly from wood, prevents the use of wastepaper from becoming more widespread in the papermaking industry other than for newsprint.

▲ Landfill is the most economic and most common option for disposal of household waste. This site produces landfill gas—methane. The gas is used by a board mill, which converts 150,000 tons (135,000 tonnes) of cardboard to packaging board every year.

◀ Glass recycling begins when the glass is delivered by truck (top left). On the conveyor belt (top right), magnets remove any iron-containing metals. Other unwanted materials are removed by hand. The glass is crushed again to release metal and plastic rings and caps, which are removed by a vacuum tube. The crushed glass (cullet) passes over screens that shake so that nonglass materials can pass through (bottom left). The glass, now graded for size and color, is piled in bays for delivery to the furnace (bottom right).

The use of wastepaper for the production of cardboard and other packaging materials appears more promising.

Metals

A significant proportion of all the metal in use today is recycled. In the United States, 67 percent of the steel industry is fed by scrap metal, as is 42 percent of the aluminum industry. At the end of their useful life, metal objects are either sold as scrap if they are large enough or simply discarded as refuse. Swarf (the offcuts from metal machining) is also sold as scrap. While most recycled metal comes from scrap-metal merchants, useful quantities can be extracted from household refuse.

In terms of quantity the most important recycled metal is iron. Scrap iron is usually melted in an electric arc furnace, and oxygen is blown in to produce an iron oxide slag. The slag is removed and carbon in the form of coke or used furnace electrodes is added to deoxidize the steel. During this process carbon monoxide gas bubbles to the surface of the molten iron. After further refining and alloying processes, which will depend on the intended use of the steel, the molten metal can be cast into whatever shape is required or formed into ingots for future use. A recently developed process, which produces good quality steel sheets suitable for drawing, makes use of scrap steel sheet from industries where stamping operations are carried out. The steel scrap is cut into small pieces, heated to welding temperatures, and rolled into sheets. One advantage of the process is that the scrap does not have to be melted.

Some scrap iron is obtained from tin cans separated from household refuse, but the quality is not high, and there are considerable metallurgical problems in obtaining steel from this source. Both the tin coating and the lead in the solder seam are detrimental to the steelmaking process; the presence of tin tends to make the final product too brittle, while lead attacks the refractory lining of the electric arc furnace. One proposal to solve this problem and at the same time increase the amount of iron recycled is to use seamless all-steel cans, while increasing use is being made of plastic linings that burn off during recycling.

Many other metals can also be recovered from scrap. Aluminum is widely used today in the manufacture of cans, and the metal is easily recycled provided the cans can be economically separated from other refuse, though at present manual sorting is the only practical means of doing so. Lead, copper, and mercury are also recovered from scrap, as of course are precious metals such as gold and platinum.

Plastics

About 90 percent of all plastics produced today are thermoplastics, in other words, they soften on heating and harden again when cooled, and it should therefore be a simple matter to reuse the plastic in discarded plastic articles. The problem is, however, that there are many different types of thermoplastic, and they cannot normally be mixed if a good quality product is to be obtained. Consequently, if scrap plastic articles are to be recycled, they must not only be separated from other refuse but also classified according to their composition. Where a relatively large quantity of plastic waste of known composition is available, recycling is straightforward. Plastic bottles, for example, are almost always made of high-density polyethylene (HDPE) or polyethylene terephthalate (PET), and provided they can be easily sepa-

rated from other refuse, the plastic can be melted and reused. However, even within the same polymer type, there may be variations in molecular weight, depending on use, that can render the mixed material unusable for its original applications. For this reason, most plastics are recycled into less-demanding products, for example, polyethylene grocery bags are turned into flowerpots, PET bottles into fibers for stuffing pillows, and polyvinyl chloride containers into traffic cones.

After sorting, the plastic is cut or ground into chips, which are then washed to remove labels, caps, and adhesives. If the plastic is from an identifiable source, then the dried chips can be extruded into pellets for immediate reuse. Mixed-source chips undergo a variety of sorting processes based on differences in density or solubility before they are reused.

It has been found that some plastics, such as chlorinated polyethylene (CPE), are able to improve the ability of other plastics to mix with each other. Such plastics, added to scrap plastic before melting, will reduce the need for classification processes. Manufacturers are also using plastics in niche applications specifically so they can be recovered and recycled.

◀ Buy-back centers and community-based recycling centers are important means of separation at source of cans, glass, paper, and bottles. Separation is the key to successful recycling, and although various types of machine are used for separating refuse into its component materials, separation at source saves time and money. Further sorting of paper can be expensive, so it is sometimes not worthwhile collecting paper unless it can be done on a large scale.

Glass

Rejected and broken glass is called cullet, and it is used in most glassmaking processes as a component of the glass batch. Glass comprises about 6 percent of municipal waste by weight, though the proportion that is reused for new glass varies between 20 and 90 percent, depending on the country. Cullet for glassmaking should have the same composition as the glass being made, and as much as 30 percent may be used in some glass batches. It is first crushed to a size of about 3 in. (76 mm) and then weighed and added to the glass batch just as any of the other raw materials. Because the cullet must have as nearly as possible the same composition as the glass being produced, it must be separated first into its various colors. Granulated waste glass can be used as an aggregate for making road surfaces, which have proved to be much harder and longer wearing than conventional tarmac surfaces.

Organic wastes

Organic materials make up the second largest constituent of municipal waste. Food wastes, yard trimmings, and contaminated paper can all be recycled by biological decomposition into compost. Tree clippings can be shredded into chips and used as a mulch.

Organic wastes from meat or fish processing are also compostable, but because they contain valuable oils and are a source of protein, they usually undergo some form of processing to turn them into animal feed.

▲ Sampling oil from a plate and frame filter press. Machine oil can be cleaned and used again, saving up to half the cost of replacement. The cleaning of lubricating and other oils widely used in industrial machines and transport is an increasingly successful area of recycling. The cleaned oil can be used for further lubrication or as a heating fuel without prior reprocessing. If the waste oil has undergone chemical change, it will have to be reprocessed before being reused.

Other materials

In other industries materials that previously would have gone to waste are now being recycled or put to some other use. In the petroleum industry, for example, refinery effluent is treated to recover any oil products it may contain. This process not only reduces wastage of oil but also cuts down pollution. Slag from coal mines is used as a foundation material in civil engineering. Waste from the textile industry finds a variety of applications: cotton waste is used as a material for upholstery, and some is respun into thread and made into high-grade paper or turned into activated carbon, which is widely used to absorb impurities out of air and water. Rubber can be crumbed and incorporated into road-surfacing materials or destructively distilled to reclaim valuable chemicals. Recycling mineral wastes from mining processes is not economically feasible as yet because mining new ores is cheap, but at some point in the future, tailings heaps may provide a valuable source of metals.

Hazardous wastes

Recycling of hazardous materials is encouraged in most developed countries as a means of minimizing the risk of pollution from industrial or manufacturing processes. Ideally this aim is achieved by promoting practices that minimize the amount of waste generated or use cleaner or less harmful materials. Hazardous waste is strictly regulated whether it is recycled or disposed of in landfill, though incentives encourage producers to manage their wastes more effectively.

Solvents, for example, can be cleaned for reuse or used as a fuel to produce heat or electricity. Substituting a nonhazardous solvent for a hazardous one in a process could also save a company a significant amount of money in disposal and regulatory compliance costs. Waste oils are another easily recyclable substance that can be burned or rerefined. Certain materials that would not be allowed disposal in a landfill are incorporated into the manufacture of products such as asphalt or paving stones that lock the contaminant in and prevent it from leaching into the soil.

Separation

The key to the successful recycling of materials contained in refuse lies in the separation of valuable components from the main bulk of the waste. In a modern refuse processing plant, the refuse is first shredded mechanically and then dried. Next it is passed to a pyrolysis furnace, where it is heated to remove the more volatile components and convert any vegetable products into char. The pyrolysis is carried out at a temperature of between 1000 and 1500°F (538–815°C) in an atmosphere containing as little oxygen as possible so that any aluminum in the waste will remain unoxidized. After cooling, the material is passed first to a rod mill, where it is mechanically fragmented, and then onto magnetic and size separators, where ferrous metal is removed and the waste is divided into streams of large and small pieces. The stream of small pieces is passed to an air classifier, where char is removed by an air blast, and the large pieces are reduced in size by means of a rod mill. Further processing, which relies on differences in density and other properties, separates out glass, and aluminum and other nonferrous metals. The glass fraction is further separated in colored and noncolored fractions in a high-intensity magnetic separator (colored glass particles are deflected by a magnetic field, whereas clear glass particles are not). The colored glass fraction is sometimes further separated into its various colors by machinery controlled by photoelectric devices.

Gas produced by the pyrolysis process can be used as a fuel, while the heat output from incineration plants can be used for such applications as district heating and power generation. An alternative approach starts by pulverizing the refuse and passing it through a system that separates out the lighter components, mainly paper, plastics, and organic materials. These materials are then compacted into fuel pellets, which may be sold or utilized within the plant. Similarly, organic wastes can be put through a composting process to give a valuable end product.

Various types of machines are used for the separation of refuse into its component materials. In a ballistic separator, pieces of refuse of approximately equal size are thrown outward into a chamber by means of a rotor, and the heavier inorganic materials are thrown further than the lighter organic ones. In an inclined plate separator, the refuse is deposited onto an inclined conveyor moving upward. The denser materials find their way to the lower end of the conveyor despite the upward movement, while the less dense materials are carried to the top. A zig-zag separator has a vertical passage; air is blown in at the bottom and separates the heavy materials, which pass to the bottom, from the lighter ones, which are recovered at the top. The shape of the passage ensures that the refuse crosses the airstream as often as possible. Another type of separator is the fluidized-bed separator in which pieces of waste material are dropped onto a bed of particles made to act as a fluid by blowing air upward through them. The heavier pieces of refuse sink in the fluidized bed, whereas the light pieces float.

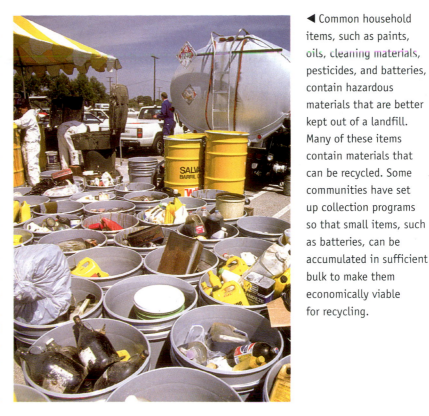

◀ Common household items, such as paints, oils, cleaning materials, pesticides, and batteries, contain hazardous materials that are better kept out of a landfill. Many of these items contain materials that can be recycled. Some communities have set up collection programs so that small items, such as batteries, can be accumulated in sufficient bulk to make them economically viable for recycling.

Encouraging recycling

Modern man produces and consumes a vast array of products every year. The comparative cheapness with which most of these products can be replaced, particularly in developed countries, has led to what has become known as the "throwaway society." However, with the costs of landfilling rising, many governments have begun to institute projects to get people to separate out the glass, paper, metal, and plastic from their domestic refuse so that it can either be disposed of at special collection points or picked up by the refuse service. Some companies also operate buyback incentives for plastics or glass or run deposit and refund programs.

The recycling loop is closed by encouraging people to buy recycled products. People may not realize that an item has been recycled—motor oil, egg boxes, synthetic carpets, cereal cartons, and car bumpers are typical examples of products that contain a recycled material. Many manufacturers indicate whether a product is recyclable or has a recycled component by the use of an approved symbol that affirms the environmental marketing claims of the manufacturer. Cutting the amount of packaging around goods and promoting the reuse of plastic bags and cardboard boxes is also helping to reduce the amount of waste being dumped every year.

 SEE ALSO: ALUMINUM • GLASS • IRON AND STEEL • PAPER MANUFACTURE • PLASTICS PROCESSING • WASTE DISPOSAL

Reflector

While all surfaces can be considered to be reflectors in the sense that they will reflect some light, their reflecting ability varies from almost zero for a matt black surface to nearly 100 percent for a highly polished mirror. A beam of light striking a rough, unpolished surface will be scattered in many different directions, and therefore, if an image of the light source can be seen at all, it will be very diffuse. A flat mirror, on the other hand, will reflect a beam of light in a single direction, the incident beam and the reflected beam making equal angles to a line perpendicular to the mirror surface at the point of reflection. As a result, the image of the light source seen in the mirror will be very sharp.

Vehicle reflectors

For many applications, specialized reflectors are used that are able to reflect light back along its original path. This type of reflector is particularly useful for making road signs and for fixing to the back of road vehicles. These reflectors are usually made of transparent plastic, which is often colored and formed into a sheet having a smooth front surface and a back surface impressed with a pattern of prisms. Light enters the front surface of the reflector, it is reflected by two of the prismatic surfaces at the back of the reflector (a process called total internal reflection), and it then reemerges from the front surface in the same direction as it entered. At whatever angle the light strikes the front surface of the reflector, it will always be reflected back along its original path or at a predetermined angle to it, depending on the geometry of the prismatic back surface. Road

◀ Reflective sheet materials, normally of plastic, are ideal for traffic signs because they have the property of retro reflection (they reflect light back in the direction of its source).

paints also include reflective glass beads to make the markings more visible at night and during periods of poor visibility.

Laser reflectors

Where laser beams are used to measure distances in applications such as surveying, it is often necessary to have a reflector that can be used as a target for alignment. The simplest reflector of this type is a transparent pyramid, or corner prism, which has four identical triangular faces. A beam entering the pyramid through its base will always be reflected back in the same direction regardless of the angle of entry. Usually, however, a reflective target will consist of many small corner prisms fixed to a flat support.

A French-built laser reflector was mounted on the Soviet lunar vehicle *Lunokhod 1*, which was landed in the Sea of Rains on November 17, 1970. A ruby laser mounted in a conventional optical telescope on Earth was aimed at the reflector. By measuring the time taken by the light beam, it was possible to determine accurately the distance between the point of projection on Earth and the reflector on the Moon.

▶ In a reflex reflector for use on a road vehicle, the incident beam is refracted at the clear, front surface and then reflected twice at the mirrored back surface to suit car and commercial vehicle drivers.

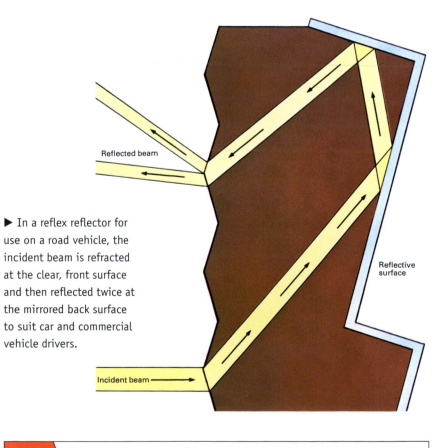

Reflected beam

Reflective surface

Incident beam

SEE ALSO: LIGHT AND OPTICS • MIRROR • PRISM • ROAD SYSTEMS AND TRAFFIC CONTROL

Refrigeration

The development of mechanical refrigeration systems began in the early 19th century and arose mainly from the needs of meat producers in the United States, South America, Australia, and New Zealand to keep their produce from spoiling during shipment to their export markets in Europe.

The first known demonstration of refrigeration was carried out in 1748 at the University of Glasgow by the Scottish physician William Cullen. This technique worked by allowing ethyl ether to boil in a partial vacuum. Following this demonstration, however, there was little experimentation until the 1830s, when many systems were devised that used the cooling effect produced by the expansion of compressed air or carbon dioxide or by the evaporation of volatile fluids, such as ammonia. In 1844, the American physician and inventor John Gorrie made a machine that used vapor as the refrigerant. This machine was never produced commercially, but its basic principles are still in common use today.

The first meat-freezing plant was built in Australia at Darling Harbour, Sydney, in 1861 by a businessman, Thomas Sutcliffe Mort, who later founded the New South Wales Food and Ice Company. This company had its own slaughterhouse, freezing plant, and cold store and used an ammonia compression freezing system.

By 1870, ships were successfully transporting chilled beef, cooled to one or two degrees below freezing point, in insulated holds cooled by ice mixed with salt (a technique that lowers the freezing point of ice and hence the temperature), but this method could be used only on the relatively short trips from the United States to Europe. The

▶ Water vapor and carbon dioxide freeze onto the delivery pipe as a bulk chemical tanker is being filled with liquid nitrogen.

first ship to be fitted with a mechanical refrigeration system for carrying chilled beef was the *Frigorifique*, which made an experimental run from Buenos Aires to Rouen in 1877. The experiment was not entirely successful, and the meat deteriorated during the journey. In the same year, however, the *Paraguay*, fitted with an ammonia compression system, successfully carried a cargo of frozen mutton from Buenos Aires to Le Havre.

The development of refrigeration systems was greatly assisted by the introduction of reliable electric motors and public electricity supplies. The first machines for homes came on the market shortly after World War I, and deep-freeze units for home use were introduced in the mid-1930s.

Basic principles

The basic principles of refrigeration are derived from the behavior of a suitable fluid when it changes its state from liquid to gas or from gas to liquid. Compressing a gas causes its temperature to rise, and if its temperature is then reduced without reducing the pressure, the gas will liquefy. On the other hand, reducing the pressure of a liquefied gas will make it vaporize.

In a refrigeration system, the refrigerant or working fluid is evaporated in the evaporator, which is placed within the refrigerated compartment, and the latent heat is drawn from within the compartment, thus reducing its temperature. The working fluid then passes to a condenser unit placed outside the refrigerated compartment, where it is condensed back to a liquid. On con-

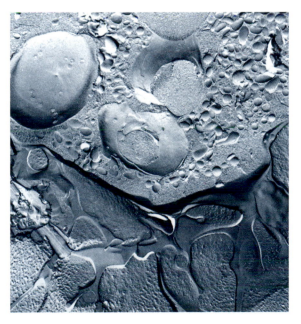

◀ A freeze-fracture replica of human red blood cells. Freeze-etching is a technique used in biological electron microscopy, enabling scientists to see cell structure with great precision.

densing, it releases its latent heat, which is the heat it absorbed from the refrigerated compartment. As the cycle continues, the refrigerant removes heat from the compartment and releases it to the surrounding atmosphere.

The temperature within the refrigerated area is regulated by a thermostat that controls the rate of circulation of the refrigerant and thus the amount of cooling.

Absorption systems

The absorption system uses ammonia as the working fluid. In its simplest form, it operates as follows. A strong mixture of ammonia and water (ammonia liquor) is heated in a boiler or generator by an electric heating element or a gas or oil burner. The ammonia, being more volatile than the water, is driven off as vapor and passed to a condenser unit. As more of the vapor is boiled off, the pressure in the condenser increases until it is high enough to make the ammonia condense into liquid ammonia.

The liquid ammonia is then passed through an expansion valve, where the pressure is reduced by about 85 percent, and into the evaporator, which is within the refrigerated area. As it enters the evaporator the liquid evaporates, absorbing heat from its surroundings and so reducing the temperature. The other end of the evaporator tube leads into

the absorber (outside the refrigerated area), which contains weak ammonia liquor circulated there from the boiler via a heat exchanger. The ammonia is absorbed into the liquor, creating low pressure in the evaporator, and the strong liquor thus formed is passed through the heat exchanger, where it absorbs some of the heat from the weak liquor leaving the boiler. The strong liquor then goes back into the boiler to continue the cycle. Circulation of the refrigerant may be by gravity and thermal siphon effects, particularly on gas- or oil-powered machines, or it may be assisted by a small electric pump.

Compression systems

A compression system uses a compressor unit to circulate the refrigerant. This unit may be belt driven by an electric motor, or it may be an integral unit containing an electric motor with the compressor fitted to the end of its shaft.

The low-pressure side of the compressor is connected to the evaporator, and the high-pressure side to the condenser. The high-pressure refrigerant vapor from the compressor is relatively hot and is condensed by maintaining the high pressure and reducing the temperature. The temperature reduction is achieved by cooling the condenser either by using a fan driven by the compressor motor to force air through it or by

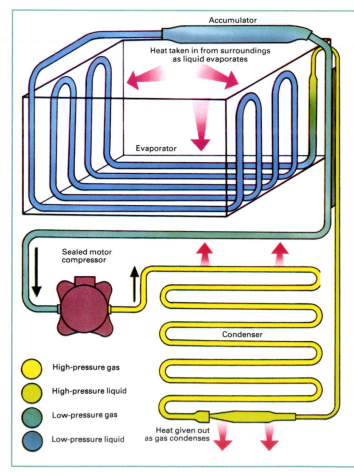

Accumulator

Heat taken in from surroundings as liquid evaporates

Evaporator

Sealed motor compressor

Condenser

● High-pressure gas

● High-pressure liquid

● Low-pressure gas

● Low-pressure liquid

Heat given out as gas condenses

COMPRESSION REFRIGERATOR

In a compression refrigerator, a compressed gas is allowed to evaporate and absorb heat from the surrounding environment, thus creating a cooling effect. First, the refrigerant passes through a compressor, where it becomes a high-pressure gas, and then into a condenser, found on the back of domestic refrigerators. The condenser is made of a long, winding tube that enables some of the heat of the compressed gas to be lost to the surrounding air. After passing through an expansion valve, the gas enters the refrigerator and travels through another series of winding tubes, where it evaporates and in the process absorbs heat from the surrounding air. As the gas evaporates it becomes a low-pressure liquid and passes out of the refrigerator through an accumulator, where it becomes a low-pressure gas. It then returns to the compressor, and so the cycle is repeated.

using a water-cooled condenser. On small systems, the heat may simply be dissipated to the atmosphere by means of cooling fins.

The refrigerant passes to the evaporator through a valve that maintains the pressure difference between the condenser and the evaporator. The refrigerant is drawn through the evaporator by the low pressure created by the compressor, and as it evaporates, it absorbs heat from the refrigerated area. In a home refrigerator, the evaporator tubes are usually built into the freezer compartment, the cooling effect spreading throughout the cabinet by convection currents set up in the air within it.

Refrigerants

A number of fluids have been used as refrigerants in compression systems, including carbon dioxide (CO_2) and sulfur dioxide (SO_2), but until relatively recently, the most widely used were the group of halogenated hydrocarbons known as freons, including freon-12 (dichlorodifluoromethane, CCl_2F_2), freon-11 (trichloromonofluoromethane, CCl_3F), freon-113 (trichlorotrifluoroethane, $C_2Cl_3F_3$), and freon-114 (dichlorotetrafluoroethane, $C_2Cl_2F_4$). Freons, however, are now known to cause damage to the ozone layer in Earth's upper atmosphere. Consequently, many alternative refrigerants are now used, such as

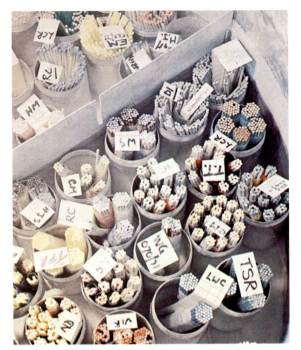

◀ Straws of frozen bull semen, stored in containers frozen by liquid nitrogen, allow a single bull to fertilize around 2,000 cows a year.

those made from hydrochlorofluorocarbons and hydrofluorocarbons. These replacements, however, also cause some environmental damage and are in turn going to be phased out in the United States and other countries. The next stage in refrigerant technology is the development of nonchlorine refrigerants that cause no damage to the ozone layer at all.

Applications

For home, catering, and retailing use, both absorption and compression refrigerators are widely used. For deep-freeze units, however, the more powerful and efficient compression system is always used. One advantage of the absorption type is that it is quieter than a compression system and can be made with no moving parts, but its use is generally restricted to small units.

Ice rinks are frozen by circulating the refrigerant through a system of copper pipes beneath the ice surface. The first rink was built in 1876 by John Gamgee in London, England. The ice was produced by a mixture of glycerine and water circulating in copper pipes and chilled by the evaporation of ether.

Freeze-drying is a development of vacuum drying, whereby food is frozen and then dried in a vacuum chamber. In this process, ice changes directly to vapor with no intermediate liquid stage. Whatever has been frozen remains a light, porous solid, retaining its original shape, color, odor, and flavor.

FACT FILE

- In 1926, the Dutch physicist Kamerlingh Onnes achieved for the first time a temperature lower than any found in nature. The lowest natural temperature is the 3 K (3 degrees on the Kelvin scale) of cosmic background radiation. Onnes achieved 0.7 K by employing a great battery of pumps on a liquid helium bath.

- Tuna clippers were the first vessels to freeze fish successfully at sea for commercial sale. From experiments that they made in the late 1930s, the tuna fishers devised a way of freezing their catch in refrigerated brine tanks.

- In 1873, an Australian newspaper editor and inventor, James Harrison, held a public banquet in Melbourne at which the meat, poultry, and fish had all been frozen for at least six months with the aid of his ether-compression ice-making machine.

SEE ALSO: COMPRESSOR AND PUMP • CRYOGENICS • FOOD PRESERVATION AND PACKAGING • FOOD PROCESSING • GAS LAWS

Refueling, In-flight

Air-to-air refueling allows aircraft to increase the distances that they can fly. It allows the military to be significantly more flexible in how they deploy and use air power in tactical and strategic roles, both operationally and economically.

In concept, in-flight refueling is not new. Early forms were used in the United States between 1923 and 1934 to enable endurance records to be set. The first British experiments were made by Squadron Leader (later Air Marshal) Richard Atcherley. A grapnel on the end of a line was deployed from a receiver aircraft, and the tanker above and slightly behind trailed a weighted line. Weaving from side to side, the tanker brought its line into contact with the receiver's line. When it was hooked, the receiver's operator pulled it in. The weighted line attached to the tanker's refueling hose was hauled down and connected to the aircraft's fuel system, and the fuel was transferred. The hose was then disconnected and hauled back into the tanker, and contact between the flights was broken off.

In 1934 Flight Refuelling Limited was set up in Britain by Sir Alan Cobham to carry out experimental and development work. The first scheduled flight-refueled service was set up in 1939 to carry mail between London and New York. The aircraft were Short C-class flying boats, and the tanker aircraft Handley Page Harrows, capable of carrying 1,000 gals. (4,546 l) of fuel. The first flight was on August 5, 1939, and 16 Atlantic crossings were achieved before the outbreak of World War II meant the service was discontinued.

The flying-boom system

The advent of the single-seat jet fighter presented the problem of establishing contact with a receiver in which an operator could not be employed. To meet this requirement, the probe-and-drogue system of flight refueling was introduced in 1949. Today it is used as standard practice by all the major military powers apart from the U.S. Strategic Air Command, which uses the Boeing flying-boom method. This method calls for an operator in the tanker aircraft to fly the telescopic boom into a location on the receiving aircraft, with the pilot of the receiver keeping station under the command of the boom operator. High flow rates are possible with this system; the boom on the McDonnell Douglas KC-10A Extender tanker aircraft has a flow rate of 1,500 gals. per min. (about 10,000 lbs./min). The KC-10A is also equipped with an 80 ft. (24 m) long hose for probe-and-drogue refueling of U.S. Navy and Marine Corps aircraft. Fuel is carried in rubberized fabric cells in the lower fuselage, which are interconnected with the aircraft's main fuel supply to give a total capacity of over 36,000 gals. (136,000 l). For maximum versatility the KC-10A is itself equipped with a receiver system so that it can be refueled in flight if required.

Probe-and-drogue system

In the probe-and-drogue system, the tanker trails a hose terminating in a reception coupling and drogue, while the receiver has a nozzle attached to a probe mounted on the nose or wing leading

▼ A U.S. Hercules refueling two Skyhawks through nose cones. The most common type of Hercules tanker is the KC-130F operated by the U.S. Marine Corps.

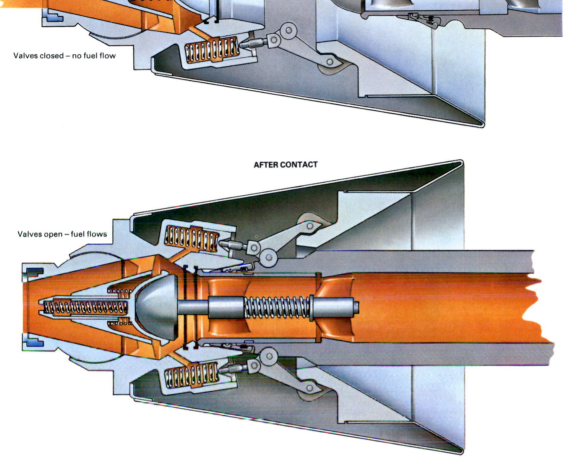

BEFORE CONTACT

Drogue reception coupling

Probe nozzle

Valves closed – no fuel flow

◄ The drogue coupling and probe nozzle of a refueling system before contact. The drogue is attached to the end of a hose trailed by the tanker aircraft above.

AFTER CONTACT

Valves open – fuel flows

◄ The drogue and probe after contact. The probe is mounted on the receiving aircraft. As the probe nozzle contacts the drogue, it compresses the springs that open the valve and allows the fuel to flow.

edge. The receiver flies the probe nozzle into the conical drogue while overtaking at 2.5–6 mph (3.7–9.3 km/h). The nozzle automatically opens its valve and that in the reception coupling, enabling the passage of fuel. On completion, the receiver pilot has only to drop back until the hose reaches its full trail position, when the probe nozzle withdraws from the reception coupling.

The tanker equipment is automatic apart from simple system selection by the tanker operator. It is best illustrated by the Mark 20 refueling pod, which can be mounted to a fighter to convert it into a tanker and can be used on single-seater planes, in which the pilot operates the tanker equipment. The Mk 20 pod has a transfer rate of up to 1,200 lbs. per min. (544 kg/min) using a 50 ft. (15.25 m) length of 1.5 in (3.8 cm) diameter hose with a working pressure of 50 lbs. per sq. in. (3.5 kg/cm²). Special-purpose tanker aircraft,

such as the British Aerospace VC10 used by the Royal Air Force, have Mk32/2800 pods mounted beneath the wings and provide a flow rate of 2,800 lbs. per min. (1,270 kg/min).

A failsafe philosophy is applied in the design of the hose unit so that, in the event of any single failure, the unit will discontinue fuel transfer and apply the hose unit arrester mechanism or wind in the hose. The main considerations are the safety of the two aircraft during the transfer of fuel. In the event of hydraulic failure, a secondary compressed air system is provided to allow the hose to be fully trailed and jettisoned—an electric failure will cause the hose to rewind and stow itself.

SEE ALSO: AIRCRAFT DESIGN • COMPRESSOR AND PUMP • FLOWMETER • GAS TURBINE • HYDRAULICS • V/STOL AIRCRAFT • VALVE, MECHANICAL

Relativity

The theory of relativity is divided into special and general theories and generalizes the laws of classical physics to situations in which high velocities are involved and the curvature of space near massive objects becomes apparent. Historically, the Special Theory of Relativity came first, in 1905, followed in 1916 by the general theory.

The Special Theory was developed independently by a French mathematician, Henri Poincaré, in Paris and the German-born physicist Albert Einstein in Zürich. During the few years before 1905, it was becoming clear that the old ether theory of electric and magnetic fields was becoming inadequate. An experiment carried out in 1887 by the U.S. physicists A. A. Michelson and E. W. Morley had failed to detect Earth's motion relative to the supposed ether, which was thought to be the medium that transmitted the vibrations of light and radio waves. The difference in the speed of light caused by Earth's motion through the ether ought to have been detectable. The Michelson–Morley experiment's failure, however, provided a startling piece of evidence: it showed that the speed of light is the same, even if the source of the light is moving toward or away from the observer at a large fraction of that velocity. This observation led to the even more surprising predictions of relativity.

Poincaré claimed that motion through the ether could never be detected. He introduced the principle of relativity, which stated that "the laws of physical phenomena must be the same for a fixed observer as for an observer who has a uniform motion of translation relative to him so that we have not and cannot possibly have any means of discovering whether we are being carried along in such a motion." During the next year Poincaré developed this new physics, while at the same time, Albert Einstein, then an unknown clerk in the Swiss Patent Office, was toying with ideas of space and time that led to the same results, the theory we now call special relativity. Today the analysis of Einstein is the one normally given in the text books and is the one to be followed in the next few pages.

Synchronizing clocks

Einstein began by asking how we can say that two events took place at the same time. This question is important, because it takes time for light to travel from an event to us, and thus, the time when we see something happening is later than when it actually happened. Of course, for nearby events, this correction is normally insignificant, but for very distant events, it is crucial for accuracy.

One way of transferring our local measurement of time is simply to use our own clock and to send out light signals to be reflected back to us from any distant object; this is known as the radar method. Alternatively, we could arrange for a network of clocks to be arranged throughout space, each clock synchronized to agree with our own, and note the time on the clock situated at the same place as the event whose time is to be recorded. But in order to follow this method, we have to synchronize the clocks to make sure they agree with our clock, and again we have to use light signals to set these clocks.

This process consists of sending out a signal that is reflected back by the distant clock and returns to the original clock. The distant clock is then synchronized with our clock if the time on the distant clock when it received the signal is halfway between the time of emission and the time of reception on our clock. If a signal was emitted at 01.00 on our clock and returned at 03.00 on our clock, then the distant clock is synchronized if it read 02.00 when it received the signal. In making this rule, or Einstein convention, as it is called, for setting clocks, we are requiring the velocity of light to be constant, the same in both outward and return journeys. Besides setting clocks by this radar method, it is also possible to measure distance in terms of time and the value of the velocity of light, 186,000 miles per second

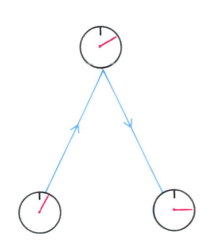

◀ Light takes an hour to travel from one clock to the other. The distance is measured by multiplying half the travel time of the round trip by the velocity of light.

(299,700 km/s), which is normally written as *c*. This formula,

$$distance = \frac{(time\ of\ reception - time\ of\ emission)}{2} \times c$$

is expressed in light seconds or light hours but can easily be turned into other units. In the example we have just used, the distance is one light hour, or 669,600,000 miles (1.13 billion km)—in the Solar System, this distance is equal to the distance between Earth and a point between Jupiter and Saturn.

Combining these rules for distance and time measurement with the principle of relativity—that the laws of physics should be the same for all uniformly moving observers—Einstein then showed that clocks synchronized for one observer were not synchronized for another moving past him or her with a uniform velocity; that is, synchronization is relative, not absolute. Time as measured by a moving observer must go at a different rate from that measured by a stationary observer.

For example, imagine that observer O has his own clock, and at the moment he passes observer A, he sets it to zero to agree with A's clock. From A, a light signal is sent out when A's clock reads 1 second. Suppose this signal reaches O when his clock reads 2, and it is then reflected back to A and then back to O. This situation is best under-

stood with the help of a space–time diagram, showing the change of distance with time.

The principle of relativity can now be used to find the time of arrival of the signal back at A. The time between O and A being together and A sending out the signal was 1 second, and the time between O and A being together and O receiving the signal is twice 1, or 2 seconds. Any relationship between O and A is equally true the other way around: a signal sent from O 1 second after A and O were together reaches A at twice 1, or 2 seconds. The signal that leaves O at 2 seconds on O's clock reaches A at twice 2, or 4 seconds, on A's clock. By the Einstein rule, A says that the signal reached O halfway between emission (at 1 second) and reception (at 4 seconds), or at a time of 2½ seconds. This is the time that would be on a clock at the reflection that was synchronized with A; but O's clock read 2 at this reflection, so O and A associate a different time with the reflection by O. O's time is ⅘ of A's time. Using the same signals, we can calculate the velocity of O relative to A. Since A finds the round-trip travel time to be 3 seconds, the signal traveled a distance of 1½ light seconds, or 1½ *c*-sec, from A to O, and it got there at a time of 2½ seconds. O therefore traveled 1½ *c*-sec in 2½ seconds, so his velocity is

$$velocity = \frac{distance}{time} = \frac{1½\,c\text{-sec}}{2½\,sec} = \frac{3}{5}\,c$$

that is, ⅗ the velocity of light.

At first sight, it seems strange that O's time is slower than A's, since by the principle of relativity, what is true between A and O is equally true between O and A. This assertion is indeed so, for if the light signal reaching A at 4 seconds is reflected back to O, it reaches him at time 8 on O's clock (again the factor of two). So O calculates the time of arrival of the signal at A by taking it halfway between emission at 2 seconds on O's clock and reception at 8 seconds on O's clock, namely 5 seconds; but A's clock reads 4 seconds, or ⅘ of O's time, just as it was the other way around. For both experimenters, the moving experimenter's clock goes slow compared with the time each assigns to the event. In fact, a device for remembering this crucial idea is the phrase "moving clocks run slow." This idea strikes many as paradoxical, for how can O be slow compared with A and A slow compared with O? There is no paradox, however; we are not comparing O's and A's clocks, but rather O's clock with A's assigned time or synchronized clocks and A's clock with O's assigned time or synchronized clocks. The relativity principle requires that the relationship between A and O be symmetrical, and it is.

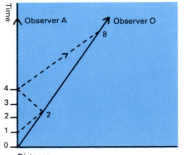

◀ A graph of time against distance traveled for two observers. An object traveling at an unvarying speed is represented by a straight sloping line: its slope indicates the speed.

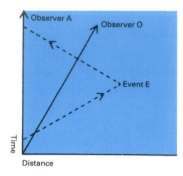

◄ Observer O travels at a fraction of the speed of light (the slope of the dotted line). When A and O compare their timings of the light traveling to a point or event at E and its reflection, they will differ.

While we have just calculated a particular example for a velocity of ⅗ c, it is possible to work out the results for any velocity, v. Signals emitted 1 second apart are then received by the other observer at intervals given by

$$\sqrt{\frac{1 + v/c}{1 - v/c}} \text{ secs.}$$

For v/c = ⅗, the result is just the factor of two that we found. The time assigned by the stationary clock and the time measured by the moving clock are found to be related by the expression

$$\frac{\text{time measured on moving clock}}{\text{time assigned by stationary clock}} = \frac{1}{\sqrt{1 - v^2/c^2}}$$

Evidence

There is now a wealth of experimental data that supports the slowing down of moving clocks, or time dilation as it is called. The simplest comes from subatomic particles called mu mesons, or simply, muons, which are produced about 6 miles (10 km) up in Earth's atmosphere, where high-energy particles from outer space known as cosmic rays smash into the atoms of the atmosphere. These mu mesons are well known from laboratory experiments, and they are unstable, living only about two-millionths of a second before they decay into other particles. Even traveling at the speed of light, they could travel only about one-third of a mile before decaying; yet we see them at Earth's surface. But as they do travel with velocities close to the velocity of light, their aging is slowed down. If their speed were ⅗ c, they would live for 20 percent longer, but if they were moving at 99.9 percent of the speed of light they would live for over 20 times longer, thus allowing them sufficient time to reach Earth's surface.

Lorentz transformations

The fundamental result of special relativity is known as the Lorentz transformation, which relates the measurements of distance as well as time by two observers moving with any speed, v. We can understand this by a calculation similar to the one that gave the time dilation, where we have two observers, A and O, moving relative to each other with velocity v and having set their clocks to zero when they passed each other. Observer A now sends out a signal to be reflected back from an event, E. On its route, the signal passes O, is reflected by E, passes O on the way back, and finally reaches A again. Observer A calculates the distance and time, say l and t, of E using his or her clock readings. O does a similar calculation using his or her clock and obtains values L and T, but because the rate of O's clock is known if the velocity is known, L and T can be expressed in terms of l and t. If this rearrangement is done, we should find that

$$L = \frac{l + vt}{\sqrt{1 - v^2/c^2}} \qquad T = \frac{t - vl/c^2}{\sqrt{1 - v^2/c^2}}$$

These are the Lorentz transformations, which were first developed by Poincaré, who corrected an error in earlier calculations by Lorentz. The transformations are represented by matrix arithmetic, by which inertial reference frames with space-time coordinates can be manipulated in relativistic terms.

▶ Mu mesons can reach Earth's surface despite their short lives because their high speed makes time run slower for them.

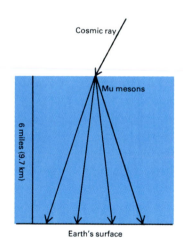

Another important result is the addition of velocities. Both Poincaré and Einstein realized that the addition law of velocities had to be changed so that the result of adding velocities below the velocity of light always gave a velocity less than that of light. Imagine, for example, that beside observer A, there is observer O moving with ⅗ c in one direction and observer Q moving with ⅗ c in the opposite direction. If simple addition were correct, Q would be moving with a velocity ⁶⁄₅ c relative to O, but this cannot be the case, since a light signal traveling at speed c can pass from O to A, and the same signal can pass

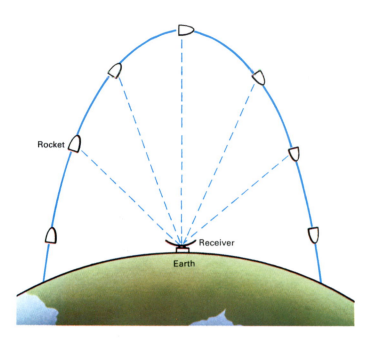

from A to Q, so O can communicate with Q. He could not do this if their separation velocity were ⅞ c, as the light signal would not reach him. The velocity of O relative to Q is calculated by considering a signal that leaves O at time 1 second on O's clock, reaches A at time 2 seconds, goes on to Q, getting there at time 4 seconds on Q's clock, getting back to A at 8 seconds and on to O at time 16 seconds on O's clock. O now calculates the distance and time of the reflection at Q as

$$\text{Distance} = \left\{\frac{16-1}{2}\right\} c\text{-sec} = \frac{15}{2} c\text{-sec}$$

$$\text{Time} = \left\{\frac{16-1}{2}\right\} \text{sec} = \frac{17}{2} \text{sec}$$

The velocity of Q relative to O is therefore given by dividing the distance by the time, giving the result ¹⁵⁄₁₇ c.

It can usually be said that, if A has a velocity v relative to O and Q has a velocity V relative to A, the velocity of Q relative to O is

▲ By launching a rocket containing the most accurate clock available, a hydrogen maser, and comparing its rate by radar signals with a similar ground-based clock, the gravitational redshift, or slowing down of clocks, can be measured.

▶ As the velocity increases so does the mass. Although negligible at speeds below half that of light, the correction then increases rapidly.

◀ The times shown are those on observer O's clock. To find the time of the reflection at Q, the average of the starting and final times must be taken.

$$U = \frac{V + v}{1 + vV/c^2}$$

This result was first discovered by Poincaré and then independently by Einstein.

Since velocities do not simply add together as in prerelativistic Newtonian physics, some correction to this theory is necessary, because the continued application of a force cannot accelerate a body beyond the speed of light. In Newton's theory, the momentum of a body (its mass multiplied by its velocity) is what changes when a force acts, and if the velocity is not to increase beyond c, then the mass must vary with velocity, becoming larger and larger as the speed approaches that of light. A simple way of looking at this theory is to consider a shell fired into armor plating and measuring how far it penetrates. This penetration is the same for an observer standing with the gun as for another observer moving with a large velocity perpendicular to the line of fire. The moving observer does not measure the same velocity for the shell, however. His clocks are slowed down, so he measures a velocity lower by the factor $\sqrt{1 - v^2/c^2}$.

It also follows from the correction to Newtonian physics that mass and energy are not

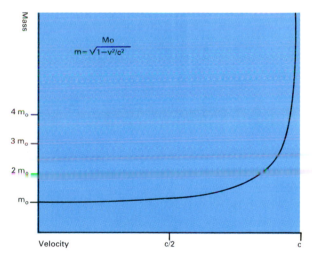

separate quantities but are essentially the same thing. This relation is expressed by the formula $E = mc^2$.

The energy E is the mass (which varies with velocity) multiplied by the square of the velocity of light. Mass, for example, is converted into energy inside the Sun and stars; to keep the Sun shining, 44 million kilograms of mass are turned into energy every second. In most cases, only a small fraction of mass can be converted into energy, as the reactions are very inefficient, but when an elementary particle collides with its antiparticle, such as an electron with a positron, their mass is converted entirely into radiant energy.

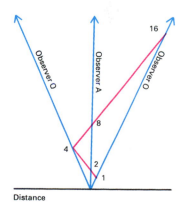

Additional insights into Einstein's Special Theory of Relativity were offered by the Russian-born German mathematical physicist Hermann Minkowski, who proposed that space and time constitute a four-dimensional continuum. This new understanding of the relationship between space and time, now often referred to as the Minkowski universe, has been important in the development of relativity theory.

General theory of relativity

The general theory of relativity, published in 1916, is a theory of gravitation developed by Albert Einstein with the help of his friend Marcel Grossman, a mathematician. Newton's understanding of gravitation required that the gravitational force acted instantaneously, but in the theory of relativity, nothing can travel faster than the speed of light. Einstein realized that a gravitational field produces effects equivalent to acceleration and, by studying the effects of acceleration in special relativity, was led to generalize the theory to include gravitational fields. As acceleration affects the measurement of time and distance in special relativity, so too do gravitational fields. As a result, the geometry found near gravitating bodies is not quite the classical geometry of the ancient Greeks, called Euclidean geometry. Einstein suggested that space–time is in fact curved and that, owing to gravitation, the shortest route between two points is not a straight line but the straightest curve possible—a geodesic.

Implications and evidence

Einstein predicted various phenomena as a result of the general theory of relativity. Among them was the change in wavelength of light toward the red end of the spectrum (called a redshift) as a result of the gravitational field around the light source; he also noted that this shift is proportional to the strength of the gravitational field. This phenomena has been observed in stars called white dwarves, which have very large gravitational fields. Another consequence of general relativity is the bending of light by large gravitational fields. This field may emanate from a source such as a star or a whole galaxy and, in the case of the latter, the size of the gravitational field may cause the light from a star to follow more than one optical path—known as gravitational lensing—resulting in multiple images of the same star. Evidence for the bending of light by gravitational fields was found only a couple of years after Einstein presented his theory, while evidence for gravitational lensing by galaxies began to appear in the 1980s. Other implications of the general theory, such as the existence of gravity waves, are

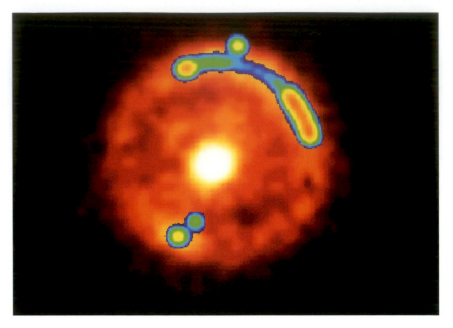

yet to be proven to the satisfaction of physicists, but research is being carried out in this area by studying the loss of energy from binary pulsars. Results seem to show that pulsars lose energy at the rate predicted by the theory of gravity waves, but more research is required before certainty is reached.

Beyond relativity

Einstein was one of the first to attempt to unite all the known forces into a single unified theory. The main difficulty for physicists has been the inclusion of gravity within unified field theories. Recent developments include string theory, which proposes that all particles, such as quarks and electrons, are made of vibrating strings, the different particles being made by different vibration frequencies. String theory has been able to include gravitation, but unfortunately, there are five different string theories available, all of which display mathematical consistency. Efforts have been made to unite these theories into a single framework called M-theory (the M either stands for mother of all theories or mystery). Much work is being carried out in this area by mathematical physicists who believe that each of the five string theories merely displays different parts of a much larger theory that relates all of the four forces found in nature—weak, strong, gravitational, and electromagnetic forces. One of the more surprising elements to this theory is that it proposes a universe made of 10 or 11 dimensions, with the extra dimensions curled up very tightly, making it impossible for us to observe them.

▲ This combined image, formed from radio and infrared data, shows Einstein rings caused by gravitational lensing, demonstrating how light can be bent by a strong gravitational field. This phenomenon was predicted by Einstein's general theory of relativity.

 SEE ALSO: BLACK HOLE • COSMOLOGY • ELECTROMAGNETIC RADIATION • ENERGY, MASS, AND WEIGHT • GRAVITY • NEWTON'S LAWS • TIME

Remote Handling

Remote-handling devices, or manipulators, enable an operator to handle or work on an object while being separated from it. Remote handling may be necessary because an object is out of reach, as in underwater salvage and space vehicles operations. Also, it may be dangerous to approach the material being handled because of radioactivity or toxicity or because the object is suspected of containing explosives.

Long reachers

In the simplest case, where the user needs only an extension of normal reach, tongs between 20 and 118 in. (50–300 cm) long and of lightweight tubular construction suffice. A simple hand grip is connected by a tensioned wire running the length of the tube to a spring-loaded claw at the remote end. Additional movements may include the ability to rotate or tilt the claw, to adjust jaw-opening limits, and to lock the jaws.

In transferring radiochemicals, for instance, from one safe container to another, where partial shielding has to be interposed to protect the operator, long-reaching tools may suffice, especially if they are angled so that the operator can work "over the wall" with them while viewing his or her work through a mirror or lead-glass window. Simple long-reaching tools can also be used for safe handling of, for example, spent nuclear fuel rods or large industrial gamma-ray sources under 16 to 20 ft. (5–6 m) of water, where they are clearly visible and can be transferred easily between transit containers or rearranged in storage racks.

"Through the wall" tools

Where the work requires full radiation shielding, whether by a sheet of Plexiglas or by 2 to 10 in. (5–25 cm) of lead bricks, it is usual to employ tools mounted on straight rods passing through ball and socket joints built into the cell wall. The operator actuates the tool by a pistol-grip handle, and by moving the handle, he or she can move and operate the tool at will anywhere within the shielded area. It is also possible to select any one of a range of interchangeable tool heads from a storage rack in the cell and clip it to the actuating rod without breaking the radiation barrier.

▲ Intensely radioactive materials are examined in caves that have concrete walls more than 3 ft. (1 m) thick. In this situation, a master-slave manipulator faithfully reproduces the movements of the operator's hand via the slave tool head. Here Mk II gas-cooled reactor fuel elements are examined in the Active Handling Building at the atomic power plant in Winfrith, Scotland.

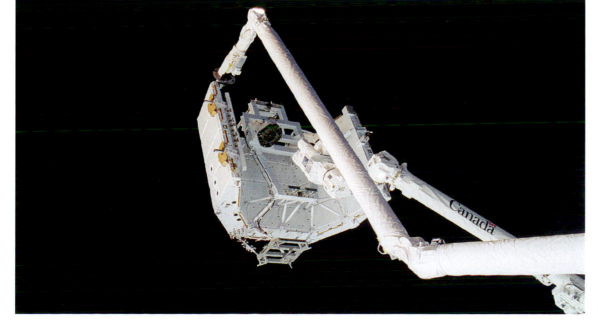

◄ The robotic arm of the space shuttle *Endeavour* takes the launch cradle from the robotic arm of the International Space Station. Both arms were being controlled by operators from the safety of the interiors of the two vessels.

Objects may be gripped and moved, rotated, cut, drilled, filed, or shaken, and small power-driven tools or engineering test equipment may even be used in the cell. If the cell walls are 4 in. (10 cm) or more thick, the ball joints are usually lubricated by compressed air fed in at the lower part of the bearing surface. This air takes the weight of the ball and provides almost frictionless movement of the tool. The operator normally views the work in progress through lead-glass windows that are thicker than the walls of the cell.

Master-slave manipulators

Where the separation between the operator and the work is great, as in heavily shielded radioactive work, master-slave systems, which reproduce the movements of the operator's hand via the slave tool head in the radiation area, are used. Intricate laboratory or workshop operations and engineering tests can be performed on dangerously radioactive specimens with complete safety.

In one widely used design, a telescopic arm hanging from a pivoted joint above the operating area terminates in a universal wrist joint that carries the operator's hand grip. The latter can be operated and closed, pivoted, twisted, and moved bodily in any direction. All these movements are mechanically transmitted, usually by tensioned steel tapes running over pulleys, to another telescopic arm, which transmits the operator's arm and hand movements through another wrist joint to the slave tool head in the radiation area.

The slave tool head consists of a simple pair of parallel-faced grippers that reproduce the grasp of the operator's hand and onto which can be locked any one of a choice of interchangeable hand or powered tools.

Care is taken to minimize friction and backlash in all mechanical movements, to provide adequate feedback or feel to the operator, and to ensure that the different hand movements do not interfere with one another (for instance, a vertical movement of the hand must not affect the tilt or grip of the tool). Additional powered or servo-assisted movements of the tool head may be provided. Glass-walled tanks filled with zinc bromide (a heavy transparent liquid) and about as thick as the concrete walls, serve as windows. Sometimes, where the situation demands, radiation-resistant closed-circuit television is used.

Advanced systems

More advanced remote handling and control systems, often using electronic or fluidic controls and with electromagnetic, hydraulic, or pneumatic actuators, have been developed for a wide variety of applications. For example, the space

▲ The Wheelbarrow, a remote-controlled bomb-disposal device used by the British army, has a small high-mobility tracked chassis controlled from a safe distance by means of electric impulses directed along wires to the vehicle. The operator can see what is in front of the vehicle by means of a television camera, which transmits the image via a control lead to a monitor.

shuttle has a 50 ft. (15.2 m) articulated arm with six joints forming elbow and wrist movements for the manipulation of payloads by an operator on the orbiter flight deck. Payloads of up to 586,000 lbs. (266,000 kg) can be maneuvered at a rate of about 2.4 in. per sec. (6 cm/s). This system incorporates a computerized coordination of the manipulator motions and uses television cameras to give the operator a good view of the working area. A similar arm is used on the International Space Station. This arm, called the space station remote manipulator system (SSRMS) is 57.7 ft. (17.6 m) long with seven motorized joints and is capable of moving payloads up to 255,000 lbs. (116,000 kg) at a rate of 0.8 in. per sec. (2 cm/s). The arm travels along tracks on the outside of the space station and is also capable of moving end over end off the track to reach less accessible areas. In addition, the SSRMS is equipped with force movement sensors, a technique often used in virtual-reality systems to enable remote sensing by the operator.

Underwater salvage systems can be controlled through cable links to surface craft, and remote manipulators are used in bomb disposal. Other developments include the introduction of feedback and virtual-reality systems and techniques that allow repeated actions to be performed under automatic control.

SEE ALSO: BOMB AND MINE DISPOSAL • ROBOTICS • SALVAGE, MARINE • SERVOMECHANISM • SPACE STATION • VIRTUAL REALITY

Reproduction

Biological reproduction is the name given to the processes by which individuals generate new individuals of the same species, encompassing organisms from the simple amoeba to the blue whale and the plant kingdom. All types of living creatures reproduce—without reproduction, life would die out. Reproduction in animals usually takes place during or after the period of maximum growth of the organism. The situation is different in plants, which continue to grow throughout their life cycle, and depends instead on environmental conditions or a particular growth stage being reached. Biology sees reproductive processes as being either asexual or sexual, and both types are found in the animal and plant kingdoms, with plants being capable of either.

Asexual reproduction may take the form of fission—the individual splits into two parts—or budding—part of the individual becomes constricted and grows into a brand new organism, either attached to or separate from the parent organism. The offspring of asexual reproduction are genetically identical to the parent.

Sexual reproduction involves two cells, called gametes, that fuse to produce a cell called a zygote. Gametes may be sexually indistinguishable, in which case the process is described as isogamous, or come from a male and a female of the species, when the process is classified heterogamous. In some species, such as aphids, the female can reproduce without fertilization, a process known as parthenogenesis. Some lower organisms and plants alternate between sexually and asexually produced generations.

Simple organisms

Simple unicellular (single celled) organisms, such as the amoeba, reproduce asexually. The process used is called binary fission, the simplest form of biological reproduction. First, the cell nucleus splits, followed by the rest of its body, producing two separate amoebas. Other simple organisms such as bacteria reproduce by binary fission. The characteristic of bacterial reproduction is its extreme speed. In suitable conditions, a bacterial cell can split every 20 minutes. In only 12 hours in these conditions, a single bacterium can produce over 600 million others.

Viruses are simpler organisms than bacteria but have a more complex reproductive process. A virus needs to reproduce inside the cells of another organism. To this end, the virus first attaches itself to the outside of the new cell. It injects a strand of nucleic acid, which then multi-

◄ Common frogs mating. Frogs lay their eggs in water where they hatch into immature offspring called tadpoles with only two front legs and a tail. As they feed and grow, the tail becomes absorbed back into the body and the rear legs develop, enabling the frog to leave the water.

plies into many strands. A new virus is formed around each of these separate strands from materials found inside the host cell. About half an hour after the initial invasion of the cell, it splits open, releasing thousands of new viruses.

Budding

Budding can be found in both the plant and animal kingdoms. Examples are the formation of potato tubers and part of the reproduction of hydras, simple multicellular animals found in ponds. Hydras consist of a cylindrical body with a mouth situated at one end surrounded by about eight tentacles. Budding takes place in the spring and summer, when the food supply is plentiful and conditions for growth are favorable. When a hydra buds, a branch grows from the side of the body. The branch develops a mouth and tentacles, and when the new hydra is fully developed, it breaks away from the parent.

Sexual reproduction

Bacteria also reproduce sexually in a process called conjugation. Two unicellular organisms fuse together and exchange part of the chromosome in their nuclei. They then break apart and reproduce by fission. In higher organisms, individuals of a species are differentiated into male and female according to the type of reproductive cell they produce. In male animals, the cell is called a sperm, or spermatozoan, and consists of a large head containing the nucleus and a whiplike tail that helps it move toward the female egg, or ovum. The female cell is much larger than the sperm and contains large amounts of cytoplasm around its nucleus. Plant cells are similar to those of animals, the male cell being known as the microgamete, and the female cell as the macrogamete.

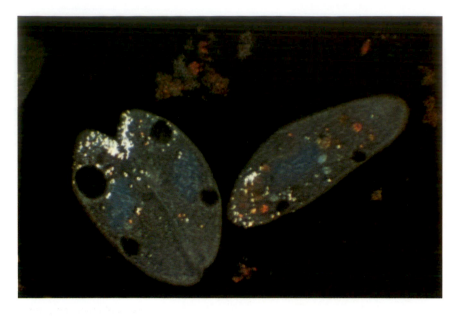

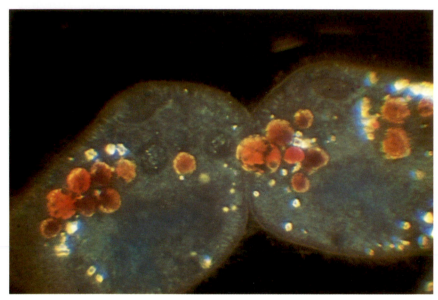

More surprising than bacteria that use sexual reproductive processes are the alternative reproductive processes of all hydras. In the autumn, when conditions are not ideal for budding, hydras sexually reproduce instead.

In the autumn, hydras develop irregularities and lumps on the side of their bodies: testes and ovaries. Each testis contains a great number of sperm, while each ovary contains a single egg. When mature, the testes and ovaries break open, and the sperm swim to the ovary of another hydra—a process called cross-fertilization. After fertilization, a hard cyst forms around the ovary to protect the developing embryo. The cyst drops from the ovary to the bottom of the pond, where the new hydra develops even after the parent hydra dies at the onset of winter. Sexual reproduction, therefore, allows the hydra as a species to survive the winter.

Some hydras are hermaphrodites and have both testes and ovaries. However, the hydra does

▲ In the upper picture, two paramecia can be seen conjugating sexually. In the lower picture, a paramecium cell splits in two to produce a new but identical individual.

not self-fertilize like some hermaphrodite organisms, because of the genetic problems that may arise through inbreeding. Hydras prevent self-fertilization by allowing the testes and ovaries to develop at slightly different times. The testes develop before the ovaries so that the sperm have already been released before the egg is ready to be fertilized.

Other hermaphrodites that cross-fertilize are earthworms. Earthworms copulate by sticking themselves together with mucus after which sperm migrate from one worm to another. Once fertilized, the eggs are laid in the soil.

Insects

All insects reproduce sexually. In insects, as in most higher animals, male–female attraction is very important. The first stage of reproduction is courtship, when the male stalks the female. Courtship is followed by mating, the act by which sperm are introduced into the female. Details of mating vary from insect to insect. For example, bees mate while flying, while some other insects mate by the male climbing on top of the female and twisting his abdomen around the female.

Fertilization does not happen immediately, but the sperm are taken into sperm sacs in the female. When the eggs are ready, they begin to pass out of her body past the sperm sacs, where they are fertilized. Some insects bury their eggs for safety when they are laid, others lay them on twigs or under leaves. Insect eggs evolved a hard shell to enable them to survive exposure to the air without drying out.

Fish and amphibians

Most fish reproduce by releasing eggs and sperm into water, where fertilization takes place. The number of eggs produced by some fish is staggering—the cod, for example, can produce some 8 million eggs at one time. In order to increase the chance of fertilization, the male aims to release his sperm as close as possible to the female's eggs. The stickleback even builds a nest where the female lays her eggs. When there are enough eggs in the nest—he may need to lure more than one female to the nest—he releases his sperm on top of them.

In the case of the frog, the male attracts a female who is loaded with eggs by croaking. Mating takes place in water, where the male grips onto the female very tightly and may remain there for up to three days in some species. Eggs pass out from the female between her back legs and are fertilized by a stream of seminal fluid from the male. Because amphibian eggs do not contain enough nutrients to allow the offspring to grow to maturity before it hatches, amphibians have to go through a larval stage, during which their bodies grow into the adult shape.

Birds

Reproduction in birds usually takes place in a number of stages. First, the male claims a territory from which he sings to attract a mate. When he is successful, the two build a nest together, or the female builds a nest alone. With the nest completed, the birds mate—male birds do not have a penis, so the birds press their reproductive openings together.

After mating, the female usually lays five or six eggs in the nest. The female sits on the eggs for a few weeks to incubate them. Once the embryo inside the egg has reached maturity, it hatches. It is usual for both parents to look after the young. Reptiles, from which birds are thought to have evolved, also lay eggs that they bury in earth or sand. Rather than incubate the eggs themselves, they rely on the heat of the soil to keep them warm until they hatch.

Mammals

Reproduction in mammals is always sexual. In most female mammals, estrus, or receptivity to mating, is limited to certain times of the year. Cats and dogs may come into estrus only once or twice a year, whereas the human female has a monthly estrus cycle. Mating normally follows courtship displays, with sperm being introduced into the female's vagina by the male's penis. It is in

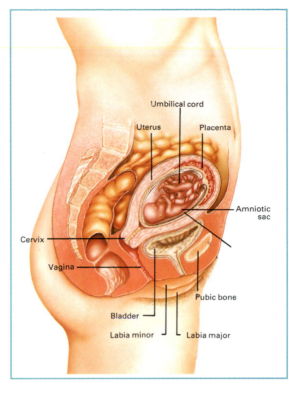

◀ During the first two weeks of a human pregnancy, the egg cell divides rapidly and implants itself in the wall of the uterus, where the placenta forms and the embryo begins to grow. The placenta allows nutrients and oxygen to pass from the mother's blood to the baby and waste products to be carried away. By day 56, all the major body organs and structures have formed. During the last six weeks of pregnancy, the baby puts on about 1½ lbs. (700 g) in weight and grows 6 in. (15 cm).

the development of the fetus that mammals show marked differences from other organisms. There are two kinds of mammals: marsupial and placental. In marsupials, the young develop in a pouch, while in placental mammals, the young develop inside the body of the mother. More unusual among mammals are the echidna and the platypus, both of which lay eggs.

The stage of development of the young when they are born varies between species. Animals born in the open where there is the danger of attack, such as antelopes or giraffes, are able to stand and run within hours. Most mammals have to spend a period of time nurturing their offspring until they can look after themselves. Human babies are dependent on their parents for food and protection for much longer than other animals.

 When it explodes, the puffball launches millions of dustlike spores. Fungi developed the spore, which begins to grow only if conditions are suitably damp.

Sex and the plant

Flowering plants use sexual reproduction. Stamens form the male part of the flower, while carpels form the female part. Stamens have a number of pollen sacs—pollen is the plant equivalent of the animal world's sperm. Carpels have slightly swollen stigmata at their tops. At the bottom is an ovary containing an egg cell in an embryosac. Pollen carried through the air by wind or by insects fertilizes the egg cell in almost exactly the same way as sperm fertilizes eggs in animals to form seeds.

SEE ALSO: Cell biology • Hormone • Obstetrics and gynecology • Population

Resistance

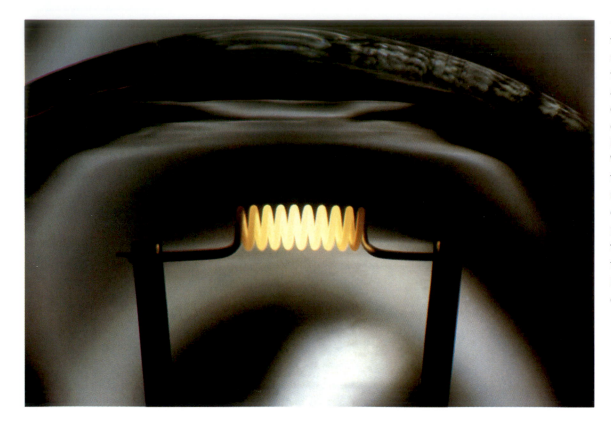

◀ Magnification reveals the structure of a high-resistance tungsten filament. This filament is a simple coil, unlike the double-coiled structure commonly used in household light bulbs. When an electromotive force is applied to the metal coil, the electric conduction that takes place causes the filament to give off energy in the form of light and heat. Energy is dissipated in the coil but not at its ends.

Resistance can be defined as an opposition to motion, leading to a dissipation of energy. Many physical systems rely on the application of some physical influence to produce some form of motion, such as the motion of electrons in an electric context or the motion of objects in mechanics.

In such circumstances the applied physical influence does not produce unlimited motion. The desired effect is limited by some internal opposition within the system.

Electrical resistance

When an electromotive force (emf, measured in volts) is applied to a metal, electric conduction takes place—an electric current flows through the material caused by the movement of negatively charged electrons.

Although a conductor of electricity allows current to flow, it does not flow with complete freedom. Collisions occur between the moving electrons and the atoms of the material to interfere with the electron flow. This phenomenon is termed electrical resistance. Materials differ in their ability to inhibit electron flow, and this property is measured by the resistivity, or specific resistance, of the material.

The total resistance of a conductor, for example, a metal wire, depends on the resistivity of the metal, the length of the wire, and the cross-sectional area of the wire. Resistance is directly proportional to length and inversely proportional to the area of cross section.

In a circuit carrying an alternating current, the total opposition to current flow is termed the impedance, which includes capacitive and inductive reactance in addition to the resistance.

In 1826, the German physicist Georg Ohm established that, in conditions of constant temperature, the current flow in a conductor is proportional to the applied voltage, the constant of proportionality (voltage divided by current) being resistance or, for alternating current, the impedance of the electric circuit. At low temperatures, the resistance of some conducting materials disappears entirely—they become superconductors.

Resistance in a capacitor

If an insulator is placed between two metal plates, a capacitor is formed. When the metal plates are at different electric potentials as a consequence of an applied voltage, the system becomes a store of electric charge, and a field of electric force is set up in the insulator between the plates. The electric field strength within the capacitor is the ratio of the voltage difference between the plates to the distance between the plates and is measured in units, such as volts per meter. The electric flux is produced as a force between opposite charges on the two plates, and the flux density is the ratio of the charge difference to the area of the metal plates. Electric flux density is measured in units such as coulombs per square foot.

The permittivity of a material is measured by comparing the flux density with the strength of field producing the flux. Comparison between materials is customarily made in terms of their relative permittivity, which is the capacitance of a system with the material between the plates divided by the capacitance of the same condenser with air between the plates.

Magnetic resistance

Magnetism is considered to have lines of magnetic force, or flux, passing through the material in which it is produced. Materials differ in the intensity of magnetization produced within them by a magnetic field. The magnetic intensity is measured as a ratio described as the susceptibility of the magnetic material.

Magnetism can be produced in a material by an electric current flowing around it (electromagnetism) or by the effect of a secondary magnetic field (magnetic induction). The degree to which a material responds to a magnetizing influence is termed its permeability. A magnetic material is usually characterized by its relative permeability, which is the ratio of the flux density produced in the material to the flux density produced in a vacuum by the same magnetic field.

By analogy with electromotive force (emf, or voltage) in an electric circuit, the effect producing the magnetic flux is the magnetomotive force (mmf), and the ratio between the magnetomotive force and the magnetic flux produced is called the reluctance of the magnetic circuit.

Mechanical resistance (friction)

When two solid surfaces are in contact, there is always some resistance to the motion of one surface relative to the other however smooth the surfaces. This resistance to motion has been explained in terms of irregularities on one surface interlocking with those on another, but now scientists believe that friction is caused by chemical bonds occurring between the two surfaces.

When a force is applied to a mechanical system in an attempt to produce motion between two surfaces, a force of friction, called static friction, is brought into play. This friction opposes motion up to a limit, depending on the contact surfaces. The friction at this limiting stage is termed limiting friction. Once motion has been established, the system requires a reduced amount of force to maintain it. The force then being overcome is termed sliding, or dynamic, friction.

The force needed to overcome friction between any pair of surfaces is proportional to the force pressing the surfaces together, and the ratio of the friction force to the force pressing them together is called the coefficient of friction for that pair of surfaces.

Resistance in fluids (viscosity)

When liquids or gases are in motion, internal friction forces cause a resistance to the fluid motion. This resistance to flow is called viscosity. Free flow is the result of low viscosity, and a less-mobile fluid has a higher viscosity. Viscosities of different fluids are compared in terms of a coefficient of viscosity, which is directly analogous to electric resistivity.

The internal resistive forces in liquids result from intermolecular cohesion forces opposing any externally applied force. When heated, the liquid molecules gain kinetic energy, and the cohesion forces are reduced—the viscosity is reduced when the liquid temperature is raised.

Overcoming resistance

When a physical influence produces movement in any situation, work is done. The performance of work requires that energy be provided. This energy must, however, overcome any resisting influences before the desired movement or effect can be achieved. So the supplied energy must be greater than the energy required to produce the desired end result, the excess energy being dissipated in overcoming the resistance of the system.

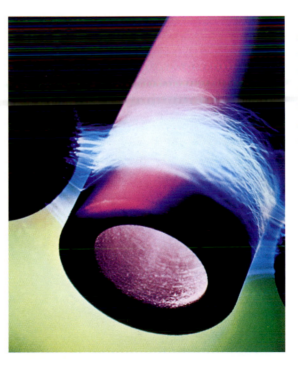

◀ A test on an insulating material shows that voltage breakdown occurs when the binding energy of the material is overcome by high temperatures and the electrons are free to move.

SEE ALSO:	Capacitor • Conduction, electrical • Electromagnetism • Electronics • Energy, mass, and weight • Insulator, electric • Magnetism • Viscosity

Resistor

A resistor is a device used to set the relationship between voltage and current in an electric circuit. The value of a resistor is known as its resistance and is measured in ohms. Most resistors are linear, that is, they obey a relationship discovered in the late 1820s by the German physicist Georg Simon Ohm called Ohm's law. This law states that the voltage in a circuit with constant resistance is directly proportional to the current in the circuit. This relationship may be expressed in the following equation:

$$R = V/I$$

where R is the resistance measured in ohms, and V and I are the voltage and current, respectively. Thus, if the voltage in a circuit remains constant, the current may be increased by reducing the resistance in the circuit. Conversely, the current may be decreased by increasing the level of resistance. Some designs of resistors, however, alter their value sharply when current is passed and are, therefore, used as protection against electric surges.

When current is passed through a resistor, power is dissipated, appearing as heat. To avoid damage to the resistor, its size and construction must be sufficient to withstand a specified amount of power (measured in watts). For this reason, there is a wide diversity of resistors manufactured, ranging from those suitable for dissipating a fraction of a watt, such as is encountered in a transistor radio, television set, or electric clock, up to very large constructions capable of handling kilowatts, for example, in power plants.

Manufacture of resistors

A large number of resistors are used in the various branches of electronics. Most of them are mass produced at low cost and have relatively poor tolerances in their values. For precise applications, more expensive alternatives are available.

The carbon-composition resistor is mass produced in extremely large numbers for a wide range of applications. The methods and materials used are cheap and simple. The resistive component consists of finely powdered carbon black dispersed in an inert filler, such as fireclay. The powders are mixed together in proportions corresponding to the final resistance values desired, and a liquid resin binder is added. The individual resistors are formed by hot pressing the mixture into rods and molding them into

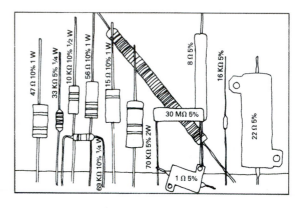

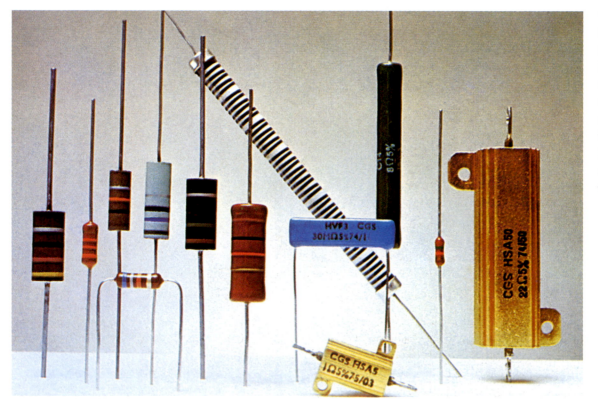

◀ A selection of resistors, showing the range in size, resistance value (above), construction, and color coding. The amount of energy a resistor can handle safely is its rating in watts. For large wattages, metal fins are added to dissipate the heat.

tively lengthening the distance between its ends and increasing the value. Very high precision resistors are also made by winding fine resistance wires onto a tubular ceramic body and then covering them with vitreous enamel to give them high stability even at extremely high temperatures.

Variable resistors, usually known as potentiometers (or pots for short), can be made in various ways. In all of them, a moving contact slides along either the surface of a resistance wire wound on a former or a resistive glaze printed onto a ceramic base.

Resistors based on glazes are known as thick-film resistors. A paste, consisting of a resistive material, usually an oxide of ruthenium, one of the rarer precious metals, glass powder, and a cellulose-based binder to give the correct flow properties, is screen printed onto a ceramic plate or substrate. Careful heat treatment at temperatures up to about 1830°F (1000°C) burns off the cellulose, melts the glass, and forms a glaze in a pattern that was defined by the screen used to print it. The method is based on two ancient crafts, screen printing as a form of art and the glazing of pottery to form porcelain. The process is inexpensive and capable of large-scale production for individual resistors and for networks of more than one component—a form of integrated circuit.

insulating sleeves with tinned copper leads. A final heat treatment hardens the casing and completes the curing of the resistive mixture. The components are then automatically tested and categorized according to the value of tolerance. The final stage of manufacture is to paint the resistor in bands corresponding to a color code. The band nearest to one of the ends represents the first number of the value, the second band the second number, and the third band the number of zeros. Gold or silver bands indicate the value tolerance of the component. The tolerance is an indication of the imperfections in the value given for a resistor, and allowances must be made for this percentage difference when designing circuits.

High-precision fixed resistors are made by deposition of a film of resistive material onto a base, usually ceramic. The film may be made from a number of materials. One of the commonest is carbon, but tin oxide is also in widespread use. For very high precision components, a thin layer of metal alloy, such as one of nickel and chromium, known commercially as Nichrome, is deposited on the base by a vacuum process.

All these types of resistor have in common the ability to dissipate considerably more power than a carbon resistor of the same size, because of the thermal properties of the material on which they are based. The values can be adjusted to within close tolerances by a method called spiraling. A shallow groove in a form similar to a screw thread is cut in the surface of the resistor body, effec-

▲ This circuit board shows just how common resistors are in modern electronics.

▶ An international color code is printed on all resistors so that their value and accuracy are readily apparent. The resistor shown above, for example, has a value of 47,000 ohms, and this value can vary by ±5 percent. The design of a circuit that includes this resistor must allow for its value being between 44,650 Ω and 49,350 Ω.

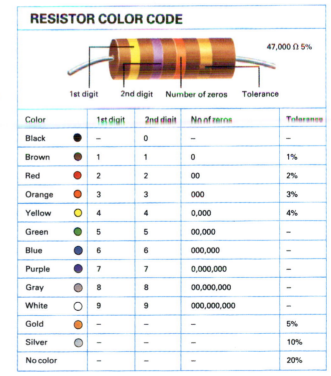

RESISTOR COLOR CODE

47,000 Ω 5%

| | 1st digit | 2nd digit | Number of zeros | Tolerance |

Color		1st digit	2nd digit	No of zeros	Tolerance
Black	●	–	0	–	–
Brown	●	1	1	0	1%
Red	●	2	2	00	2%
Orange	●	3	3	000	3%
Yellow	○	4	4	0,000	4%
Green	●	5	5	00,000	–
Blue	●	6	6	000,000	–
Purple	●	7	7	0,000,000	–
Gray	●	8	8	00,000,000	–
White	○	9	9	000,000,000	–
Gold	●	–	–	–	5%
Silver	●	–	–	–	10%
No color		–	–	–	20%

SEE ALSO:

ALLOY • CERAMICS • ELECTRICITY • ENERGY, MASS, AND WEIGHT • INTEGRATED CIRCUIT • POTENTIOMETER • POWER • RESISTANCE • SEMICONDUCTOR • SWITCH

Resonance

Resonance is a large increase in the amplitude of a vibrating system in response to a series of imposed vibrations at a certain frequency. It is a characteristic of all oscillators. In many physical systems, particles disturbed by some external influence or force vibrate or oscillate about their original position. When left alone after the initial disturbance, the range of movement each side of the rest position (the amplitude) gradually decreases as the particle energy is dissipated in overcoming the resistance to motion. This decrease of amplitude is termed damping.

The number of oscillations that a particle performs in one second is termed the frequency of vibration, and any such physical system has a certain characteristic, or natural, frequency of vibration called the resonant frequency of the system. It is determined by the physical quantities involved, namely the type of medium and the physical dimensions of the system.

If the system is disturbed in a regular repetitive manner, instead of being allowed to vibrate naturally, it will be forced to vibrate at the frequency of the disturbing force rather than at its own natural frequency. If, however, the frequency of the applied force coincides with the natural frequency of the system, then the amplitude of the vibration becomes large, and the energy supplied by the forcing vibration becomes a maximum. This condition of maximum energy transfer is termed resonance, and it has many important consequences, particularly in mechanics, acoustics, and electronics.

Mechanical resonance

A simple example of resonance in a mechanical system is that of pushing a child on a swing. Resonance and maximum amplitude are achieved if a push is applied to the swing at the same frequency as that with which the swing is oscillating—if it is pushed each time it reaches the end of its path. Any attempt to push the swing at any other frequency will be comparatively inefficient, because the push may miss the swing occasionally or oppose the momentum of the system. The principle is the same as that of a pendulum.

Another simple example is that of a diver on a springboard. As the diver jumps up and down to gain height for the dive, a stage is reached where the frequency of the periodic downward force practically coincides with the natural frequency of the board. The amplitude of vibration then becomes large, and the periodic force is said to have set the board in resonance.

The energy absorbed by a system at resonance can be destructively large when periodic forces act on the structure. For example, soldiers marching in step over a bridge can provide a periodic forcing influence at a frequency coincident with the natural frequency of the structure, in which

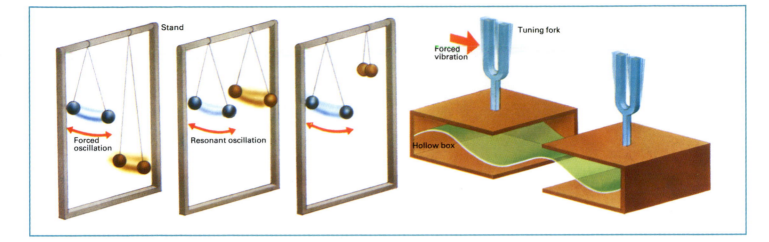

case, excessive energy is transferred to the bridge, producing resonance, and the resulting large amplitude of vibration can cause collapse.

There are several recorded instances of bridge collapse, and it has long been established practice for soldiers to break step when crossing a bridge. Probably the most famous and most dramatic bridge collapse resulting from resonance was of the suspension bridge across the Tacoma Narrows in Washington State in 1940. In this instance, the destructive resonance was induced in the bridge by wind gusting at the critical frequency.

A recent example of resonance occurring on a bridge is the lateral sway induced on the London Millennium Bridge by pedestrians. Engineers have long been familiar with vertical resonance in bridge structures, but problems with lateral resonance have rarely been observed. When the Millennium Bridge opened in 2000, it had to be closed again quickly owing to a large swaying motion that caused pedestrians to fall from side to side. Investigations later showed that this swaying was due to slight sideward motion caused by large numbers of pedestrians. To maintain their balance, the pedestrians compensated for this lateral movement by stepping slightly sideways as they walked, thus increasing the sideward motion. Gradually, nearly all of the pedestrians were stepping in time with the lateral resonant frequency of the bridge, thus creating a much larger and unacceptable level of side-to-side motion. Engineers hope to solve this problem by installing dampeners under the bridge.

Acoustic resonance

If a vibrating tuning fork is held near an open air cavity, or column, of which the natural frequency, determined by its geometry, equals the frequency of the vibrating fork, a much louder sound comes from the mass of air than from the fork itself.

This increase is the result of standing waves, produced in the cavity. When the cavity length is tuned to the wavelength of the vibration, the sound waves are repeatedly reflected from the cavity ends, resulting in resonance. The effect of resonance is to produce an amplification of the the sound volume. If the cavity end is closed, reflection occurs at the point in the standing wave of minimum displacement—the node. An open end gives reflection at the point of maximum displacement—the antinode.

This phenomenon in air columns is of prime importance in the design of wind instruments. The pitch of a note emitted by an air column is controlled by altering the length of the resonating cavity. An organ consists essentially of a large number of pipes of different resonant frequencies that can be separately selected. In brass instruments, the column length is increased by the opening of valves, giving access to further sections of tube, and in woodwind instruments, although the physical length is fixed, the effective length is varied by opening and closing holes or valves.

The suppression or avoidance of unwanted resonances is a major consideration in the design of loudspeaker enclosures and in the acoustic design of rooms and halls for various purposes.

▲ Left: Three views of moving pendulums. If the pendulums are of different lengths, motion in one has little effect on the other. Resonance (maximum swing) occurs when the pendulums are the same length. Right: Resonance can occur between identical tuning forks mounted on separate hollow boxes, the open ends facing each other. Sound from one tuning fork travels to the other box, inducing vibration in the other fork.

▼ Left: A column of air resonating in a tube. The tube is closed, so air at the ends is stationary, forming nodes. Midway between the nodes the air has maximum movement. Right: The ends of an open tube will always be places of maximum air movement. This tube is shown resonating at its second harmonic (with two nodes within the tube).

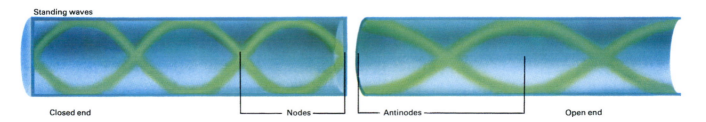

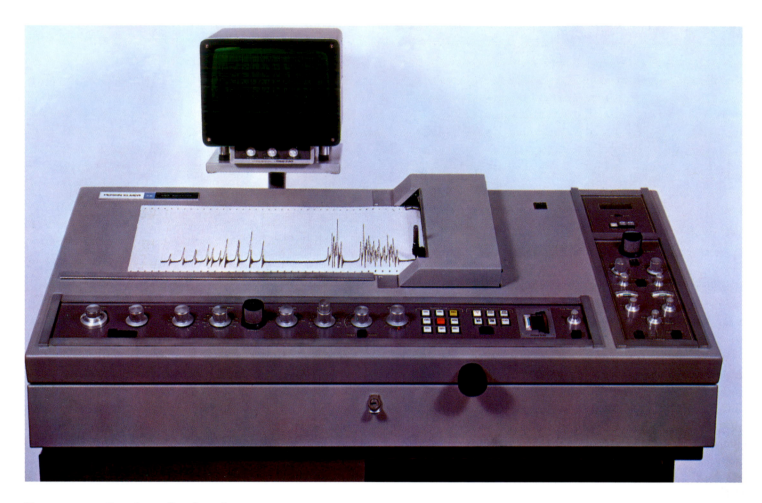

Resonance in electric circuits

The phenomenon of resonance finds important use in electric-circuits applications, such as the tuning of a radio receiver. Tuning involves the absorption of energy from the transmitted radio waves, but only waves of a frequency corresponding to the desired station are of interest.

While the resistors in an electrical circuit offer the same resistance to signals of any frequency, the inductors (coils) and capacitors have an effect that depends on frequency. This frequency-dependent opposition to current flow is called reactance. Inductors provide a reactance that is zero at zero frequency and increases as the frequency increases, while capacitors have infinite reactance at zero frequency but very little reactance at high frequencies. When an inductor and capacitor are connected together in parallel, a resonant circuit results. In this case there is one resonant frequency at which the reactances combine to yield a maximum value opposing current flow. When an inductor and capacitor are in series there is one resonant frequency at which the reactances cancel each other so that there is minimum opposition to current flow.

This frequency becomes the resonant frequency of the circuit, and current flow is maximized, resulting in the receiver having a selective response to waves at the frequency of interest. So the circuit accepts a particular frequency preferentially and is frequently referred to as an acceptor tuning circuit. If the circuit elements are joined in parallel instead of in series, then a similar condition occurs on tuning, except that voltage is maximized and the current minimized. This effect minimizes the response of the receiver to the particular resonant frequency, and the circuit is termed a rejector. Acceptor and rejector circuits are often used in conjunction to tune a desired frequency response free from nearby interfering frequencies.

Other resonance applications

Any physical system capable of vibration will resonate under the action of an impulse of the appropriate frequency. Atomic or molecular systems, which consist of vibrating particles, for example, electrons, will resonate.

A range of techniques has been developed in which resonance effects between such systems and suitable periodic impulses are used for the identification and structure determination of complex molecules; they can also provide detailed information regarding the atomic characteristics of an examined material.

▲ Resonance of the atomic nuclei in a magnetic field with a radio frequency signal is used in a nuclear magnetic resonance spectrometer. The resonant frequencies of a sample are plotted to help determine the chemical composition.

 SEE ALSO: ACOUSTICS • BRIDGE • CAPACITOR • INDUCTION • NUCLEAR MAGNETIC RESONANCE • OSCILLATOR • SOUND • WAVE MOTION

Rifle and Shotgun

A rifle is a firearm with spiral grooves cut into the inside of its barrel that impart a spinning motion to its projectile for greater accuracy. Shotguns, however, are smooth bored and use many small pellets, or shot, rather than a single projectile.

The earliest hand-held guns were all made for military purposes, but it was not long before they were being made for sporting use also. It was soon popular among the rich and influential to own a gun for shooting game, and there are many remaining examples that were made in the second half of the 15th century. The earliest rifles also date from this period. It was not until the 18th century that sporting guns became cheap enough for the ordinary citizen to own, and from then on, progress in design and construction was rapid.

Although early guns would fire both single bullets and multiple shot, the shot-firing guns gradually evolved as a distinct pattern. Rifles developed separately into guns used both by the military and for hunting. Today rifles are distinctly different from shotguns, and their manufacture is a different skill altogether.

Rifle

In general usage, the word *rifle* has come to mean a shoulder-controlled weapon capable of being carried and used by one person and firing a relatively small-size high-velocity projectile.

The spiral grooves (rifling) cut into the inner surface of the rifle's barrel engage with the projectile on its way to the muzzle. The rotation so acquired continues during flight, giving gyroscopic stability, which reduces the tendencies to erratic flight arising from any irregularities in the shape or density of the projectile.

Before the invention of gunpowder, projectiles—such as arrows—were usually fin stabilized in flight. The spin stabilization of rifling is normally ineffective for long, thin projectiles and much more effective for short, fat ones. This fact can be demonstrated easily by spinning a top and a pencil. The top will be quite hard to pull out of line, but a pencil would have to spin on its end at incredible speeds to stay upright. With the advent of short, fat projectiles fired from guns, rifling became worthwhile. Short, fat projectiles, however, do not penetrate as easily as long, thin ones made of dense material, so smooth-bore guns that fire fin-stabilized projectiles are used once more in the antitank role.

Originally, rifles were used mainly for sport, though small numbers were introduced into all armies. These rifles were all muzzle loaders, and

the drawback to the muzzle-loading rifle lay in the difficulty of getting the ball to fit the rifling and of clearing the rifling grooves of powder fouling. Most muzzle loaders used a tight-fitting bullet, which was rammed or even hammered down the barrel, an operation that took much time and was acceptable for game shooting but not in war.

The breech-loading systems, which were invented in the 1860s, changed the whole aspect of rifling. The bullet no longer had to be forced down the barrel, because it could now be introduced to the rifling at its beginning, just in front of the breech. Soon bullets became cylindrical in shape and more efficient, and with the invention of high-pressure powders at the end of the 19th century, the final form of the rifle was completed.

Bolt-action rifles

All older rifles were hand operated, and they used a diversity of mechanisms, some of which have survived today. By far the most practical mechanism and also one of the earliest to be used is the bolt action. With this type of action, the breech is closed by a device similar to the domestic barrel bolt found on household doors. The rifle bolt has a small hole drilled through its length to accommodate the firing pin. The action is arranged so that on opening the bolt, the firing pin is withdrawn and cocked, ready for the next shot.

▲ Some of the best shots in the world enjoy the sport of target shooting. The shooter on the left is using a sling to support his arm and a stiff glove to strengthen his hand. The man on the right is using a palm rest. Target shooting is a popular sport, requiring the greatest coordination and judgment.

The first bolt-action rifles were single shot, each cartridge having to be put into the bolt way and the empty case pulled out and discarded. It was not long before repeating rifles were made, in which there was a magazine of several rounds of ammunition and a system of feeding the rounds successively into the breech. Enormous ingenuity was displayed in the design of repeaters, but the bolt system has proved to be the best and simplest for general use. A magazine is placed below the bolt, and the rounds are pressed upward by a spring. As the bolt is pushed forward by the shooter, it strips a cartridge off the top of the magazine and runs it into the breech. An extractor pulls out the empty case. Speed of firing depends on how fast the bolt is operated.

Bolt-action rifles are used in large numbers for sporting and target shooting, and a few are retained by armies for sniping. Practically all these rifles are of a similar size and weight, being about 10 lbs. (4.5 kg) together with ammunition, and they all shoot bullets of about 0.30 in. (8 mm) caliber. A rifle of this type can fire a bullet to a range of more than 6,000 ft. (1,800 m) and will be capable of hitting a target 2 ft. (0.6 m) square at half a mile (0.8 km).

Self-loaders

Normal military rifles are no longer hand operated, and all use some type of self-loading system, which requires the firer only to pull the trigger. The mechanism is operated by the force of recoil or, more usually, the gas generated by the propellant powder. The firer has only to take fresh aim and pull the trigger after each shot and so can shoot far more rapidly with less effort than with a hand-operated rifle, since the firer's hand need not be taken off one part to operate another. Self-loading systems are more complicated and more expensive, but for military needs the inconvenience is worthwhile.

Heckler & Koch G11

Many innovations in rifle technology have occurred as a result of the changing needs of the military. One such development occurred in the late 1960s, when the West German army, the Bundeswehr, began thinking about their next generation of small arms and circulated to manufacturers an unusual invitation. Provided the weapon met the standard requirements regarding range, reliability, and accuracy, it would be prepared to accept any design, however outlandish, on condition that it would guarantee to place a three-shot burst with an accuracy of 1.2 to 2 mils. One mil is one-thousandth of any given range, so three shots would have to fall within a 2 to 3 ft. (0.6–1 m) circle at a 1,640 ft. (500 m) range.

This sort of accuracy is impossible with a conventional type of rifle or machine gun, because the recoil force after each shot lifts the barrel and disturbs the aim so that successive shots are spread around. Heckler & Koch, the German weapons manufacturer, came to the conclusion that a rifle with a gentle recoil was required (so as not to throw it off target), one with a flat trajectory and high velocity (to reduce the time of flight of the bullet) and a rate of fire in excess of 2,000 rounds per minute for the three-round burst. Heckler & Koch collaborated with Dynamit

▼ The AR-18 is a gas-operated weapon that uses a rotating bolt similar to that on the M16. The rifle has a conventional gas piston arrangement although it differs slightly in that the piston wraps around a hollow cylinder and is blown backward by the gas pressure, hitting the bolt carrier. As the carrier moves back, it compresses the return springs and unlocks the bolt. The carrier and bolt then go back together, extracting the spent case, and the springs drive the assembly back to chamber a fresh round. The hammer is cocked during the bolt carrier movement, so that as the carrier completes its forward stroke the bolt is locked and the rifle is ready to fire again.

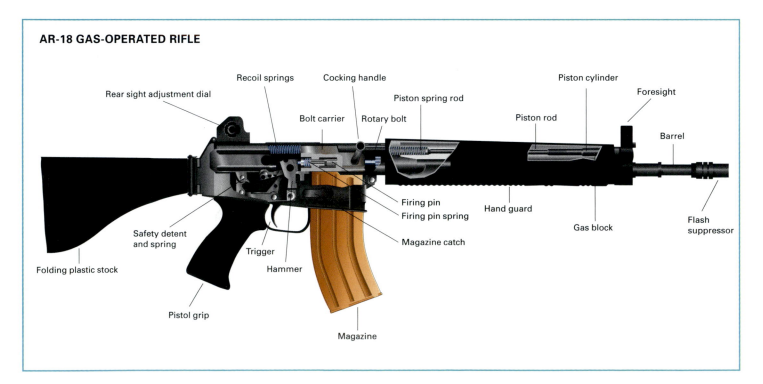

AR-18 GAS-OPERATED RIFLE

Rear sight adjustment dial — Recoil springs — Cocking handle — Bolt carrier — Rotary bolt — Piston spring rod — Piston rod — Piston cylinder — Foresight — Barrel — Flash suppressor — Gas block — Hand guard — Magazine catch — Firing pin spring — Firing pin — Magazine — Hammer — Pistol grip — Trigger — Safety detent and spring — Folding plastic stock

Nobel to develop a caseless round with a 4.7 mm bullet. This bullet is embedded in a solid block of propellant explosive, a percussion cap being embedded in the other end.

The heart of the rifle is an unusual rotating breech block containing the firing chamber. This chamber is a metal drum, bored to accept the cartridge, that rotates behind the rifle barrel. In the firing position, the chamber is in line with the barrel: to reload, the drum turns through 90 degrees so that the chamber is vertical and a fresh cartridge can drop in.

The entire mechanism—barrel, breech, magazine, and gas system—is concealed inside a reinforced plastic housing. This housing is shaped to form the butt and pistol grip and also to form a carrying handle, which conceals an optical sight. The magazine, a long box containing 50 cartridges, is inserted horizontally above the barrel so that the cartridges feed downward into the breech. Except for the muzzle, there are no apertures that allow water or dust to enter the weapon, the trigger and magazine being sealed by rubber flanges. The sight is also provided with battery-illuminated cross wires for firing in poor light.

On firing, the mechanism, including the magazine, recoils inside the plastic housing against a spring so that the recoil felt by the firer is more like a gentle push than a sharp blow. The chamber revolves and is reloaded during the recoil movement, and the rifle is ready to fire again immediately. A change lever above the trigger permits selection of either single shots, three-round bursts, continuous automatic fire, or a safe position. On changing to three-round bursts, the unique nature of this weapon becomes apparent. During the recoil stroke, the breech rotates and loads a second round, which is immediately fired, and the recoil force of the second shot adds to the movement of the mechanism. Now the breech rotates again, reloads, and fires the third shot of the burst; once more, the recoil force adds to the movement, and at last, the mechanism is permitted to complete its rearward stroke and return to the ready position. The recoil of the three shots is buffered, and the force felt by the firer is relatively mild. The important thing, however, is that all three shots leave the barrel before the firer feels the recoil shock and before the barrel begins to move off target. So the three shots fly close together and strike the target well within the designated spread. A single shot fired in combat by an average soldier has, perhaps, a 50 percent chance of hitting the target, depending on factors such as wind strength. Three shots fired rapidly and with a small spread improve the chance of hitting the target to about 90 percent.

◀ The action mechanism plate of a side-by-side shotgun. When the trigger is pulled, the tightened mainspring drives a hammer against the firing pin to pierce the primer in the cartridge.

Further developments

The present U.S. Army rifle, the M16, was introduced in 1964 and has been continually improved and updated since. The small caliber, however, has remained the same—0.223 in. (5.56 mm). Lighter, smaller rounds such as these are used because researchers at Johns Hopkins University discovered that infantry rarely engage targets at more than 1,000 ft. (300 m) in battle, and this range can be attained by a smaller, lighter bullet fired from a lighter rifle.

Another development in the military rifle has been the use of modular components that can be used in a variety of arrangements to provide the optimum weapon for different situations. One example of this is the Heckler & Koch G36, which can, for example, have different barrel lengths, sights, and triggers. This rifle is made of a lightweight carbon-fiber reinforced polymer and has the same caliber as the U.S. Army's M16.

Shotgun

Shotguns are primarily used for shooting flying birds or small ground game such as rabbits. A flying bird is almost impossible to hit with a rifle, but the shotgun launches a large number of pellets, which spread out to form a distinct pattern in the air, and this pattern allows the shooter to be less exact in aim than when firing a rifle. The effective range is usually quite short, not much more than 100 ft. (30 m), and the pellets fall to the ground in a couple of hundred yards. The danger area is therefore quite small.

Most shotguns fire about 1 oz. (28 g), or slightly more, of lead pellets. These pellets are graded in size by a numbering system that is more than 200 years old. The smallest size has the highest number, which in practical terms is 8 or 9. The largest has the lowest number, about 3. For most game, shooting size 5 or 6 is preferred. With number 6 shot, there are 280 pellets to the ounce (10 per gram).

The usual criterion of the quality of a gun is the number of pellets that it can fire into a circle 30 in. (76 cm) in diameter. A good gun, firing 1⅛ oz. (31.9 g) of number 6 shot, should put 240 pellets into the circle (the rest are lost outside the circle), allowing for one pellet every 3 sq. in. (20 cm²). Thus, anything inside that circle is certain to get at least one if not more pellets. One pellet can kill most birds and small animals.

Clay-pigeon (trap) shooters fire at thin baked-clay disks, shot rapidly into the air by a spring device, that break into fragments on being hit. These clay disks are difficult to hit, and the shooter usually uses number 8 shot so as to increase the density of the pattern.

The bore of a shotgun is described by a number, which is the number of spherical lead balls of a size to fit the bore that will add up to 1 lb. (454 g) in weight. Thus, the diameter of a bore that would accept a ball ¹⁄₁₆ lb. in weight (that is, 1 oz.) is a 16 bore; one that accepts 12 balls to the pound, a 12 bore; and so on. The method is very old and universally used. The popular 12 bore is actually 0.73 in. (1.85 cm) in diameter.

Shotgun barrels are usually tapered internally. A parallel-sided barrel is called a cylinder. One with a taper is said to have a choke. Choking a barrel makes the shot fly in a closer pattern and so improves the chance of hitting at longer ranges when the shot from a cylinder barrel would have spread so widely as to pass around the target. Choking does not increase the velocity. Shotguns rarely have the same degree of choke in both barrels. The right hand one, which is always fired first, has less choke because the target is near; the left barrel is fired second and has more choke to make the shot fire closer together.

Double-barreled shotgun

The earliest shotguns were single-barreled, but sports enthusiasts were soon asking for a second, quicker shot. This request brought about the double-barreled gun, with the barrels side by side for the convenience of the primitive flintlock firing mechanisms then used. The side-by-side gun is still strongly favored, but there are other patterns. Clay-pigeon shooters frequently use over-and-under barrels. A few people still prefer a single barrel. There are self-loading guns and semiautomatic loaders.

Semiautomatic guns have a magazine and are reloaded and recocked by the shooter moving some part of the gun by hand. Usually it is the front hand guard that is pumped to and fro, giving rise to the nickname of pump guns or trombone guns. Self-loading guns use the same principles as a self-loading rifle and employ recoil or gas action to operate the mechanism. The magazine of sporting shotguns can hold up to five cartridges.

Shotgun cartridges are all parallel-sided cylinders, made of cardboard or plastic, with a thin brass base. They generate low pressure, by rifle standards, and the usual muzzle velocity for the shot is just above the speed of sound. As a result, the barrels can be made quite light, and a good double-barreled gun weighs less than 6 lbs. (2.7 kg). Shotguns are loaded by pivoting the barrel forward and downward, an action known as breaking, which ejects the spent cartridge and allows rapid reloading.

Shotguns are made in many countries, but it is generally accepted that the finest are made in England. A gun from a top English gun maker can be very expensive and will be fitted to the buyer as carefully as a tailor-made suit of clothes to ensure that the barrels are exactly in front of the shooter's eyes when he brings the gun to his shoulder so that he does not have to pause to take a sight. Shotguns are aimed by instinct, and there are no sights, except on some trap-shooting and military combat shotguns.

Shotguns have also been designed for military use. In jungle- and house-clearance operations, adapted shotguns can deliver more stopping power at close range than rifles or submachine guns. In fact, their limited range means that ricochets or stray shots provide less danger to comrades or passers-by in a confusing situation. For military applications, shotguns are made more rugged and compact, with folding stock, large-capacity magazine, sights for firing solid rifled slugs, and a high rate of fire.

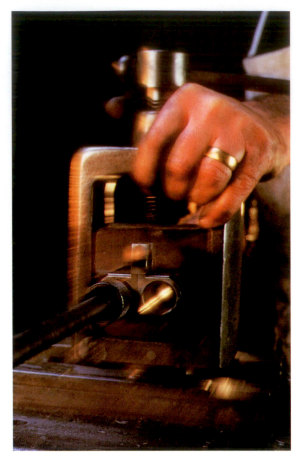

▲ Checking the choke in a 12-gauge barrel. Choking fires the shot in a closer pattern than a parallel-bored rifle.

 SEE ALSO: AMMUNITION • ANTIAIRCRAFT GUN • AUTOMATIC WEAPON AND MACHINE GUN • GUN • MORTAR, BAZOOKA, AND RECOILLESS GUN

Riot Control

A riot is generally defined as a public disturbance caused by three or more people acting with common intent to breach the peace. Riots can arise from diverse situations, including peaceful demonstrations and sporting events. They can endanger the welfare—or even the lives—of peaceful participants at such events, and they can result in collateral or intentional damage to public or private property.

In democracies, the main intention of law enforcement agencies at riots is to avoid harm to people and property to as great an extent as possible. At the same time, it is important to respect the right to demonstrate peacefully and the entitlement to enjoy a sporting event, for example.

Preventative measures

A great deal can be done to prevent riots or minimize their severity by the use of intelligence and surveillance techniques. In recent years, the Internet has increasingly been used as a means of coordinating civil disorder; hence, the monitoring of information available by Internet has become increasingly useful in planning countermeasures against potential riots. Similar information can also be obtained by using plain clothes officers to infiltrate troublemaking groups.

Even when little formal evidence is available, preventative measures can be taken at events where the potential for a riot exists. In Britain, the police regularly segregate groups of rival sports enthusiasts, escorting them by separate routes from bus and rail depots to their respective fenced-off sectors of the sports arena. Sensitive political and economic summits are also protected by establishing security cordons around their venues and participants' accommodations, again with the intention of keeping potential rioters away from the target of their aggression.

Security forces maintain databases containing photographs of people with previous convictions for riotous behavior, and they are used by trained undercover spotters to establish whether known troublemakers are present at the location of a potential riot. Attempts are currently being made to automate this process by using optical recognition systems in conjunction with closed-circuit security cameras. In such systems, a known offender triggers an alarm if he or she enters the field of view of a camera, and the name and criminal file of that person is displayed on a screen.

In some cases, security databases are used as a basis for temporarily suspending a person's right to travel to foreign events, such as sports matches, where they might incite a riot. In such cases, the individual in question is informed of the temporary suspension, and any attempt to enter the out-of-bounds country will be declined when that person's travel documents are processed.

Crowd control

If intelligence and countermeasures fail to prevent a riot or if a riot occurs without warning, law enforcement agencies generally have two options

RIOT-CONTROL HARDWARE

While the conventional use of firearms is avoided in most riot-control maneuvers, a standard revolver can be fitted with a grenade launcher, such as the .38 Special Mighty Midget (1), or used to fire rubber bullets, such as the Tru-Flite TM 37 mm (2).

Hand-thrown grenades that contain rubber projectiles (3) may be used, as may handheld pepper or Mace sprays (4). Pepper spray, tear gas, Mace, or smoke-generating compounds are often delivered in hand-thrown continuous-discharge grenades (5).

for ending a riot: dispersal or containment of the rioting crowd. In practice, however, one or other of these options might be made unfeasible by such factors as the geographical layout of the riot scene or political considerations. Dispersal of a rioting crowd in an urban area might widen the field of harm to people and property, for example, whereas mass arrests of political activists might lead to allegations of political oppression.

Whether the intention is to disperse or to contain the rioting crowd, the riot-control team must take measures to move groups of people against their will. In one approach, officers form a line across the rioters' path. Each officer carries a full-length transparent polycarbonate shield or half-length metal shield, and the officers advance en masse with their shields touching to form a continuous barrier against bricks or other missiles that might be thrown at them by the rioters. Body armor and helmets with visors provide additional protection, and each officer might carry a rubber or wooden baton for personal defense.

Nonlethal weapons

Under most circumstances, the use of conventional firearms against rioters is considered excessive and liable to cause injuries as a result of the mass panic that might occur after a shot is fired. For this reason, the advancing front line is usually backed up by officers who hurl CS (tear gas), CN (Mace), or pepper-spray grenades into the crowd

in order to debilitate and disorient the rioters. If such weapons are used, the officers must wear appropriate filter masks so as not to be incapacitated by the clouds of irritating fumes that ensue. Smoke grenades can disorient rioters and conceal police surprise tactics. Alternatively, officers might fire plastic or rubber baton rounds at the floor in front of the crowd to cause light but painful injuries as they ricochet into the crowd.

A high-pressure water cannon mounted on an armored truck is an effective crowd-control measure, capable of knocking people off their feet and pushing them away. The water can be mixed with dyes that mark rioters' skin and clothing and make subsequent follow-up and arrest easier. Riot-control gases can be added to the water to make it more effective against crowds.

Armored vehicles

Apart from their use as mobile platforms for water cannons, armored vehicles can be used to bulldoze barricades or to carry armed snatch teams into the midst of rioters, where they can arrest key individuals. Full-scale tanks can also be used to intimidate crowds with their bulk, but their weaponry is poorly suited to crowd control.

SEE ALSO: AMMUNITION • ARMOR • ARMORED VEHICLE AND TANK • GAS AND DUST MASK • GUN • NONLETHAL WEAPON • PROTECTIVE CLOTHING • RIFLE AND SHOTGUN

Road Construction

Although many early civilizations built roads, it was the Romans who were the first great road builders. Designed for the speedy movement of troops, the roads were built to such high standards that some examples, including bridged sections, still exist. In addition, many Roman routes have been followed by modern roads. Following the decline and fall of the Roman Empire, however, much of the road system fell into disrepair. Throughout the Middle Ages in Europe, the packhorse was the main means of land transportation, and little road building was undertaken.

Elizabeth I of England made it one of the duties of the justices of the peace to ensure that the local roads were kept in repair. Later, turnpike trusts were set up to maintain the roads and charged tolls on travelers. In 1716, the French king Louis XV took over responsibility for maintaining his country's roads. Men of ability then began to take an interest in road building. The engineer Pierre-Marie-Jérome Trésaguet in France and later, toward the end of the 18th century, the British engineers Thomas Telford and John MacAdam, began to apply sound scientific principles to road construction.

Road building in France and Europe was encouraged by the emperor Napoleon, who required good, direct roads to move his armies. Several roads over the Alps were built at that time. These improved roads produced the heyday of the stagecoach, but the advent of the railways in the 1830s slowed the road-building boom.

Early in the 20th century, the development of motorized transportation required the improvement of road surfaces, which was achieved using tarmacadam (blacktop). Between the world wars, the growth of the U.S. automobile industry quickened the pace of road building, and in Germany, the Autobahnen formed the first national express highway system.

Road design

Traffic planning is the first stage in the design of a new highway, long-range forecasts being made of the traffic requirements for the region concerned. These forecasts have to take into account factors such as probable increases in traffic flow, the volume and type of existing flows, and the nature of the country to be crossed. Consideration also has to be given to the way funds will be raised for construction. Once the highway authority has decided to construct a new major road, it will employ either its own engineers or a consulting engineer to survey the alternative routes and carry out the road design. Information required for each of the possible routes, that is the detailed ground levels of the terrain, can be obtained nowadays by aerial photography accurate to 6 in. (15.2 cm). Details of the types of materials needed for the construction of embankments and of geological strata must be obtained from trial pits and boreholes taken along the line of the route and at bridge sites. Local climatic conditions, such as fog, frost, and rain, must also be established. In developed countries, information is required about land values and various environmental factors that may involve public inquiries in addition to consultation with interested parties. The question of environmental impact has become increasingly important with modern highway projects; special measures are therefore taken in sensitive areas, and environmental impact assessments are required in, for example, Europe. A highway may be hidden from sight by running it through a cutting, or its design modified to reduce the effects of noise.

From the survey information, the line and level of each of the possible roads will be chosen in accordance with the standards of gradient, sight lines, and other factors laid down by the traffic authority. This planning should minimize the amount of material that has to be excavated and carried to fill the adjacent embankments. It is

▲ The construction of roads is a major undertaking. Millions of tons of rock and soil may need to be excavated before engineers can begin to lay the foundations. Siting of bridges and intersections requires careful planning so that there is minimum disruption to the surrounding area after the road has been built.

◀ This type of interchange to link freeways is a familiar sight in the developed world. Often, the interchange is constructed while traffic continues to use neighboring roads, and accurate planning is necessary to keep disruptions to a minimum.

also important to keep to a minimum the size of the bridges needed to cross railways, rivers, and other roads. Taking into account these factors, the choice of route is made and the design carried out.

Arrangements are then made to purchase the land on which the road will run. Detailed drawings, specifications, and estimations of cost are prepared so that contractors can bid, normally in competition with each other, for the construction of the work. The consulting engineer or highway authority will usually provide a resident engineer and site staff to ensure that the work is carried out by the successful contractor in accordance with the drawings and specifications. Within the requirements of the design, the contractor will be responsible for deciding upon the methods of construction to be used, including the design of temporary works, and will also be responsible for formulating a program of order. The length of the contract is usually decided by the client's consultant or the client itself, if it is acting as consultant on the project, though in some countries and under some types of contract the contractor will be involved in this decision.

Site preparation

The route of the new road is staked out, cleared, and fenced where necessary. Trees are cut down and stumps and roots are grubbed up by crawler

dozers or, where necessary, blasted out by explosives. It may also be necessary to build temporary haul roads and bridges or fords at river bridges.

The bases of embankments and the slopes of cuttings must be protected from the action of groundwater, which could cause them to collapse. A primary drainage system is therefore constructed before starting earthworks along the length of the road to divert the natural groundwater and prevent it from entering the works. Draining is usually done by digging a shallow cut-off ditch with a hydraulic excavator. At the low point of the natural ground, the water flowing in these ditches is taken across the road line in piped or reinforced-concrete culverts and allowed to flow away through existing streams or ditches. If the ground underneath the new embankments is weak and waterlogged, band drains are laid before the embankments are placed to alleviate the possibility of subsidence after the road is built.

Earthworks

The topsoil is first stripped and stacked for spreading on the slopes of cuttings and embankments toward the end of construction. This work is usually done with caterpillar-tracked tractors towing box scrapers. The main cutting and embankment work is then started using rubber-tired scrapers. These scrapers are single- or twin-engined machines with a horizontal blade that can be lowered to cut a slice of earth from the ground and collect it in the bowl of the scraper. When the scraper bowl is full—some machines can carry up to 100 cu. yds. (75 m^3)—the blade is raised, and the loaded scraper travels to the deposition area on the embankment. If the ground is hard, it may be necessary for the scraper-loading operation to be assisted by a pusher crawler, which pushes the scraper while it is loading in order to speed up the operation.

For certain types of material, such as chalk, which may soften in wet weather, or when the excavated material has to be carried for more than 2 miles (3 km), the excavation may be undertaken using face-shovel, or back-actor, excavators (which have buckets faced so that they pull rather than push the earth in) loading into dump trucks. When rock is encountered, it is first shattered with explosives and ripped by the tractor and then loaded by face shovel.

At the embankment, the earth is spread by the scrapers into a thin layer about 12 in. (30 cm) thick, which is leveled by bulldozers and then compacted by caterpillar tractors towing rollers or by self-propelled rollers. It is essential that the successive embankment layers are properly compacted so that the final embankment will be stable.

Road drainage

On completion of the earthworks, further shallow drain trenches, about 4 ft. (1.2 m) deep, are constructed to keep the top layer of the cutting or embankment free from water, which would weaken it. Perforated pipes are laid in these trenches, which are then filled with gravel. In or adjacent to these trenches, further pipes are laid to carry the water collected in the road gullies away from the finished road surface.

Carriageway construction

It is necessary to phase the bridge construction period so that the bridges are completed ahead of the paving operations, and the existing roads diverted over or through them. Where possible, prefabricated bridge units are employed to reduce site work and construction time, although in some European countries complex concrete pours using elaborate shuttering are common. The roadway-paving operation then begins by the top layer of earth—the formation—being accurately trimmed to a 2 in. (5 cm) tolerance by scrapers or a grader. A grader is a wheeled machine that has a steel blade mounted horizontally between its four wheels. This blade can then be accurately raised, lowered, or tilted by the driver to cut a precisely level and accurate surface.

If the expected traffic loads are light, the graded soil surface can act as the roadway. For slightly heavier traffic conditions, a loose surfacing of gravel, or a similar material, may be used. In both cases, grading is repeated periodically to maintain the profile. Soil stabilization may be carried out by mixing dry cement into the top layer of the earth, damping it and compacting it with rollers. The base produced this way can then be used directly or surfaced with a blacktop coating.

Where larger volumes of traffic are involved, a more substantial form of construction is needed to increase the load-bearing capacity. A sub-base of gravel or crushed rock is spread over the graded earth surface to a thickness of 12 in. (30 cm) or so (depending on the design load) and compacted. This sub-base is then normally covered with a further layer around 5 in. (12.5 cm) thick that forms the actual base of the road, which is then paved with flexible tar or rigid concrete or in some cases concrete covered with tar.

Blacktop roads

Bitumen and stone are heated and mixed together in a site mixing plant and brought hot, by truck, to the laying point. The material is then tipped into a paver, which spreads it in succeeding layers of road base, base course, and wearing course. These layers are compacted by road rollers to give a firm surface. The accuracy of each successive layer until the final wearing course (usually of asphalt) provides the accuracy of the finished road surface. The total blacktop thickness can be up to 12 in. (30 cm), depending on the traffic load. To improve the skid resistance of the road, bitumen-coated stone chippings are spread over the top surface and rolled into it while it is still hot, a method called flexible construction. For a composite construction, the road base is constructed of dry, lean concrete instead of bituminous material. Porous asphalt may also be used to reduce spray from rain-wet surfaces and lessen the noise of tires on the carriageway.

Concrete roads

If the final surface is to be concrete, then the road will consist of a concrete slab approximately 10 in. (25 cm) thick. The actual thickness will depend upon whether the concrete is reinforced. Joints will be incorporated in this slab at about 15 ft. (4.6 m) intervals to enable expansion and contraction of the concrete to take place.

Conventionally, the concrete is laid between temporary steel road forms, which support the edge of the concrete slab, by a concrete train, which consists of a series of machines that run on rails supported on the road forms. The forms and thus the rails are accurately laid to level well ahead of the train and provide the level control for the finished road surface. The first machine in the train is a placer spreader, which puts the concrete, transported by truck from the concrete mixing plant, between the road forms. The concrete is then compacted and trimmed to true level by successive machines. To provide a skid-

▼ A typical composite construction blacktop highway usually consists of four layers of compacted soil, granular material, concrete, and flexible tar.

ROAD STRUCTURE

— Black top
— Rolled black top
— Concrete base
— Granular sub-base
— Soil

resistant surface, the wet concrete is then lightly brushed or otherwise grooved to a shallow depth. Pockets for reflectors, which mark either the center of the road or the road edges and junctions, are also formed in the wet concrete at this stage.

In recent years, so-called slip-form machines have been developed, and by using these machines to form the concrete slab, it is possible to eliminate the lengthy process of accurately laying out road forms. These slip-form pavers incorporate traveling side forms within the body of the machine itself. The degree of vibration used when compacting the concrete is much greater than with the conventional train so that after the moving forms—which are approximately 15 ft. (4.6 m) long—have slipped past, the fresh concrete is able to stand up without any further support. Cracking is controlled by the addition of steel reinforcement, which enhances the tensile strength of the concrete and ensures that any cracks are fine and evenly distributed. Transverse joints are also used to minimize cracking.

The surface level of the finished concrete is formed by the same machine and is controlled, both for level and direction, by means of electronic or hydraulic sensor controls that follow string lines placed at each side of the machine along the roadway. With this paver, is possible to achieve lay rates of up to 6 ft. (1.8 m) per minute.

Road finishings

Once the roadways are completed, the verges are filled with subsoil and then topsoil, and the cutting and embankment slopes are seeded with grass. Safety barriers can be erected in the central reserve between the roadways or in the edge verges wherever the height of embankment justifies them. Reflectors are laid on the roadway to

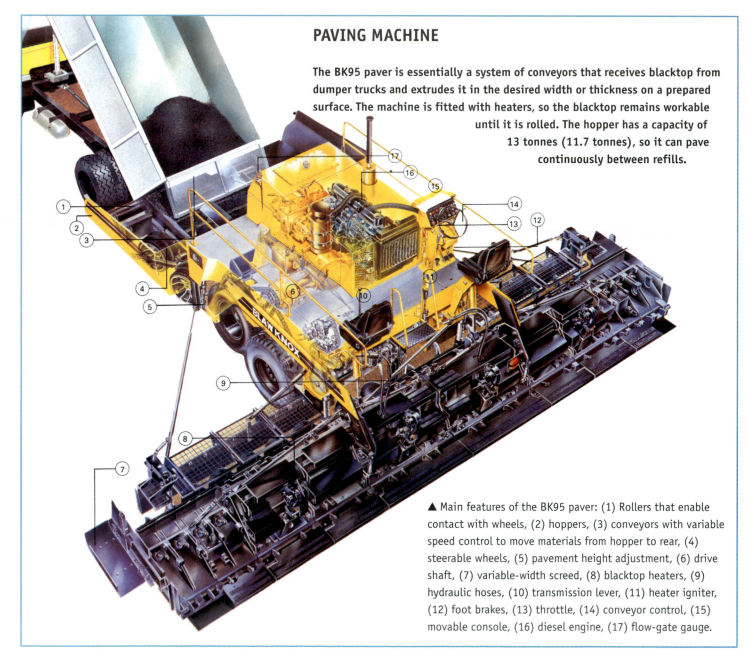

PAVING MACHINE

The BK95 paver is essentially a system of conveyors that receives blacktop from dumper trucks and extrudes it in the desired width or thickness on a prepared surface. The machine is fitted with heaters, so the blacktop remains workable until it is rolled. The hopper has a capacity of 13 tonnes (11.7 tonnes), so it can pave continuously between refills.

▲ Main features of the BK95 paver: (1) Rollers that enable contact with wheels, (2) hoppers, (3) conveyors with variable speed control to move materials from hopper to rear, (4) steerable wheels, (5) pavement height adjustment, (6) drive shaft, (7) variable-width screed, (8) blacktop heaters, (9) hydraulic hoses, (10) transmission lever, (11) heater igniter, (12) foot brakes, (13) throttle, (14) conveyor control, (15) movable console, (16) diesel engine, (17) flow-gate gauge.

◀ A jackhammer being used to break up rock to prepare the foundations for a new freeway.

may also be installed. Speed cameras use a set of regularly spaced lines on the carriageway as a distance measure to judge if a vehicle is speeding and then take a picture of the number plate. The photograph can be used to prosecute a speeding driver without the need for the police to be present when the offence is being committed.

Traffic-monitoring cameras are frequently placed at extremely busy junctions and critical road intersections, and pictures from them are fed back live to police control centers so that action can be taken to ensure that traffic disruption is kept to a minimum.

Closed-circuit television (CCTV) cameras are an important addition to roads running through enclosed spaces, such as tunnels, where traffic build-up and carbon dioxide levels have to be monitored as a way of determining whether the tunnel's jet fans need to be switched on to prevent drivers from suffering adverse effects from traffic fumes. Fog monitors may also be deployed on roads where there is a known risk of fog. They consist of a beam emitter and receiver. The receiver measures the intensity of the beam, and if it drops by a set level, a signal is relayed to the traffic-control center, which can then send the information to the relevant variable traffic signs to enable them to display fog warnings.

Information and road safety are now integral parts of road construction. For instance, the impact of a crash can be considerably reduced by using so-called soft signs and light poles designed to give on impact and by the use of guardrails and impact attenuators placed to protect roadside objects such as bridge piers, railway embankments, and freeway exit ramps.

In countries where earthquakes are common, safety measures would include the reinforcement of bridge decks, piers, and roadways, which have to be designed to resist the enormous lateral and shaking forces generated. Sophisticated traffic signaling also helps reduce risk in any emergency by coordinating speed reductions and overhead information provision so that drivers can be confident of arriving at their destinations safely.

indicate the traffic lanes and ramp entrances together with white lines. These white lines are composed of small spherical glass beads (called ballotini) contained in a soft plastic paint that is sprayed onto the road surface so that the lines are easily visible in daylight or when lit by headlights.

Street lighting and signposts are erected at the intersections and where traffic joins or leaves the new road. In towns and foggy areas, overhead lighting is often installed for safety reasons. Emergency telephone cables connected to telephones placed at intervals along the route are frequently installed in the verges. In urban areas, it is possible to reduce the level of noise from traffic on the road by erecting light screens about 8 ft. (2.4 m) high continuously along and close to the edges of the road.

On major roads, more complex types of signing are employed including variable messaging, overhead or roadside gantries that provides information to drivers on the state of the road or weather (such as fog) ahead, reduced speed limits, and lane closures. Other devices such as traffic-speed cameras and traffic-monitoring cameras

▼ Steel beams being placed on concrete piers for a bridge.

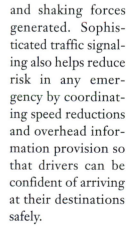

SEE ALSO: BRIDGE • CIVIL ENGINEERING • CONCRETE • EARTHMOVING MACHINERY • ROAD SYSTEMS AND TRAFFIC CONTROL

Road Systems and Traffic Control

Road systems underpin the principal transport networks of developed nations. In 2000, an estimated 2.7 trillion miles (4.3 trillion km) were traveled in the United States alone—1.6 trillion miles (2.6 trillion km) of that total being traveled in urban areas. Road systems carry passenger transport—private and public—as well as freight, and they both penetrate and interlink centers of population. Roads also stimulate settlement in the land through which they pass, making tracts of land accessible by automobile and their users constituting a market for hotel accommodation, for fuel and food retailers, and for mechanics.

The principal aim when designing a road system is to cater to the volume of traffic that is likely to wish to travel between the nodes of that system—its intersections and termini. For a stretch of road that connects two centers of population, that volume is usually proportional to the product of the populations of those two centers, divided by the square of the distance between them. For more complex networks, a prediction of the volume of traffic that will use a new route can be obtained by conducting a census of vehicles using the existing roads between the two points that the proposed road will link. This result will be less than the true volume, since a faster or more direct route encourages road travel between two centers of population.

Once a prediction of traffic volumes has been made, the road design should have a sufficient number of lanes to carry the maximum predicted vehicular flow. If not, delays due to overcrowding of the highway will occur, causing a cost to the economy in terms of wasted fuel and working hours as well as inconveniencing road users.

Safety and the environment

While catering for the volume of traffic on a road, special consideration must be given to the safety of road users and pedestrians around the road and to the environmental impact of a road. Studies of accidents show that road design and the behavior of road users are the most important factors in the occurrence of accidents. Vehicles themselves cause accidents less often, but their construction and safety features have a great influence on the resultant injuries.

Adequate road capacity is not only important for saving time and money, it also helps avoid increased hazards that occur when frustrated drivers act rashly in overcrowded conditions. The consequences of such situations range from collisions to acts of aggression, or road rage.

In situations where vehicles and pedestrians are in close proximity to one another, such as city streets, the use of speed limits, light-controlled crossings, and traffic-calming measures minimize the hazard to pedestrians and—if well designed—reduce pollution from noise and exhaust gases. Often the construction of a new bypass, tunnel, or elevated road significantly reduces the traffic density in populated areas by carrying through traffic, while only local traffic populates the road in the immediate vicinity of pedestrians. These solutions are costly, however, and elevated roads in particular can have strongly detrimental visual impacts. Nevertheless, such approaches are often the only practical options for reducing street traffic in densely built-up urban areas.

In many countries, the number of vehicles on roads has been successfully reduced by establishing exclusive lanes for multiply occupied cars, buses, and taxis. Such lanes are generally lightly occupied, so those entitled to use them enjoy faster journey times while reducing the number of

▼ Road systems at busy intersections are highly complicated structures designed to enable traffic to move from one side of a city to another without being stopped by traffic signals or held in long backups in urban streets.

vehicles on the road. Priority lanes for cycle and motorcycle users encourage people to use forms of transport that are more environmentally friendly and that occupy less space in the road.

Major highways

Freeways, expressways, and other major highways offer short journey times and are without delays under favorable conditions. Their road alignments, junction layouts, and signage are all designed to simplify the decisions taken by drivers and provide enough time for those decisions to be made correctly and safely. The design and limited number of access points, combined with the absence of pedestrians and parked vehicles, keep the number of accidents per unit distance traveled to around half the rate for other classes of road.

One of the key factors to the good safety record of major highways is the absence of extreme curves and the parabolic alignment of the curves that are present. A parabolic curve tightens gradually, encouraging drivers to slow to an appropriate speed if necessary to handle the curve. Where poorly aligned curves have been realigned in this way, cuts in accident rates as

great as 80 percent have been achieved. Superelevation—a gradual increase in vertical height from the inside to the outside edge of a curve—facilitates steering on curves by providing a lateral force due to gravity that naturally drives a vehicle around the curve if traveling near the intended speed. This force reduces the need for adhesion and makes for a comfortable ride.

Wherever possible, intersections are graded—the separate streams of traffic pass at different vertical levels—often with a rotary junction joining access and exit roads at an intermediate level. Alternatively, a clover leaf of access and exit roads provides links between two crossing highways.

As a rule, the major highway is at the lowest level, so the downward gradients of access roads help vehicles accelerate to the pace of the through traffic on the highway; conversely, the upward gradients of exit roads slow traffic as it heads toward the minor road. Further inducement to reduce speed, particularly when approaching a rotary, is provided by curves that become progressively tighter or by ridges in the road surface that cause audible beats and are spaced at increasingly closer intervals toward a junction.

Conflict between through traffic and vehicles that are leaving or entering a highway is avoided by the provision of acceleration and deceleration lanes, which allow traffic that is moving at a different pace to stay out of the main flow. Similarly, additional crawler lanes on steep upward gradients allow slow-moving, heavy vehicles to keep out of the way of faster moving traffic.

Median strip

A characteristic of major highways is the median strip that separates the opposing traffic flows of a divided highway. The principal virtue of a divided highway is the great reduction in the frequency of severe and fatal head-on collisions when compared with roads where the two opposing streams share a single strip of pavement. Work in the United States has shown that the width of the central median has a direct effect on the rate of crossover accidents on highways where there is no central barrier. The standard specification for the U.S. Interstate highway system requires a median width of 50 ft. (15 m). In Europe, where land is more expensive, the preference is for narrower medians, usually with central barriers.

Crash barriers and arrester beds

The purpose of a central barrier is to prevent out-of-control vehicles from straying into oncoming traffic, but their use is not always advisable. On divided highways where traffic densities are low, crash barriers can cause collisions—between

STREET LIGHTING

The purpose of street lighting is to increase the nighttime visibility of any vehicles, pedestrians, or obstacles on a public or private road. Its primary goal is to reduce the likelihood of road-traffic accidents, but it also acts as a deterrent against assaults and other crimes. Around one-third of all accidents occur during darkness, and the installation of street lighting on an unlit road can reduce night accidents by between 30 and 50 percent.

One approach to street lighting uses silhouette vision, whereby the road and surroundings appear lit, while vehicles, pedestrians, and stationary obstacles appear as silhouettes. This approach requires a substantial amount of light to reflect off the road surface and sidewalk, so surfacing materials with good reflective properties must be used.

In a second approach, high-efficiency discharge lamps produce higher lighting levels. Objects on the road and sidewalk are then directly illuminated.

The most widely used light sources for street lighting are high-pressure sodium and mercury-vapor discharge lamps, both of which give good color rendering as a result of their near-white light outputs. Low-pressure sodium discharge lamps, which produce a monochromatic orange light, are used in some countries outside the United States, where their use is restricted owing to the color of their light.

The light source is contained in a weatherproof globe, and shaped reflectors and refractors direct its light downward in a well-defined T-shaped pattern. In so-called cutoff lamps, the light spreads over angles up to 65 degrees either side of the vertical, giving good glare control. The illuminated footprint under the lamp is quite narrow, so cutoff lamps have to be closely spaced. The favored pattern is to have lamps at regular intervals that are staggered on either side of the road.

Semicutoff lamps cast light up to 75 degrees from the vertical and have a longer tail to their T-shaped footprint than that found in cutoff lamps. Their glare control is less than that of cutoff lamps, and they illuminate in silhouette as well as directly. For this reason, semi-

cutoff lamps are used in conjunction with smooth, highly reflective road surfaces. The broader footprints of semi-cutoff lamps means they can be more widely spaced than cutoff lamps.

The heights of streetlamps vary to some extent but are typically around 30 ft. (9 m). On wider roads, lamps may be positioned opposite one another, and on four-lane or six-lane highways the favored system has pairs of lamps on columns installed in the median strip.

High-intensity lighting from masts up to 150 ft. (46 m) high can be used at complex multilevel junctions to reduce the number of conventional lamp columns, which would otherwise present a collision hazard. This type of high-mast lighting works by direct illumination.

In tunnels, roof-mounted fluorescent strips or discharge lamps provide high-intensity lighting throughout. During the hours of daylight, additional lamps near the entrances and exits of tunnels create a gradual transition between the external and internal light intensities. This enables drivers' eyes to adjust to the changing light intensities as they pass through.

◀ The semi-cutoff street lamp is typical of the lamps used to illuminate highways and urban roads. A mask around the lamp ensures that the amount of glare that reaches drivers' eyes is kept to a minimum while also reducing the light pollution that strays into the night sky.

◀ The mask is designed such that the patch of light cast onto the road surface can interlock with similar patches from other lamps. Then patches of light from appropriately spaced lamps on alternate sides of the road form a reasonably uniform carpet of light over the entire surface of the roadway.

Economy dictates that street lamps should operate only when the ambient light intensity falls below levels that are acceptable for safe driving. In one of the more basic control systems, called the solar-dial time switch, a synchronous motor drives a clock that switches the power supply to the lamp on and off at predetermined times. Those times vary in accordance with the changing times of sunrise and sunset throughout the year, but the system fails if the power is cut.

More sophisticated streetlamps are switched on and off by photoelectric cells. These switch on the power supply when the light intensity falls below a threshold level for safe driving and switch it off again when the light intensity rises above that threshold. Photocells have two main advantages over time switches. First, they do not rely on motor-driven clocks, so they return to normal operation as soon as the power is restored after a power cut. Second, they respond directly to light intensity, so they switch on if night falls early owing to overcast conditions or if fog or a heavy rainstorm severely reduces light intensity during normal daylight hours.

vehicles and the barrier—when straying vehicles would otherwise be likely to come to rest on the median strip or on an empty stretch of highway. Where traffic densities are high, however, the increased likelihood of meeting oncoming traffic makes the installation of crash barriers imperative. Also, a crash barrier blocks glare from the headlights of oncoming traffic at night.

The construction and form of crash barriers varies and has an influence on their function. Reinforced-concrete barriers, cast as the road is laid, perform the basic function of preventing vehicles from crossing into oncoming traffic. More sophisticated barriers consist of toughened steel strips mounted on posts along the median. If a vehicle collides with such a barrier, the strips deform as they absorb the energy of the impact, thus reducing the rate of deceleration and consequently the likelihood of serious injury.

In some cases, crash barriers are placed around the bases of lighting masts and other obstacles on the shoulder or median of a highway. They provide some protection in the event of impact with such obstacles, but the preferred approach is now to build lightweight aluminum or steel lighting masts with weak points near their bases. Such masts snap on impact without causing excessive damage to the colliding vehicle. In some cases, several lamps are strung from catenary wires above the median, thereby reducing the number of columns necessary for lighting. This approach is favored particularly in Europe.

Support columns for bridges cannot be built with weak points, but they can be protected by surrounding them with plastic drums that contain sand. A vehicle on collision course with a bridge column then decelerates at an acceptable rate to avoid injury—around five times acceleration due to gravity—as it hits progressively fuller barrels.

Sand or gravel can also be used in roadside arrester beds. They tend to be built alongside roads on prolonged downward gradients. In the event of brake failure, the driver of a vehicle can steer into the bed, which then slows the vehicle at an acceptable rate as it plows into the bed. These beds are of such a depth and size that they are able to stop a free-rolling truck in safety.

Road surface and drainage

An effective road surface must be smooth enough to give a comfortable ride but not so smooth as to become slippery, particularly when wet. The most popular road surfaces are made by embedding gravel aggregate in bitumen. The surfacing material is applied hot, when the bitumen is soft. On cooling, the bitumen hardens and holds the aggregate in place, while points of the aggregate protrude from the bitumen to form a sufficiently rough surface for tires to grip. Such surfaces become polished after a while—the aggregate gets worn down to the level of the bitumen, so the surface becomes smooth—and have to be replaced periodically. Alternatively, the surface can be made from concrete, in which case a surface pattern provides the necessary grip.

Advanced surfacing materials have been developed for sites where heavy braking is frequent. One such surface is a calcined bauxite in a resin base, which provides high skid resistance even when wet and does not polish significantly with use. On experimental sites, it has given a reduction of more than 30 percent in accidents. It is, however, an expensive material, and use is generally restricted to high-risk areas, such as junctions.

Effective drainage is essential to prevent the accumulation of rainwater, which would otherwise reduce adhesion. It is particularly essential in regions where long hot spells can cause the road surface to be covered in a thin layer of rubber from tires and subsequent heavy rainfall then results in a greasy road surface.

Surface water presents the additional hazard of aquaplaning at traffic speeds greater than around 50 mph (80 km/h). In this effect, a wedge of water intrudes between the moving tire and the surface, eventually eliminating direct contact between the tire and the road surface and causing almost complete loss of adhesion. Modern tires are designed to eject water from the road surface as they move, but the problem can be further reduced by use of a porous road surface that allows rain to soak in without having to run off into gutters at the sides of the road.

▼ A truck leaves a toll plaza on the Governor Thomas E. Dewey Thruway, which connects New York City and Buffalo in New York State. Funds from tolls go to road building and maintenance.

Road signs and markings

Information about hazards, restrictions, and road layout should be delivered to drivers with the utmost clarity while causing as little distraction as possible. One type of road marking that meets these criteria in a particularly elegant way is the cat's eye, which consists of one or more reflective beads in a rugged but flexible mounting. At night, cat's eyes embedded along lane divisions reflect light from headlights to reveal the course of a road without requiring lighting masts to illuminate the painted markings. On some divided highways, amber cat's eyes mark the edge of the roadway closer to the median strip, while red cat's eyes mark the outer edge. At junctions, the red cat's eyes give way to green ones that mark where vehicles can safely leave the main flow.

Rumble strips are useful for alerting a driver whose vehicle is straying off the roadway. These strips consist of a resinous material whose surface is ridged. When a tire passes over the strip, the ridges cause a loud rumbling noise. The nonvisual nature of this warning is particularly appropriate, since drivers are most likely to stray off the road as their eyes close at the onset of sleep.

The majority of information has to be conveyed using signs, however. The most appropriate means of conveying information, with the exception of directions and speed limits, is by pictorial signs, because their information is easy to assimilate and does not require a driver to be literate or familiar with the local language. Images that depict such hazards as road narrowings and maintenance, for example, have become standardized between North America and Europe, so drivers need not be bewildered by a host of unfamiliar signs when they travel in foreign countries.

Signs must be large enough and appropriately mounted to be visible for a sufficient time for drivers to assimilate their information while traveling at the intended speed on a given roadway. They must also be at a sufficient distance from the junction or condition to which they refer for drivers to take appropriate action, such as by changing lanes near an intersection. On major rural highways, for example, large reflective signs become illuminated by vehicle headlights, or are lit from the front at night. In urban areas, backlit signs can be used to overcome the high ambient light intensity. On multilane highways, it is often necessary to mount such signs on gantries over the roadway; each sign then gives information specific to the lane over which it is mounted, thus helping avoid driver confusion.

Variable signs are used to convey information such as temporary speed limits and lane closures. Such displays typically consist of matrix arrays of small lamps that can be used to spell out a number

▶ At left, the upper portion of this matrix array indicates a temporary speed limit of 40 mph (60 km/h). The lower portion advises of slippery road conditions over the next 2½ miles. At right, the same sign warns of a temporary closure of the right-hand lane for road maintenance in 7 miles. Signs such as this are useful for warning of a variety of deviations from the normal road condition.

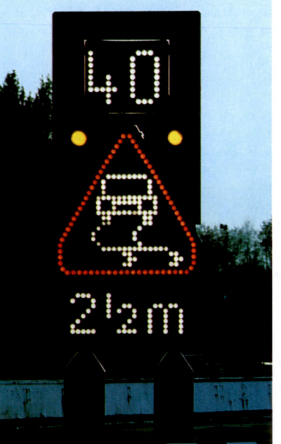

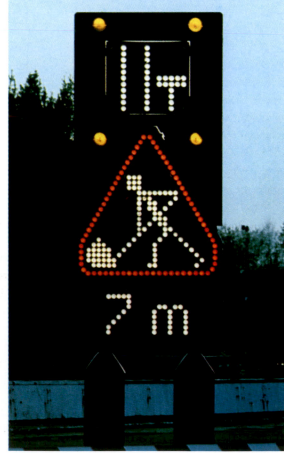

STOP SIGNALS

Road networks are safest when traffic moves in parallel lanes and pedestrians are kept away from vehicular traffic. Where this ideal condition is not possible, stop signals help manage the movements of vehicles and pedestrians so as to avoid accidents and prevent obstructions where traffic streams cross or merge or where a pedestrian route crosses a road.

Stop signals work by allowing one or more parallel traffic streams to proceed while those streams that would cross are kept waiting. After a while, the priorities reverse so that the traffic that was held can proceed through the junction.

In most cases, three colors of lights control vehicular movement: red stops traffic, green allows it to proceed, and yellow indicates an imminent change between red and green. A sole yellow light indicates an imminent change to red, while in some systems, simultaneous red and yellow lights indicate an imminent green light. Various forms of signal are also used to control pedestrian traffic.

Each light assembly consists of a light source, a reflector, and a colored Fresnel lens that directs light toward the drivers in its path. In some cases, an arrow filter on the Fresnel lens of a green light allows traffic to proceed in one direction while vehicles bound for other directions are held on red. To prevent misleading sightings, hoods and sometimes louvre screens are fitted to restrict the angle from which the signal can be seen by drivers.

High-intensity lights are used to ensure good visibility in sunlight, and photoelectric sensors reduce the light intensity at night to avoid dazzle.

The simplest form of control system uses fixed timing, with each traffic stream being allowed a predetermined flow time in a repeating sequence. Several timing patterns may be programmed to allow for different traffic patterns during the day. In older designs, the timing mechanism consisted of an electric motor driving a set of timing dials that actuated switches for the appropriate lights. Now, electronic controllers use microprocessors to give a range of operating cycles, and relays or solid-state switches control the supply of power to the lights. Timing periods vary according to the traffic density but are typically 30 to 150 seconds.

More sophisticated control systems use induction-loop sensors to count the vehicles at each approach to the junction. In extreme cases, the lights for the main road stay green until a vehicle is detected on a side road, when the priority switches for a limited period; more often, the times for which each route has priority are adjusted according to their relative traffic volumes.

In some cases, additional inputs to the control system come from pole-mounted buttons on the sidewalk. Pedestrians press these buttons to signal their desire to cross the road, and the control system stops traffic on the appropriate routes while they do so. A preset minimum time for the traffic routes to have priority ensures that pedestrian phases do not cause excessive disruption to traffic flow.

On major routes and in urban centers, several sets of signals are controlled by a central computer, and the control signals reach the lights by cable or radio signals. In such systems, the green phases of lights can be coordinated so traffic that moves at a predetermined speed will always reach a green light. This type of coordination, called a green wave, reduces pollution by minimizing the number of times drivers have to stop and accelerate their vehicles. Green waves also encourage drivers not to exceed the speed limit, since they will encounter red lights if they drive faster than the green wave moves. Normal operation of coordinated systems can also be disrupted temporarily to allow emergency vehicles to pass freely along their route to the scene of an emergency.

In the United States, the Manual of Uniform Traffic Control Devices (MUTCD) lists eight minimum warrants for traffic signals to be installed. At least one of them must be completely satisfied before traffic signals can be installed.

Warrant 1 states that the traffic level must meet certain minimum requirements, determined by the physical condition of the roadway, for around eight hours of the day. Warrant 2 looks at the interruption to

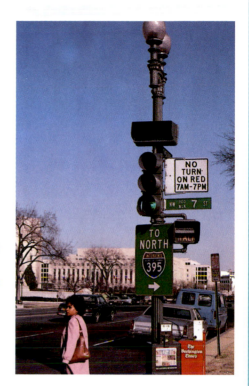

▲ This stoplight controls the movements of vehicles and pedestrians at an intersection. Without it, more accidents would occur and traffic flow would become chaotic.

continuous traffic that traffic signals might cause: proposed traffic signals must be likely to help traffic flow. Warrant 3 combines the pedestrian and vehicular flow figures and compares the result with the number of pedestrians crossing the road, looking for the minimum pedestrian volume. Warrant 4 considers the special case of school crossings and applies a mathematical formula to determine the danger to students from traffic. Warrant 5 looks at progressive movement of traffic to determine whether the flow could be improved by platooning (dividing traffic into groups of vehicles). Warrant 7 examines the condition of the roadways at the proposed site—for example, whether it lies on major trunk routes, freeways, or important routes connecting areas of traffic generation. Warrant 8 contains conditions for when a proposed site does not completely satisfy minimum requirements for signalization. It looks at combinations of warrants; for example, if warrants 1, 2, and 3 are satisfied to the 80 percent level, then warrant 8 is satisfied.

► This census unit, which is embedded in a road surface, collects data from vehicle detectors and sends it via cable to a traffic-control center.

► In the traffic-control center, operators use data from census units and video cameras to provide information for roadside signs and radio broadcasts.

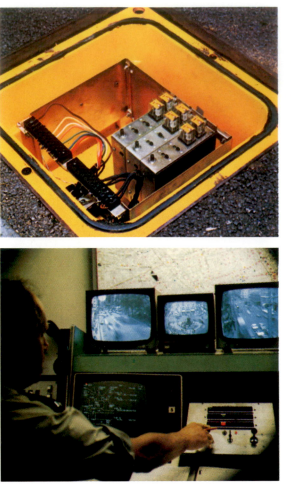

of messages, and they are operated from a central control. More sophisticated signs can carry information about traffic congestion, recent accidents, or recommended alternative routes.

Speed limits

The principal goal of a speed limit is to improve safety for road users and pedestrians. Since the fuel crisis of the 1970s, fuel economy has been another reason for imposing speed limits, and the reduction in noise when a speed limit is reduced in urban areas is an environmental bonus.

When choosing a speed limit for safety reasons, the aim is to ensure that all traffic flows at roughly the same speed. When vehicles move at different speeds on the same roadway, the increased incidence of potentially hazardous maneuvers, such as sudden braking and overtaking, leads to errors of judgement and accidents. The imposition of a speed limit helps avoid such hazards by reducing the number of vehicles traveling much faster than the average speed.

One technique for choosing an appropriate speed limit, used particularly in the United States, is to measure the distribution of speeds in the traffic stream in the unrestricted condition. The speed limit is then fixed around the 85th percentile level—the speed exceeded by 15 percent

of all vehicles. This procedure is sound in that it suits the expectations of most road users and consequently results in a speed limit that is adhered to by the vast majority of drivers. Such a policy demands that the speed limit change frequently with every curve and straight stretch of road but is effective in improving safety.

Safety can also be improved by imposing minimum speed limits, so as to narrow yet further the band of speeds on a given highway. Slow-moving vehicles are prohibited from using the highway, and drivers who are not confident of driving above the minimum speed limit are encouraged to find a route that suits their pace. Typical minimum limits are around 40 mph (60 km/h)

The ideal speed limit varies with light and weather conditions. In some cases, reflecting signs show a higher speed limit in daylight and a lower speed limit when illuminated by headlights at night. It is also common in some countries to have two speed limits shown on each sign on a highway—the lower limit applying in rain or fog. The problem with such signs is the occasional ambiguity regarding the limit that should apply; this ambiguity is eliminated by the use of matrix arrays to show the prevailing speed limit.

Speed limits can also vary at times of heavy traffic, because the average spacing between vehicles decreases as the volume of traffic increases. When the average spacing drops below the safe distance for the normal speed limit, cautious drivers attempt to increase their distance from the vehicles in front by slowing down, while more reckless drivers tailgate, leading to bunching and increasing the risk of accidents. Smoother flow can be achieved by imposing a speed limit that corresponds to the safe spacing for a given traffic load.

Traffic monitoring

Traffic-monitoring devices are used to provide information as a basis for imposing temporary speed limits and changes in stop-signal sequences. It can also be used to compile information on trends in traffic densities when planning maintenance or the construction of new roads.

An early device for counting traffic was the road tube, an inflated pneumatic tube stretched across a road surface near a junction or crossing, for example. When a vehicle passed over such a device, the weight of its tires would increase the pressure within the tube. An electromechanical device would then convert that increase in pressure into an electrical signal fed to a counter. Such devices were prone to rapid wear and failure on heavily trafficked roads. A modern and more rugged variation on the same theme uses a strip of piezoelectric material embedded with resin in a indentation in the road surface to emit an electrical signal in direct response to a passing vehicle.

Road tubes and piezoelectric strips count axles rather than vehicles, so that vehicle counts can be distorted by vehicles with more than two axles, such as trucks. Nonetheless, some instruments work with software that recognizes two pulses in rapid succession as a double axle, for example. When such software is used, the count can be classified into standard and multiple-axle vehicles.

One type of instrument that detects vehicles—rather than their axles—is the inductive loop. An inductive loop is a coil of insulated wire that can be embedded in an indentation or buried under a road surface. It forms part of a tuned electrical circuit that has a characteristic resonant frequency. When a conducting mass, such as the engine and transmission of a road vehicle, passes near the loop, the inductance and resonant frequency of the loop decrease—in effect, an inductive loop acts as a metal detector. Inductive loops can be used singly, simply to count vehicles, or they can be used in pairs that measure speed from the time difference between pulses from the two coils. In the latter case, detection of excessive speed can trigger a flash camera that records the vehicle's license for subsequent prosecution.

Devices related to sonar and Doppler radar equipment can detect stationary and moving vehicles from roadside posts or overhead gantries. Such equipment has the advantage that it can be installed without cutting the road surface or interrupting traffic. The sonar-type device uses ultrasound to detect vehicles that are stationary at stoplights, whereas inductive loops can only sense moving vehicles as they approach a junction. This information can be used to trigger a change in the stoplight sequence. The radar-type device uses microwave pulses to detect moving vehicles. Doppler analysis separates frequency-shifted pulses bounced off moving objects from unshifted pulses reflected by stationary objects; this information can then be used to capture on camera the license plates of vehicles that pass through stoplights at red, for example.

Highway monitoring

Traffic-monitoring devices can be used in conjunction with mast-mounted remote-controlled video cameras to monitor the condition of traffic on major highways. When inductive loops detect high traffic volumes, for example, a control-room operator can impose a temporary speed limit to be displayed on matrix arrays along the highway. In the case of tidal-flow highways—roadways that have reversible central lanes—the flow direction

of the tidal lanes can be switched according to fluctuations in traffic density. At changeover, traffic is first blocked from both directions using stoplights and signs on overhead gantries. When the tidal lanes are clear, as can be confirmed using video surveillance, traffic is allowed to enter the tidal lanes in the direction of heavier flow by setting the appropriate stoplights to green.

Sudden falls in average speed can be an indication that an accident has occurred. When such falls are detected from inductive loop data, the control computer can alert the operator to the troubled stretch of highway for a video inspection of what has happened. The appropriate warning and lane-closure signs can then be activated, and emergency rescue teams called if necessary.

Highway-control centers can send information about delays and congestion to roadside signs near access points, to radio stations that issue traffic broadcasts, and to systems that work with onboard route-planning computers. Drivers can then plan alternative routes to avoid trouble spots, thereby easing congestion at those points.

An experimental scheme on Highway 401 in Ontario, Canada, uses radio listening posts at crucial points to detect the signals cellphones send to their base stations even when on standby. By correlating the count of cellphones on the highway with the proportion of drivers who carry cellphones, the total number of vehicles can be estimated. This is a cheap and easy way of monitoring traffic density—much cheaper than installing inductive loops—and it could make viable complete coverage of a nation's entire highway network. Additional benefits could be gained by connecting the control computers of such detector networks to roadside maps that automatically display heavily congested stretches of highway.

▼ These elegant twin streetlamps and their streamlined support column show how fixtures designed to improve road safety can also contribute to the aesthetic of the urban environment.

Robotics

The term *robot* comes from the Czech word *robota*, meaning "forced labor." It was first used in the play *R.U.R.: Rossum's Universal Robots*, written in 1920 by the Czech author Karel Capek, in which humans used robots to perform tasks for them. A robot can be broadly defined as a task-performing machine that resembles a human in one or more respects, and robotics is the study, construction, and use of such machines.

Early robots

The forerunners to modern robots were industrial machines designed to move standard workpieces from one station to the next on automated assembly lines. These devices consisted of mechanical grippers mounted on movable arms. They could perform specific tasks but could not be programmed to perform various functions.

An early industrial robot had a grasping "hand" fixed to the end of an extendible arm. The arm could tilt up or down to a maximum angle of 60 degrees from the horizontal and could be rotated through 360 degrees around a vertical axis. The "wrist" joint between the arm and the hand could also be rotated, and all movements were effected by hydraulic motors and jacks. The robot was programmable: it could be set to move between a total of up to 45 predetermined positions in a specified sequence and to spend a selected time in each position.

The next stage in the evolution of the robot incorporated data-processing capability based on computer technology and had improved dexterity compared with the first robots. Early Unimate robotic arms had six basic movements: arm extension and retraction, movement of the arm in a vertical plane, hand rotation about the wrist axis, hand pivoting at right angles to the wrist axis, gripping, and movement of the whole arm along a slide. Gripping was accomplished by a set of pneumatically operated fingers, achieving a maximum force of 359 lbf. (1,600 N). The Unimate places objects to an accuracy of 0.04 in. (1 mm).

The arm's movements are controlled hydraulically by means of a servo valve, a servo amplifier, and a comparator. The comparator receives sequence information—the instructions to which the robot responds—from a computer. Early robots of this type required large mainframe computers to provide their instructions; with time, desktop microcomputers became capable of performing the task, then onboard microprocessors. Sequence information is stored on magnetic or optical media. Some robots of this type use simple

▲ The EPA Japan SDR-3X soccer-playing humanoid robot. The movement skills of this playful prototype may some day be used in an advanced android.

feedback to monitor the effect of instructions, so an increase in pressure within the pneumatic rams of the fingers indicates that they have grasped something, for example.

Industrial robots

Robots find most of their applications in the manufacturing industries, where they perform simple and repetitive tasks with an unerring precision that surpasses the ability of even the most skilled human worker. Because they can work quickly, thoroughly, and without breaks, well-programmed robots increase the productivity of a given work station while practically eliminating the production of substandard articles.

Although they boost productivity and can cut production costs, the initial outlay when installing robots is great. Apart from the cost of the machines themselves—an amount that increases with the complexity and versatility of the model—the factory owner must pay for specialist installation, ancillary equipment, and lost production during installation and fine tuning.

The basis of most industrial robots is a robotic arm. Devices called end effectors take the place of the hand, and they range from mechanical grippers or vacuum cups to tools such as welding torches, spray guns, and machine tools.

The simplest industrial robots are basic units that are programmed to perform a simple task repeatedly. Examples include robots that feed granules of plastic into injection-molding machines and cut apart sets of injection-molded components in a toy-component factory. At the other end of the scale are the enormous machines that work on automobile assembly lines. One such machine makes hundreds of spot welds on each body shell within a few minutes, its long, jointed arms reaching into and under the car, and the entire assembly moving some 30 ft. (9 m) during the operation. A similar machine uses arm-mounted spray guns to apply a uniform layer of paint across the whole body, inside and out.

All the examples discussed so far are of first-generation robots, which account for the large majority of industrial robots. They perform according to simple preset instructions and cannot vary greatly from a single type of task. However, simple modifications, such as those required to cater for different automobile models, can be made by changing the instruction set. While being relatively unsophisticated machines, they bring considerable benefits to humankind: they spare humans from having to twist in and out of car bodies to weld and from working in environments where they could get burned or inhale hazardous paint fumes, for example.

Remotely operated vehicles

Remotely operated vehicles, or ROVs, extend the range of circumstances in which first-generation robotics can serve humanity. They are self-propelled vehicles that move—usually on tracks or wheels—under remote steering via radio or cable communication. More often than not, they have one or more video cameras that report their view to a monitor screen at the remote control.

The video link enables an operator to guide and use tools mounted on robotic arms on the vehicle. In this case, signals from hand controls or pedals at the remote control replace preprogrammed instructions, making for a much more

▲ A robotic installation for polishing sink units. The polishing sequence consists of 200 positions.

versatile robot—they are, in effect, human representatives in environments that might be hazardous for a human to occupy.

ROVs find use in inspecting and repairing the highly radioactive cores of nuclear reactors, in bomb disposal, close to active volcanoes, and in chemically contaminated areas. As well as being used on land, ROVs can also be used in locations that range from deep sea to outer space.

Second-generation robots

As their name implies, second-generation robots are more advanced than the first generation. Instead of relying on laboriously created instruction programs, a second-generation robot is capable of learning tasks—creating its own instructions from a demonstration of a task. An example is the paint-spraying robot: the trainer in this case is a human who performs the spraying routine using a spray gun wired with sensors and transducers that report every action. Once such instructions have been created, they can be used by any number of identical robots to perform the same paint-spraying routine, all with the same technique as a highly skilled human operator.

There are two subclasses of second-generation robots: continuous path (CP) and point-to-point (PTP). Programming a continuous-path robot is simple: the operator leads it through an operation, and the robot's processor records each part of the movement, storing the movement as a huge number of small steps. To reprogram the robot, the operator leads it through a new set of movements, and new instructions are written.

Point-to-point robots, although initially "taught" in the same way as CP robots, translate the operation into a series of points through which the manipulator passes. These points are recorded as coordinates in three-dimensional space. To reprogram the robot, the operator need only make the appropriate alterations to the coordinates of the manipulator's reference points that are stored in the robot's processor.

Robotic senses

Although a robot might seem to "know" what it is doing with uncanny accuracy, it must be remembered that basic robots perform purely according to fixed instructions. Hence, a car-spraying robot, once triggered, will go through its spraying routine whether a car body is present or not.

A great deal of robotics research concentrates on making robots that can sense their environment and adapt their routines accordingly. These sensing mechanisms correspond to the five human senses—hearing, sight, smell, taste, and touch—but their mechanisms are different.

Smell. Robots with sensing equipment have been around for some time: as early as 1983, the Austin Rover motor company's Maestro production line at Cowley, England, used robotic sensors to check for leaks. The car body would be filled with helium gas, and two sniffer heads would then move over every seam, seal, and aperture in the body checking for the gas, whose presence indicated a leak. The system was flawed, however, since not all leaks let out enough helium to be detected under the test conditions, and the Maestro acquired a reputation for leaks.

One sniffer method uses gas chromatography to identify chemical substances by the amount of time they take to be swept through a fine glass tube by an inert gas, such as nitrogen. In broad terms, the longer this time—called the retention time—the heavier the molecule, and substances can be identified by reference to values of retention times stored in a database.

Taste. The human sensation of taste arises when certain types of chemicals stimulate the taste buds. When stimulated, the taste buds send electrical signals through nerves to the brain, and the brain interprets combinations of these signals from the different types of taste buds as flavors. The equivalents of taste buds for robots are chemical sensors and biosensors.

A chemical sensor, such as a pH electrode, uses an electrochemical reaction to measure the concentration of hydrogen ions in a solution. This property characterizes its acidity—the chemical equivalent of sourness. Similar electrodes can detect the ions that constitute common salt—sodium and chloride ions—and indeed many other types of ions. A robot could therefore be equipped to measure the salt content of a sample of food, for example. This ability falls a long way short of being able to determine whether the food tastes right, but it could form part of a sampling procedure to determine whether more salt should be added.

More complex biochemicals, such as sucrose (sugar), can be detected using highly specific biosensors. Biosensors use other biochemicals—typically enzymes—that react in some way with the target compound to produce a change, such as the release of an ion or an increase in temperature. That change is then detected by a transducer that responds by producing an electrical signal. While it is unlikely that a robot will ever be able to taste in the way humans do, the ability to measure chemical composition has various applications, such as sampling soil for contamination.

Sight. An early example of a seeing robot was developed by the FIAT motor company of Italy. The robot used a video camera, interfaced with a microprocessor and preprocessor, to locate the bolt holes for fixing a hinge to a door by scanning the edge of the door. The system analyzed an image of the approximate location of one of the sets of bolt holes, splitting that image into 250,000 picture elements (pixels). The preprocessor then graded each pixel as black or white, forming a checkerboard pattern that resembled a high-contrast, grainy black-and-white photograph of the area. The computer then compared that image with a standard image in its memory to pinpoint the centers of the two bolt holes. That positional information then formed the basis for instructions to guide the arm holding the hinge and bolts toward the bolt holes.

More sophisticated vision systems use binocular vision to form a stereoscopic image—just as the human system does. At the Laboratory of Agricultural Systems Engineering at the University of Okayama, Japan, researchers have

▼ This Fata welding station has two robotic arms fitted with welding end effectors. Each arm moves along a slide, can extend and retract, and has three rotary joints.

developed a tomato-harvesting robot that uses stereoscopic vision to locate tomatoes for picking. The system distinguishes ripe tomatoes from unripe fruit and foliage by analyzing the red, green, and blue components of the image. A processor interprets the stereoscopic image to produce coordinates for the position of ripe fruit. An end effector then harvests the fruit, using two mechanical fingers to secure the bunch, while a suction cup plucks the ripe fruit.

At the Computational Sensory-Motors Laboratory of the Johns Hopkins University, Baltimore, researchers are investigating an imaging system that is more akin to a bat's "sonar" system for imaging its environment. The system uses an array of microelectromechanical microphones etched into a single silicon chip. A separate ultrasound source emits pulses that "illuminate" objects near the detector. A processor analyzes the echoes registered by the microphone array to calculate the ranges and angular positions of reflectors. It then uses this information to build up a three-dimensional image. The intention of the project is to produce equipment that lets submarine robots "see" in murky water.

Hearing and speech. The human sense of hearing and the related ability of speech have been mimicked with various degrees of success for many years now. Voice-recognition software is used to accept spoken instructions for some telephone-answering services, for example, while voice-synthesis programs create spoken warnings for computer users. Voice recognition also has a role in security, since a program can distinguish the voices of those authorized to give commands.

Touch. Human touch has two functions that are of value to robots: it indicates when first contact is made with an object—thus helping avoid damage to the object and the toucher—and it characterizes surface textures. While the latter function is under investigation for robots, the ability to sense contact and pressure has more applications and has developed further.

Robots use a number of sensors to determine the proximity of nearby objects ranging from photosensors to sonar. There are also various forms of force sensor, based on load cells, that measure the pressure exerted by an end effector on a surface. However, the type that most resembles skin consists of a layer of elastomer backed by an array of ultrasound emitters and detectors. The ultrasound system measures the thickness of the elastomer—which corresponds to the pressure exerted on it—from the time taken for ultrasound to travel through the elastomer and bounce off the opposite side. The film can detect forces equivalent to 0.04 oz. (1 g) and has a surface reso-

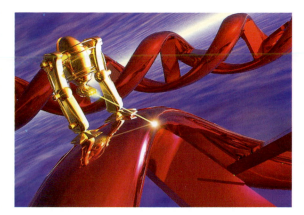

◀ Conceptual computer illustration of a nanorobot repairing DNA with a laser. One day, tiny robots like these could help the body repair its DNA.

lution of 0.07 in. (1.8 mm). This resolution enables it to produce reasonable maps of held objects to help in their identification.

Androids

An android is a mobile humanoid robot. Most robots work at fixed stations or roll along fixed, level paths that are marked out by buried signal-transmitting wires, marked tiles, or similar guidance devices. They use infrared or ultrasound ranging devices to spot objects in their paths and negotiate their way around them. Nevertheless, this motion does not resemble that of a human.

Numerous prototypes of robots have been developed that can walk or at least crawl on multiple "legs," but the first public demonstration of a humanoid robot walking on two legs was that of the Honda Motor Corporation's P-2, in 1996. The P-2 was 6 ft. (1.82 m) tall and weighed in at 463 lbs. (210 kg); it was followed by the more lightweight and compact P-3, which was 5 ft. 3 in. (1.6 m) tall and weighed only 287 lbs. (130 kg).

The walking ability of the P-2 and P-3, as well as of the earlier secret P-1, was achieved by close analysis of human motion and by matching the geometry and weight distribution of humans. These robots also impressed with their ability to perform key tasks, such as operating switches.

With basic physical dexterity conquered, it is possible that androids will be capable of performing simple household and workplace chores, such as cleaning, by 2010. It will be many more decades before the processing power is available and compact enough to support an android that can react to and learn from its environment and show basic human reasoning skills. Some experts believe that such a machine would have to process around one trillion instructions per second—an amount of processing power that, by current trends, should be available by 2050.

SEE ALSO: ARTIFICIAL INTELLIGENCE • COMPUTER • MASS PRODUCTION • TRANSDUCER AND SENSOR • VOICE RECOGNITION AND SYNTHESIS

Rocket and Space Propulsion

1990

The launch of the *Friendship 7*, the first U.S. manned orbital space flight in 1962. The space race was used during the cold war as a means of developing rocket engines for missiles in a seemingly nonthreatening way. Much of the expertise behind the early space-launch vehicles came out of the work done by German scientists on the V-2 bomb during World War II.

The term *rocket* applies both to a jet engine that functions without relying on atmospheric oxygen and to a vehicle such an engine propels. Small rockets that carry scientific instruments on short parabolic flights to the edge of the atmosphere are called sounding rockets. Multistage devices designed to carry spacecraft into orbit are more correctly called launch vehicles, and their propulsion units are usually described as rocket engines (if liquid-fueled) or rocket motors (if solid-fueled). The terms are flexible, and rocket engine can infer a large propulsion unit—based on liquid or solid propellant—whereas rocket motor refers to a smaller device.

Basic principle

Newton's Third Law of Motion—that for every action there is an equal and opposite reaction—is the basis of rocket propulsion. Turn up the water flow through a garden hose, and watch the nozzle jump back. Cover half the nozzle with your thumb, and feel the extra strain on the nozzle as the water suddenly streams farther and faster. Likewise, eject anything from the rear of a rocket, and the rocket will experience a forward thrust.

A rocket will accelerate if sufficient mass is ejected at sufficiently high speed to create a thrust greater than opposing forces, including gravity or air resistance. So the escape of expanding gases through a constricted nozzle propels a rocket engine in the opposite direction.

History

The first known form of rocket appeared in the early 13th century in China, shortly after the invention of gunpowder. These first rockets consisted of arrows lashed to tubes of gunpowder. The development of stick-stabilized rockets was rapid, as was the spread westward, and by the mid-13th century, first the Mongols and then the Arabs were using rockets in battle.

Not all rockets are used for space flight. This is an example of a surface-to-surface rocket weapon that can be launched from its self-propelled amphibious mobile launching pad.

The French crusaders brought rockets to Europe, and French troops under the command of Joan of Arc defended Orléans with rockets in 1429. At this time, however, cannon and small arms were more accurate and effective than rockets, and the rocket faded from the military scene—if not the festive one—for 350 years.

In 1792, British troops fighting in India were heavily assailed by small metal-cased rockets with an effectiveness that revived British respect for the military potential of such devices. It was the director of Woolwich Arsenal, Colonel (later, Sir William) Congreve, who, by 1804, developed this device into an efficient and destructive naval weapon with an incendiary or explosive warhead.

The accuracy of rockets, however, remained far from satisfactory until the mid-19th century, when the British engineer William Hale used spin stabilization to steady rockets in flight. Hale used angle exhaust nozzles to cause rockets to rotate around their central axis; the gyroscopic effect of this motion then resisted deviations from a flight path that coincided with that axis.

Range was still limited in relation to size until 1855, when the British firearms specialist Colonel Boxer stacked two rockets together in a line-carrying rocket for life saving. In Boxer's design, which was the forerunner of modern multistage rockets, the first stage burned to completion before an explosive separation charge jettisoned the spent first stage and ignited the second stage. In fact, Boxer was reviving an invention of two centuries earlier, when a German fireworks maker, Johann Schmidlap, created a display rocket that climbed higher than other rockets of the time by using a large first stage rocket to start its ascent before a smaller second stage took over.

The first true rocket theoretician was Russia's Konstantin E. Tsiolkovsky, who developed theories to explain the significance of high exhaust velocity, the importance of mass ratio—the ratio of launch weight to engine burn-out weight—and the relationship between these two factors in increasing vehicle velocity. In 1895, Tsiolkovsky published papers expressing his view that rockets could be used to power space flight and, by 1898, had proposed the necessity for liquid propellants for successful rocketry. These papers—coupled with his extensive studies of multistaging techniques using parallel and tandem arrangements of rocket stages—earned Tsiolkovsky the reputation as one of the first pioneers of space flight.

20th-century rocketeers

The work of Tsiolkovsky inspired numerous other pioneers of modern rocketry, notably in the former Soviet Union, in Germany, and in the

WERNHER VON BRAUN AND THE V-2

Wernher von Braun was born March 23, 1912, in Wirsitz, Germany. His interest in space and related topics was stimulated when, as a child, his mother presented him with a telescope. That interest was further nurtured in his early teenage years by the science fictions of Jules Verne and H. G. Wells and by the nonfictional *Die Rakete zu den Planetenräumen* (The Rocket to Interplanetary Space), written in 1923 by the Romanian-born German astrophysicist Hermann Oberth.

Von Braun's fascination with rocketry was not without setbacks: one day in 1925—the year he read Oberth's book—he tied six firework rockets to a wooden cart and set them alight. The cart hurtled through the streets of Wirlitz until the rockets exploded and set fire to the cart, getting von Braun into trouble with the police. More productively, von Braun's determination to understand the math and physics of rocketry was such that he transformed himself from an underachiever to class leader in these two topics.

In 1929, von Braun entered the Technische Hochschule (Technical College) in the Charlottenburg district of Berlin. There, he became a member of the German *Verein für Raumschiffahrt* (Society for Space Travel), a group of rocket enthusiasts that counted Hermann Oberth among its members. Within five years of being captivated by Oberth's book, von Braun was assisting him in his experiments with primitive rockets, which included tests at the Reinickendorf military test ground.

By 1932, the German army had set up a rocket research group in a laboratory near Kummersdorf, Germany. In the same year, the *Verein für Raumschiffahrt* demonstrated a rocket—the *Mirak*—to the head of the group, then-Captain Walter Dornberger. Despite giving a lukewarm reception to the group, Dornberger was impressed by the talents of Wernher von Braun. At the time, the Nazi government was set to prohibit any civilian rocket research, and von Braun signed a contract to start rocket research on November 1, 1932. In the same year, he started an army-sponsored Ph.D. in physics, which he completed in two years.

At Kummersdorf, von Braun started work on the *Aggregat* series of liquid-propellant rockets. The first of these, the A-1 (*Aggregat* 1) was followed by the A-2 and A-3. Tests moved from Kummersdorf to the North Sea coast, and in 1935, the whole group moved to a site near Peenemünde, on a German island in the Baltic Sea. At that time, the group was headed by von Braun and had 80 members including former members of the *Verein für Raumschiffahrt,* such as Hermann Oberth.

At Peenemünde, work started in earnest on the development of an *Aggregat*-based weapon, and the group eventually grew to some 4,000 researchers and support staff. After years of work, a fourth-generation *Aggregat* was successfully launched at Peenemünde on October 3, 1942. This rocket—the A-4—later gained the designation *Vergeltungswaffe* 2 (Vengeance Weapon 2)—or V-2—when in 1944 it started to be deployed as a long-range rocket missile.

The V-2 had a range of around 200 miles (320 km). This range enabled it to reach important targets such as Antwerp, London, and Paris from German-occupied soil. The first launch as a weapon was on September 6, 1944, against Paris.

The V-2 used ethanol as its propellant and liquid oxygen as an oxidant. The two liquids burned in a combustion chamber to develop thrust. The rocket would fly vertically for one mile (1.6 km) after takeoff, then its graphite vanes would tilt it to around 45 degrees under gyroscopic control. After a burn time of around 60 seconds, earlier V-2s would follow a ballistic trajectory—essentially that of a thrown stone—reaching a maximum altitude of 60 miles (97 km) before dropping on targets at three times the speed of sound. Later V-2s followed radio guidance.

In spring 1945, facing invasion by Soviet forces and chaos among the crumbling Nazi command, von Braun set about moving the members of the Peenemünde group toward southern Germany. They took vital equipment and paperwork with them. That summer, they surrendered to U.S. forces near Austria.

Wernher von Braun and some 120 other scientists accepted an offer to work on U.S. missile development. Von Braun would eventually become head of NASA's Marshall Space Flight Center, where he developed the immense Saturn V launch vehicle that powered the Apollo missions to the Moon. Von Braun died in 1977.

◄ An artist's impression of a wartime V-2 launch. The red flame shown here is misleading, since the ethanol–oxygen mixture used to fuel such craft burned with a white flame. The white clouds are realistic, however, and they would consist mainly of steam—one of the combustion products. The checkerboard markings served to highlight roll (spin) in films of early V-2s in flight, thereby helping analyze test flights of the rocket. Later V-2s were camouflaged in ragged and wavy patterns of cream, brown, and olive-green batik to protect them from airborne attack while awaiting launch.

Some 3,000 V-2 rockets were built between August 1944 and February 1945. The production site was a web of tunnels cut through a mountain in Nordhausen, Germany. Assembly took place in a main tunnel, and parts arrived through a parallel access tunnel and minor link tunnels. Completed rockets emerged at one end of the main tunnel.

United States. In the Soviet Union, rocketry was given official status from the start in 1929, when research began at the Gas Dynamics Laboratory (GDL) in St. Petersburg—then called Leningrad. In 1933, GDL united with Moscow's Group for Jet Propulsion Research (GJRD) and, with military financing, built liquid-fueled rockets that flew as high as 3.5 miles (5.6 km).

Germany's pioneer was Hermann Oberth, a theoretician whose concepts in liquid-fuel rocketry prompted a group of young engineers to form in 1927 the *Verein für Raumschiffahrt* (Society for Space Travel, or VfR). The VfR's practical experiments laid the foundation for Germany's wartime lead in rocketry when the VfR was forced to disperse by the Nazi government, military research absorbed some of its members, notably Wernher von Braun, who would develop the V-2 rocket and later head the U.S. Apollo program (see the box at left).

Before Wernher von Braun's arrival in the United States, the leading U.S. rocketry expert was the U.S. physicist Robert Goddard, whose research group struggled on limited private financing from the early 1920s. The Goddard group launched the world's first liquid-fueled rocket in 1926 and continued its research work until Goddard's death in 1945.

After World War II, the combined spectres of the V-2 and the atomic bombs that devastated the Japanese cities of Hiroshima and Nagasaki created a new fear: that of a nuclear weapon that could be delivered by ballistic missile. The Soviet Union and the United States—two great military powers of the time—had grown increasingly mistrustful of one another during the war, and the climate of tension between those two states became known as the cold war—a poorly defined period during which displays of military supremacy took the place of outright battles. Both superpowers were driven on in the development of ever more powerful and far-reaching intercontinental ballistic missiles, or ICBMs, by the fear of domination by an opposing ideology.

With both sides knowing that the first to show proficiency in space flight would most certainly be capable of delivering a nuclear warhead from one continent to the other, space flight became the arena in which technological supremacy could be demonstrated without overt hostility. The result was the start of the massive investment in space programs that created artificial unpiloted Earth-orbiting satellites, lunar probes, piloted missions that culminated in humans landing on the Moon in the U.S. Apollo and Soviet Soyuz programs, and then to reusable space vehicles (space shuttles) and deep-space probes.

Propulsion systems

Several different propulsion systems have been used during the development of rocketry, but all conventional systems rely on combustion reactions between two components: propellant and oxidant. The propellant is the equivalent of the fuel of a jet engine, while the oxidant takes the place of the atmospheric air supply.

There are various criteria that apply when choosing propulsion systems—the combination of liquid hydrogen and liquid oxygen might be favored because its exhaust is pure water, for example. Nevertheless, the deciding factor is often simply the amount of boost available per unit mass of propulsion system.

In scientific terms, the boosting power of a propulsion system is called its specific impulse, or I_{sp}. The first thing to note about specific impulse is that it is crucially different from thrust. The thrust developed by a rocket engine at any given time is the amount of matter it ejects in a given time multiplied by the speed at which that matter is ejected. In other words, it is the rate at which the rearward momentum of ejected matter increases, and consequently the rate at which the forward momentum of the rocket-powered vehicle increases (this acceleration is required by conservation of momentum). A propulsion system of any design has a maximum thrust, which is the rocket equivalent of how fast a given model of car accelerates with the gas pedal pushed right to the floor.

Specific impulse is defined as the number of seconds for which a given rocket-motor system can get 1 lbf. (4.45 N) of thrust from 1 lb. (0.454 kg) of fuel. In terms of an automobile engine, it is related to how long a car can operate at a given power level without needing to refuel. Since it is currently impossible to stop off for refuelling in space, a large I_{sp} is highly desirable.

Specific impulse is directly related to the speed at which matter leaves a rocket motor. An I_{sp} of about 102 seconds corresponds to an exhaust velocity of 0.62 miles per sec. (1 km/s), for example. Also, the higher the I_{sp}, the less the mass of fuel needed for any specific thrust level.

Chemical rockets

High-thrust systems, in which thrust greatly exceeds the engine weight, are necessary where gravity must be opposed, as in planetary lift-off and soft landing. The main practical contenders are chemical rockets based on solid or liquid fuel. Both produce exhaust through combustion and must therefore carry their own oxygen supply.

Solid-fuel systems are basically powder-packed tanks whose charges are mixtures of a solid fuel, such as rubberlike polyisobutene, and an oxygen-rich solid, such as ammonium perchlorate (NH_4ClO_4). Once ignited, the mixture burns inside the fuel tank until depleted, the combustion gases escaping through a nozzle at one end of the tank. Such systems are simple and reliable, but the fact that the whole tank must withstand combustion calls for robust construction, and thus implies additional weight. Furthermore, such rockets cannot be switched on and off at will, so they are used only as single-burn boosters.

Liquid-fuel rocket engines pump a liquid fuel, such as hydrazine or liquid hydrogen, and an oxidant, such as liquid oxygen, into a small combustion chamber from separate tanks. Such engines can be stopped, restarted, and throttled at will by controlling the flow of the two liquids to the combustion chamber. Some combinations of propellant and oxidant are hypergolic—they ignite spontaneously on heating; others have to be ignited by sparks, for example.

Liquid-fuel engines are more complex and less reliable than those that use solid fuel, however. A good compromise is to use a solid propellant and liquid oxidant. The oxidant passes through channels in the fuel during burn cycles, but burning can be stopped by cutting off the oxidant supply.

The specific impulses of chemical rocket systems are all of the order of a few hundreds of seconds. Solid-fuel boosters such as the two strap-on boosters of NASA's space shuttle, have I_{sp} values of around 245 seconds, while the same vehicle's

liquid-fuel rockets burn liquid hydrogen together with liquid oxygen to give an I_{sp} of over 450 seconds in the vacuum of space. The five massive stage-one engines of the Saturn V launch vehicle of the Apollo mission burned kerosene with liquid oxygen at an I_{sp} of around 245 seconds.

Not all rockets need to provide the high levels of thrust required for takeoff and soft landing. Others provide the relatively minor impulses necessary to power orbit changes, interplanetary course corrections, and changes in attitude for probes and satellites and for rocket-stage and payload separation. Small solid-fuel rockets are used if only one burn is needed, as is the case for stage separations of multistage launch vehicles. Spacecraft control thrusters tend to be liquid-fuel rockets based on monopropellants—mixtures of fuel and oxidizer in a single fluid—or hypergolic combinations of liquids. Tank pressurization forces the propellants into the chamber under the control of simple valves but without the need for pumps. The I_{sp} values obtained for such systems tend to be low, but this lack of efficiency is compensated for by good reliability and the minimum number of weighty parts.

▲ NASA's *Deep Space 1* probe before its launch in 1998. The probe was assembled in clean-room conditions to protect its sensitive equipment. NASA has been experimenting with new propulsion methods to power its spacecraft with the ultimate aim of sending manned vehicles over long distances in space.

Nuclear propulsion

One of the options explored in the quest for improved I_{sp} values for high-thrust engines was that of nuclear power. Both the former Soviet Union and the United States ground tested so-called solid-core fission devices consisting of solid fissile cores containing perforations through which hydrogen gas was pumped. Heat from the fission reaction superheated the hydrogen gas, causing it to expand through a nozzle. I_{sp} values of 600 to 1,500 seconds were measured.

In the early 1950s, the U.S. Project Orion examined the use of controlled nuclear explosions to launch a space vehicle. Nuclear means were abandoned in favor of less efficient chemical rockets when it became clear that large stretches of Earth's atmosphere could be contaminated with radioactive material. Such contamination might be tolerable in space, however, and greater attention is being given to the idea of streaming nuclear bomblets behind a thrust shield, where they would be held in position by a magnetic field and detonated by laser beam. This detonation could provide the hard acceleration necessary for quick orbital escape or entry, for example, with I_{sp} values around 1,000 seconds.

Ion propulsion

The highest I_{sp} values available at present are those of ion-propulsion systems, whose I_{sp} values are around 3,000—some ten times the values associated with chemical rockets and greater even than those of the proposed nuclear propulsion systems. Unfortunately, the thrust available from such systems is tiny, so ion propulsion could not be used for launches, for example. Nevertheless, over an extended period of operation—typically months—ion propulsion can boost space probes to speeds much greater than attainable with chemical rockets, so it is an attractive option for long-term unpiloted probes into deep space. Furthermore, the high I_{sp} of ion propulsion means it requires a smaller mass of fuel than a comparable chemical propulsion system. This weight saving can be used to reduce the amount of thrust required at launch, or to increase the mass of equipment included in a space probe.

Ion propulsion uses electricity generated by arrays of solar panels, which explains its alternative name—solar-electric propulsion. This electrical energy acts first to rip electrons out of xenon atoms, forming positive ions. These are then accelerated to around 19 miles per sec. (30 km/s) by an electrical field produced by a grid electrode. The speeding ions pass through the grid and stream from the back of the space craft, producing the reaction force that equates to thrust. At the same time, a pointed electrode emits a stream of electrons from the engine that prevents negative charge from accumulating on the craft, which would otherwise experience a backward electrostatic attraction to the cloud of positive ions behind the craft.

NASA's *Deep Space I*—the first space probe to use ion propulsion—was launched on October 24, 1998, with 180 lbs. (81.5 kg) of xenon gas. Its solar arrays generate up to 2.5 kW of electrical power, of which up to 2.1 kW goes to the propulsion system (the thrust available from an ion propulsion system depends on the rate at which the solar arrays deliver energy). This rate of power supply would exhaust the xenon supply in around 20 months of continuous operation, resulting in a final speed of 2.8 miles per sec. (4.5 km/s). The unit can operate at thrust levels between 0.0043 and 0.0208 lbf. (19.0 and 92.7 mN), taking 0.42 to 2.28 kW of electrical power. The I_{sp} under these conditions ranges from 1,800 to 3,200 seconds.

Future systems

In a proposed electromagnetic, or plasma, rocket, a fuel such as hydrogen would be converted to an electrically ionized gas by an electric arc and then accelerated out of the rocket by a magnetic field. Nuclear fission is also under study for this category in the form of a gaseous core rocket, in which fuel would pass through a gaseous fission reactor, suspended in a chamber by magnetic fields. This concept, like others that use magnetic

▼ *Deep Space 1* was the first craft to use ion propulsion, seen here under test. The glow is due to positive ions combining with electrons and releasing their excess energy as light. One purpose of the mission was to evaluate whether this process would interfere with radio communications or measurements. In practice, these problems were not observed.

fields for containment and position, faces the major technological hurdle of achieving accuracy in magnet-field control.

Of all the exotic ideas under discussion—including photon drive, which uses a beam of light particles for thrust, the space ramjet, and laser radiation—only hydrogen fusion shows promise of succeeding. Using a nuclear pulse motor, a rapid succession of deuterium-originated nuclear explosions would be a spacecraft's power source. Such an engine, if built, would have an exhaust velocity of 6,000 miles per sec. (10,000 km/s), which is several hundred times that of the most advanced ion-drive engine and certainly powerful enough for interstellar travel.

Fuelless propulsion

The ideal propulsion system would require no fuel, so its I_{sp} would effectively be infinite. Energy cannot be created from nothing, however, so such systems would have to derive the energy for thrust from an external source.

One system that has already been used is known as gravity assist, or the slingshot effect. In this approach, the course of a space probe is chosen so that the probe passes behind a planet as it progresses through its orbit around the Sun. The gravitational field of the planet then pulls the craft along behind the planet for a while, accelerating the craft at an angle to its original trajectory.

In a currently proposed system, a space probe would use huge metallic sails to reflect the photons of sunlight falling on it, just as a conventional sail catches momentum from the molecules of the wind. As with ion propulsion, the thrust available from such a system would be small. The final speed, developed over many years, would nonetheless be much greater than that available from ion propulsion. A major drawback of solar sailing is that the available thrust decreases with the distance from the sun. Further, reversing the direction of flight would require an internal power source or gravitational assistance.

Construction and launch

Much present rocket research focuses on chemical engines, searching for better propellants and more efficient ways of exploiting them. The main challenge is in the materials required to cope with ever-increasing extremes of operating temperature and pressure and to achieve the necessary combinations of flexibility, rigidity, lightness, purity, and thermal conductivity. Heat-resistant copper alloys tend to be used for the linings of combustion chambers, for example, whereas strong, low-density aluminum alloys are used in the construction of most stress-bearing elements.

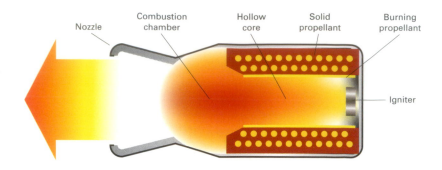

Nozzle • Combustion chamber • Hollow core • Solid propellant • Burning propellant • Igniter

In the United States, engines are usually designed specifically for a particular booster stage, each stage being a self-contained rocket. NASA pays specialist firms to produce competitive preliminary designs so that the best can be selected. Usually, one of the major aircraft companies builds the structures, tanks, and controls and installs the engines. Different stages of a booster are often built in different parts of the country. The stages are brought separately to the launch site by air, road, or water, and assembled vertically on the launch pad. The largest rockets in history, the Saturn V launch vehicles for the Apollo missions, were stacked in Cape Canaveral's Vertical Assembly Building—the world's largest building—and then carried erect on a huge crawler transporter to the launch pad 1.5 miles (2.4 km) away. The Soviet Union's space programs mainly used the Standard S launch vehicle, which would be assembled horizontally, carried to the launch pad by rail car, and erected piecemeal on the launch pad.

Countdown can begin days before launch to schedule in complex fueling, checkout, and contingency operations; an automatic final ignition sequence usually starts from around three minutes before launch. Ignition is induced by electrical sparks or an explosive charge; in the case of a hypergolic fuel mix, ignition is spontaneous. Restraining arms hold the rocket for a few seconds until full thrust has built up. As the rocket ascends, the exhaust flame becomes broader in the thinning air, and upper-stage engines that operate purely in space have long, narrow engine bells to contain the exhaust flow.

Directional control is often achieved by swiveling the bell. During ascent, power is sometimes reduced to ease acceleration loads either by early cutout of one engine in a cluster or from burnout of small, strap-on, half-stage rockets. Each rocket is jettisoned by a small explosive charge at the end of its burn time.

▲ In a solid-fuel rocket, a blend of oxidant and propellant burns from the center of the rocket to its edges. The rate of burning is controlled by a factor such as the fineness of grain of the solids and cannot be stopped until the fuel is depleted.

 SEE ALSO: Ballistics • Ion and ionization • Missile • Space shuttle • Space station • Space suit • Space weapon

Rubber, Natural

◄ Most of the world's supply of rubber comes from the tree *Hevea brasiliensis*. The rubber is obtained by cutting shallow diagonal strips out of the bark. A milky fluid called latex is collected over two or three hours in a small pot attached to the tree. It is then collected for processing at a central plant serving the whole plantation.

Natural rubber is a material derived from the hevea tree, a native of Brazil, and from certain other trees and shrubs. The rubber is present as latex, which is a milklike fluid found in a distinct area within the tree's normal sap system, between the bark and the trunk. When the bark is cut or damaged, latex seeps out; as it dries, the rubber in it forms a protective film over the damaged part.

The natives of the Amazon region called the tree *cahuchu*, or *cauchu*, meaning "the tree that weeps." This name is still preserved in *caoutchouc* and *Kautschuck*, the French and German names for rubber. The English name is descriptive of the first use that was found for the material, in the mid-18th century: rubbing pencil marks from paper. A primitive industry in Brazil produced rubber footwear by coagulating latex, layer upon layer, onto clay formers smoked over a fire. Waterproof tents and cloaks were made by drying out latex sandwiched between two sheets of cloth.

The first industrial use of rubber copied these primitive techniques. The rubber came mainly from the state of Para, where it was collected in the form of roughly spherical masses about the size of a man's head, produced by dipping a wooden pole or paddle into the latex and then holding it over the smoke from a fire. In this way, the rubber was built up in a series of thin layers until it reached the required size, when it was cut free from its support. The solid rubber was dis-solved in coal tar naphtha, and the solution was used to make dipped goods such as galoshes and gloves and for impregnating fabrics to make them waterproof. These garments, called Mackintoshes after their inventor, were waterproof but sensitive to heat, being hard and brittle on cold days and sticky and smelly when it was hot.

Goodyear in the United States and Hancock in England, in 1839–1840, found out how to stabilize rubber by combining it with sulfur. Depending on the percentage of sulfur added, a range of products could be made, from soft extensible rubber bands or sheeting to hard inextensible ebonite or vulcanite. This vulcanized rubber was stable over a wide range of temperatures and could be molded into commercial articles with well-defined permanent shapes in the process of vulcanization by heat.

In 1876, the British government sent Sir Henry Wickham to Brazil to collect rubber seeds for shipment to Malaya and Ceylon. After wintering in the orchid houses at Kew, London, the plants were taken out to form the basis of the organized rubber plantations of today.

On plantations today, latex is collected by cutting inclined grooves into the bark of the hevea tree and allowing the latex to run down these channels to collect in a cup attached to the tree near its base. After collection, the latex is purified by filtration and passed to tanks where it is diluted with water. Coagulation is then induced by adding a chemical such as formic or acetic acid (it must be added within 24 hours of collection of the latex). The rubber comes out of suspension as crumbs, which are dried and pressed into sheet form in a mill. Part of the output is smoked in wood-fired drying rooms, while the remainder is used to form yellow crepe shoe soles.

Chemical composition

Rubber is an unsaturated hydrocarbon, of basic formula $(C_5H_8)_n$, where n is about 3,000. The basic unit in the molecule is isoprene, $CH_2{=}CH{-}C(CH_3){=}CH_2$, which occurs in turpentine. The composition of rubber was proved in 1860, when it was broken down into isoprene on heating, and confirmed in 1884, when the British chemist W. A. Tilden produced rubber by accidentally polymerizing isoprene that had been left to stand in a bottle.

The outstanding property of rubber is its ability to stretch to four or five times its original length and then to recover when released. This property is true of the form of the molecule that

◄ Newly coagulated latex being pressed into sheets in a Malaysian rubber-processing plant.

has a long chain of carbon atoms as its backbone. A carbon atom bonded by four single bonds behaves as if it were at the center of a tetrahedron, or four-faced pyramid. Successive bonds between carbon atoms can be considered as being formed by joining the pyramids point to point. As a long chain is formed, it turns at random, depending on the point of each tetrahedron at which the bond is made. A model can be made of the molecule by bending a wire randomly at the appropriate angle. The wire coils back on itself, and this property demonstrates how a rubber molecule can be distorted and then recover its original shape.

Uses of rubber

The bulk of the world's production of natural rubber soon came from the plantations, which spread beyond Malaya and Ceylon notably into the Dutch East Indies. Today the world produc-

▼ Dried latex crumbs being compressed into bales. The traditional method of processing latex is to coagulate it by adding a chemical such as formic or acetic acid; the latex emerges from this process in crumb form. The crumbs are then dried and either pressed into sheets or compacted into bales.

tion is approximately 6.8 million tons (6.2 million tonnes) per annum. Over 90 percent is in the form of dry rubber, and the rest is concentrated latex for the production of rubber foam and dipped goods, such as rubber gloves.

The largest use of rubber came with the development of road transportation. First came tires, in solid form, for carriages and bicycles. After Dunlop's reinvention in 1890 of the pneumatic tire, the air tire developed rapidly, first for bicycles and later for automobiles, trucks, aircraft, tractors, and earth-moving machines.

In the 1920s, scientists found that the resistance of a tire tread to wear could be increased many times by adding carbon black to the rubber—sulfur mixed in the plastic state before vulcanization. This material, which has a very fine particle size, is formed when natural gas or oil is burned under controlled conditions with a restricted amount of air. Other materials are milled into the rubber on steel roller mills at this stage. They may include resins, tars, clay, colorings, and organic rubber chemicals to speed vulcanization, retard aging, or modify physical properties.

Some products, such as waterproof clothing and footwear, gloves and surgical goods, take advantage of rubber's resistance to water. Good air retention leads to its use in air beds, inflatable boats, and life rafts. Its electric resistance makes it valuable as a sheathing for insulation of cables.

Synthetics have replaced many uses, but rubber is still used for the largest truck and earth-mover tires, as it gives the coolest-running compounds.

FACT FILE

■ In the 18th century, a French explorer sent specimens of rubber to France from South America and described waterproof shoes made by local natives from single pieces of rubber. He also described how they made flasks using liquid rubber and molds.

■ Although most natural rubber is made from the collected latex of the hevea tree, in northern Mexico, rubber is derived from the high-altitude guayule shrub. The whole shrub, which contains 20 percent rubber, is shredded and mixed with water so that the rubber floats to the surface.

SEE ALSO: Polymer and polymerization • Rubber, synthetic • Tire • Water-repellent finish

Rubber, Synthetic

A synthetic rubber is an elastic substance that consists wholly or in part of an industrially manufactured polymer. Such materials emulate to some extent the properties of rubber compounds made from the latex of rubber trees—particularly *Hevea brasiliensis*—but they do not rely on the availability of that material for their manufacture. Furthermore, the exact chemical and physical properties of synthetic rubber depend on the blend of monomers used to make it.

Methyl rubber

The need for a synthetic replacement for natural rubber first arose during World War I in Germany, which was at that time isolated from supplies of latex from the outside world. Chemists had already decomposed natural rubber to reveal that it was a polymer of isoprene—2-methyl-1,3-butadiene, $CH_2=C(CH_3)-CH=CH_2$—but there were at that time no polymerization methods capable of producing rubber from isoprene. Instead, the Germans set about producing rubber from a related compound: 2,3-dimethylbuta-1,3-diene, $CH_2=C(CH_3)-C(CH_3)=CH_2$. In this reaction, the two double bonds open to form one double bond at the center of the molecule and two single bonds to the rest of the chain:

$$nCH_2=C(CH_3)-C(CH_3)=CH_2 \rightarrow$$
$$-(CH_2-C(CH_3)=C(CH_3)-CH_2)_n-$$

The polymerization of 2,3-dimethylbuta-1,3-diene was performed at around 160°F (70°C), and the process took between three and six months to complete. The product—methyl rubber—was inferior to natural rubber, but around 2,750 tons (2,500 tonnes) were nevertheless produced for the manufacture of solid tires for wartime transportation. After the war, Germany ceased production of methyl rubber and returned to using rubber derived from natural sources.

Buna rubbers

In the period that led up to World War II, German scientists invented a process for making the Buna rubbers, so named for buta-1,3-diene and Natrium, the German name for sodium. The process uses a small amount of metallic sodium to convert some butadiene molecules into anions from which polymer chains grow.

The appeal of butadiene as a starting material was its availability from a number of sources, such as the modification of products from coal or petroleum distillation. Butadiene can even be made from ethanol (C_2H_5OH), which can be obtained by the fermentation of sugar-containing plants if petroleum-derived buta-1,3-diene or ethanol become unavailable or expensive.

The disadvantage of rubber made from pure butadiene is its lack of resilience in comparison with natural rubber. This deficiency was compensated for by the inclusion of some styrene (phenylethene, $C_6H_5-CH=CH_2$) in the monomer blend. The presence of phenyl (C_6H_5-) groups along the polymer chain mimics the effect of the methyl (CH_3-) groups present in natural rubber by impeding the relative movement of polymer chains and thereby increasing hardness. The resulting polymer, called Buna-S, entered large-scale production in Germany in 1933 and is still one of the largest-volume synthetic rubbers.

A second type of Buna rubber, Buna-N, is made by copolymerizing acrylonitrile (propenonitrile, $CH_2=CH-CN$) with buta-1,3-diene. The presence of nitrile groups adds toughness and makes the material more resistant than natural rubber to softening by solvents, gasoline, and vegetable oils. Buna-N—also called nitrile rubber—is used as a flexible lining material, particularly where exposure to solvents might occur.

Other butadiene synthetics

An alternative process for manufacturing elastomeric copolymers of styrene and buta-1,3-diene uses soaps to disperse the monomers and catalyst in water. The process produces suspensions of polymers whose molecular weights are

▼ Synthetic rubber latex being applied to the back of a carpet. When the water in the latex has evaporated, the rubber will form a tough underlay.

PRODUCTION OF STYRENE–BUTADIENE RUBBER (SBR)

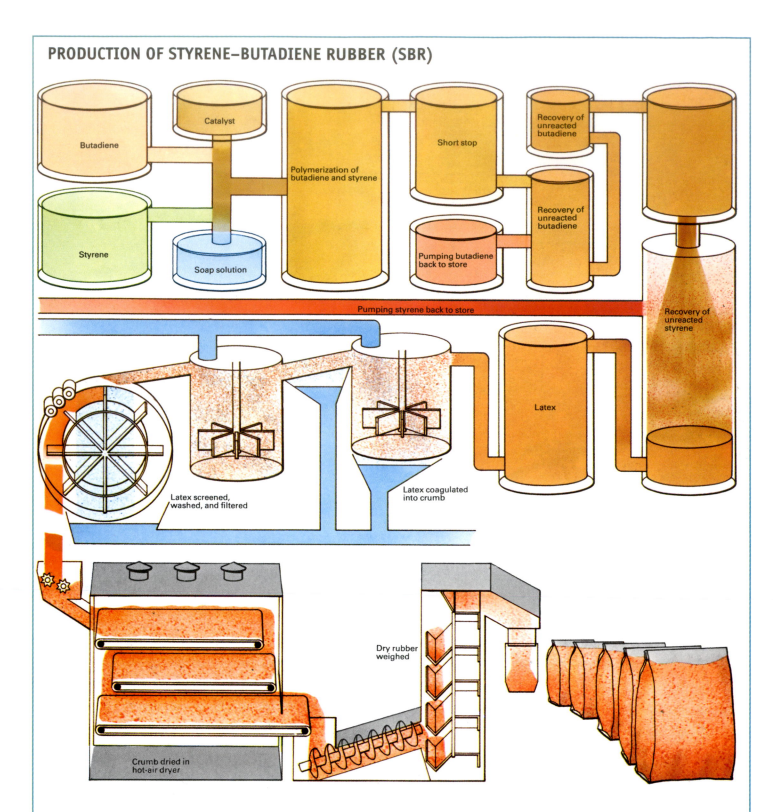

Butadiene

Catalyst

Styrene

Soap solution

Polymerization of butadiene and styrene

Short stop

Recovery of unreacted butadiene

Recovery of unreacted butadiene

Pumping butadiene back to store

Pumping styrene back to store

Recovery of unreacted styrene

Latex

Latex screened, washed, and filtered

Latex coagulated into crumb

Dry rubber weighed

Crumb dried in hot-air dryer

Styrene–butadiene rubber production starts with the copolymerization of a small proportion of phenylethene (styrene, $C_6H_5–CH=CH_2$) with butadiene ($CH_2=CH–CH=CH_2$). The reaction is done in water, which dissolves neither the starting materials nor the final polymer. A soap disperses the monomer droplets in water.

Polymerization is initiated by heating, which makes the catalyst active, and the droplets of monomer gradually become suspended particles of copolymer. From the polymerization reactor, the mixture passes to a short stop tank, where the drop in temperature rapidly renders the catalyst inactive and stops the reaction.

Unreacted butadiene—a gas at room temperature—then evaporates from the mixture and is collected for reuse. Styrene, which is less volatile, is collected for reuse by spraying the mixture into a tower, where the styrene evaporates.

▲ The three main stages of SBR production are polymerization (top), coagulation (center), and drying (bottom). The dried rubber crumb is then weighed and packed.

Agitation with coagulating agents causes the copolymer to coagulate—clot together as a crumbly solid—so that most of the water can be removed by screening. The remaining water content is removed by evaporation in a hot-air dryer.

high but whose viscosity is low, because the water forces the hydrophobic polymer molecules to coil up, so they do not tangle with one another as they would if they were dissolved in solution. Styrene-butadiene rubber (SBR) produced in this way is the largest-volume synthetic rubber, its main use being for producing pneumatic tires.

In recent years, copolymers of acrylonitrile, buta-1,3-diene, and styrene (ABS) have gained widespread use in the manufacture of high-resilience components, such as vehicle fenders. The good resilience and solvent resistance of these materials are conferred by the presence of nitrile and phenyl groups in the polymer.

One of the earliest synthetic rubbers, but still one of the most widely used, is neoprene. Neoprene is a polymer of 2-chlorobuta-1,3-diene (chloroprene, $CH_2=CCl–CH=CH_2$); it is particularly resistant to the effects of fire and solvents and is stable at high temperatures. The high tensile strength and abrasion resistance of neoprene make it a suitable material for manufacturing conveyor belts and divers' wet suits.

Synthetic natural rubber

Although their name might seem contradictory, synthetic natural rubbers are so called because they are artificial polymers of isoprene, the basic structural element of natural rubber. Analysis of natural rubber shows that it consists of repeating $–(CH_2–C(CH_3)=CH–CH_2)–$ units and that the $–CH_2–$ groups that form the polymer chains both lie on the same side of the double bond in each repeat unit. This structure, called the *cis* configuration, is crucial to the elastic properties of natural rubber. It is also the factor that thwarted early attempts to mimic natural rubber.

When isoprene is made to polymerize using standard catalysts, the product tends to have the *trans* configuration, in which the $–CH_2–$ groups that form the polymer chains lie on opposite sides of the double bond in each repeat unit. As a consequence, such polymers have little elasticity, and they are inadequate as substitutes for natural rubber. In the 1950s, however, the development of Ziegler–Natta catalysts for polymerizing ethene ($CH_2=CH_2$) and propene ($CH_3–CH=CH_2$) offered the possibility of producing *cis*-polyisoprene, because these catalysts hold isoprene in the correct configuration as it adds to the growing chain. The product is effectively a duplicate of natural rubber.

Other types of polymers

A number of synthetic materials exist that have elastic properties similar to those of natural rubber but that are based on repeating units other than the butadiene-based structure of the types of synthetic rubbers discussed so far. The simplest of these is butyl synthetic rubber, a copolymer of methylpropene (isobutylene, $CH_2=C(CH_3)_2$) and styrene. This material blocks the passage of gases better than natural rubber does, and its main use is in the manufacture of tubing.

Polyurethane rubbers are characterized by the urethane linkage ($–NH–CO–O–$). They have great mechanical strength and resistance to wear, and they can be produced as foams for padding furniture and bedding, for example.

Silicone rubbers have backbones of alternating silicon and oxygen atoms. They have great flexibility and chemical resistance, and they are useful over extreme ranges of temperature. Silicone rubbers are also biologically inert, so they can be used in implants without risk of rejection.

Thiokol is a polymer made by the reaction of 1,2-dichloroethene ($CHCl=CHCl$) with sodium polysulfide (NaS_x, where x is between 2 and 5):

$$(n + 1)CHCl=CHCl + nNaS_x \rightarrow$$
$$Cl–(CHCl–CHCl–S_x)_n–CHCl–CHCl + nNaCl$$

Thiokol is nonflammable and resistant to chemical attack and softening by solvents, and it can be used over a wide range of temperatures.

Vulcanization

Vulcanization is the process that toughens rubber by introducing cross-links between adjacent polymer chains. In the case of natural rubber, heat treatment with sulfur introduces polysulfide links ($–S_x–$) between double bonds in adjacent chains. This process is also effective in toughening butadiene-based rubbers for tire manufacture, for example. Neoprene can also be vulcanized by heat treatment with zinc oxide (ZnO).

◄ Here, a neoprene lining is inflation tested before insertion into the fuel tanks of a jet. As the fuel burns away, the lining deflates to prevent air locks from interrupting the flow of fuel to the engines.

SEE ALSO: HYDROCARBON • POLYMER AND POLYMERIZATION • RUBBER, NATURAL • SILICONE

Rudder

◀ The rudder of a ship is located directly behind the propeller. Its surfaces are designed to give maximum turning force and minimum resistance to water flow. On merchant ships, the rudder is normally expected to operate at angles of up to 35 degrees from the centerline to port or starboard, so the critical angle—the angle of attack at which the rudder force is suddenly reduced—is important. A reduction of force within the working range could be disastrous, especially if the ship is maneuvering in a harbor or in crowded shipping lanes.

The earliest form of ship rudder was simply an oar or paddle that was used to propel the stern of the ship in a sideways direction. Later, the paddle was secured to the side of the ship and provided with a lever at the upper end of its handle to act as a tiller. It is not known with certainty when the first sternpost rudder was invented, but it was in general use in the 12th century C.E. Aircraft rudders came into use with the development of flight at the beginning of the 20th century.

Action of ship rudders

The passage of a ship through water causes the water to flow past the rudder, and the angle at which the rudder is inclined to the direction of flow is called the angle of attack. The steering action is dependent on the pressure distribution between the two hydrodynamic surfaces of the rudder. Pressure on the downstream side is less than the static pressure of the surrounding water, while the pressure on the upstream side is greater. The result is an outward force on the downstream side of the rudder, which can be regarded as being made up of a lift force at right angles to the direction of flow and a drag force directly opposing the direction of flow. The variation of the lift and drag for different angles of attack is extremely important in rudder design, as it is the lift force that creates the turning effect. At a certain angle of attack, called the critical angle, the rudder stalls: a phenomenon called burbling occurs and the rudder force is suddenly reduced. Burbling is caused by a breakdown in the streamlined flow on the downstream side of the rudder into a swirling irregular eddying flow. Rudders on merchant vessels are normally expected to operate up to an angle of 35 degrees from the centerline to port or starboard, and so the critical angle is important, as a reduction of rudder force would be undesirable within the working range.

Results from model tests with rudders in open water must be interpreted with care and cannot be directly applied to a ship, as the rudder action is modified by the flow of water around the hull interacting with the propeller slip. Reliable results can be obtained only from full-scale ship tests, and then the model information must be corrected by a suitable factor for further rudder design.

When a ship's rudder is turned, the ship first moves a small distance sideways in the opposite direction to the intended turn and then moves around a circular path until it eventually faces the opposite direction. The distance moved forward from the point at which the rudder was turned to the point at which the ship is at right angles to its original direction is called the advance. Transfer is the sideways distance between these two points, and the diameter of the circular path followed by the ship is called the tactical diameter. During the turn, the bow of the vessel lies always inside the turning curve so that a drift angle is formed between the center line of the vessel and the tangent to the turning curve. The tactical diameter is a measure of the ability of the rudder to turn the vessel. This diameter is important for warships, because they are frequently required to execute complicated turning maneuvers.

Rudder design

With a simple rudder arranged to turn around the edge nearest the ship, the force produced by the rudder will act to return the rudder to the straight-ahead position, and this force has to be resisted by the steering gear to maintain the turn. To avoid excessive steering forces, a balanced rudder arrangement is employed with the turning

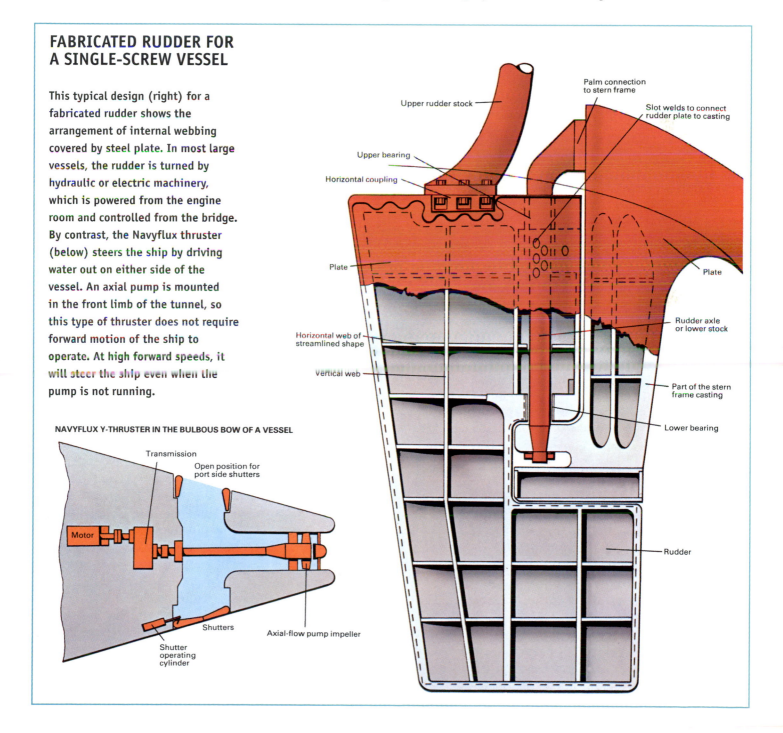

FABRICATED RUDDER FOR A SINGLE-SCREW VESSEL

This typical design (right) for a fabricated rudder shows the arrangement of internal webbing covered by steel plate. In most large vessels, the rudder is turned by hydraulic or electric machinery, which is powered from the engine room and controlled from the bridge. By contrast, the Navyflux thruster (below) steers the ship by driving water out on either side of the vessel. An axial pump is mounted in the front limb of the tunnel, so this type of thruster does not require forward motion of the ship to operate. At high forward speeds, it will steer the ship even when the pump is not running.

Upper rudder stock
Palm connection to stern frame
Slot welds to connect rudder plate to casting
Upper bearing
Horizontal coupling
Plate
Plate
Rudder axle or lower stock
Horizontal web of streamlined shape
Vertical web
Part of the stern frame casting
Lower bearing
Rudder

NAVYFLUX Y-THRUSTER IN THE BULBOUS BOW OF A VESSEL

Transmission
Open position for port side shutters
Motor
Shutters
Axial-flow pump impeller
Shutter operating cylinder

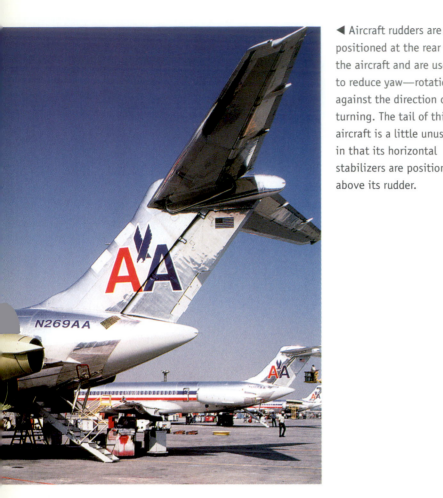

◀ Aircraft rudders are positioned at the rear of the aircraft and are used to reduce yaw—rotation against the direction of turning. The tail of this aircraft is a little unusual in that its horizontal stabilizers are positioned above its rudder.

axis positioned some way along the rudder near to the center of pressure of the turning forces. In a semi-balanced rudder, the proportion of the rudder area in front of the turning axis is 20 percent or less, whereas for a fully balanced design, the value will be 25 to 30 percent.

A number of different arrangements are used to support the rudder and allow it to turn, with most using tapered pintles (pins on which moving parts turn) working in bearings. These bearings are often water lubricated, although oil lubrication is also used. In some cases all the support is provided by the upper bearing on the ship's hull, and in others, there is a lower bearing beneath the rudder. The turning motion is provided by the rudder stock, which is made from cast or forged steel and bolted to the rudder. The upper end of the stock passes into the ship's hull through a trunk with a watertight seal and is connected to the steering gear. Normally the steering gear is power operated and the stock is turned by hydraulic rams supplied with oil from electric pumps and controlled from the steering position on the bridge.

The rudder itself is generally made from steel plate and the sides are stiffened by internal webs or a cast frame. A drain hole is provided, but in some designs, the interior of the rudder may be filled with foam.

Types of rudders

Many different designs of rudders have been developed, the simplest being the fully movable type, where the whole rudder moves as one unit. A development of the fully movable design is the Schilling rudder, which has a special hydrodynamic profile and is fitted with upper and lower plates to guide the water flow. These modifications result in an increased deflection of the water flow from the propeller (which is immediately in front of the rudder), giving a rapid response and increased maneuverability and allowing a vessel to turn in its own length when starting from rest.

Another design suitable for vessels that have to be highly maneuverable, such as ferry boats, fishing vessels, and offshore supply boats, is the Becker, or articulated, rudder. It consists of a main rudder of conventional profile with a pivoted fin mounted on the rear edge. A pivoting mechanism turns the fin through an angle around twice that of the main rudder to increase the deflection of the water flow. At low speeds, the articulated rudder produces a greater force and thus a more positive turning effect. Somewhat similar is the flapped rudder, though in this case, the movable flap on the trailing edge of the main rudder is operated by hydraulic rams within the main rudder. Minor steering corrections under way can be carried out by use of the flap alone, while with the flap set centrally, the complete unit acts as a conventional rudder.

An active rudder has a propulsion unit fitted into the rudder body and a fixed or variable-pitch propeller at its trailing edge. When the rudder is turned, the propeller will produce thrust at an angle to the center line of the vessel, causing a greater turning effect than the rudder alone. To operate, the rudder is not dependent on the forward motion of the ship.

Airplane rudder

Airplane rudders and ship rudders function slightly differently as the former are used, not to turn the aircraft, but to help control the turning initiated by the ailerons on the wings. When an airplane turns, it also has a tendency to rotate around its vertical axis in a direction opposite to the turn, a phenomenon called yaw. The rudder counteracts this tendency by making the nose turn in the correct direction. The controls in the cockpit may be connected to the rudder by mechanical wires or rods or may be linked using electrical wires connected to electric motors.

SEE ALSO: Aircraft-control engineering • Aircraft design • Propeller • Sailing • Ship • Warship

Safe

Safes are designed to be secure not only from burglars but also from natural disasters such as fires and flooding. Some safes survived the Chicago fire of 1871 after falling through burning buildings, but the survival of the safe does not mean the survival of its contents if the safe is warped by heat.

In the United States, safes are tested by prolonged exposure to heat and by dropping them from heights, and they are divided into categories according to the protection they offer. Record safes offer protection from fire, money safes from burglars, and the third category comprises a money safe inside a record safe.

Safes used to be made of case-hardened steel, but carbide-tipped drills were soon developed that could cut through it. Today steel alloys are used that cannot be penetrated by drills; in addition, solid, hardened particles are mixed in the steel during its molten state. Trying to drill such a plate results in stress that will chip or shatter the tip of a drill. The steel plates are made three-layers thick, comprising a sandwich of hard steel alloy, seam welded all the way around to make a single structure, with a layer of a hard, fireproof composite material in the center to prevent the successful use of oxygen flame-cutting equipment. Some safes are cast in a single piece, so there are no seams.

Lock

The lock of a burglarproof safe is nearly always a combination lock, because there is no keyhole into which explosives or lock-picking tools can be inserted and because a four-ring lock, for example, with 100 numbers on each ring offers more than 100 million possible combinations. Also, the combination can be changed at the convenience of the safe's owner.

When locked, the door of the safe must fit as snugly as possible all the way around its edge. Consequently, there are many bolts around the edge of the door. In the past, these bolts were all thrown by the lock and were only as secure as the lock itself; the safecracker's technique was to knock off the outside of the lock and drive out the spindle. Modern safes, however, have a mechanism in the lock that breaks the connection between the lock and the bolts when the lock is upset by heat or tools.

Lock mechanisms are protected by additional layers of drill-resistant steel; by key-operated dial-check locks, which prevent unauthorized manipulation with the combination; and by anti-observation shields, which make it difficult to observe the combination being dialed.

During a wave of bank robberies in the United States before World War II, time-lock devices began to be used, with which the combination lock cannot be opened during certain hours, making it pointless to kidnap or torture bank employees to make them reveal combinations. Combination locks are also fitted with a device that transmits an alarm to police if the dial is turned after business hours.

Vault

A vault is a room, usually below ground, that is protected in much the same way as a safe. Vaults in Hiroshima survived the atomic blast there in 1945, only 300 yards (274 m) from the point below the explosion.

Vault doors are often round, because it is easier to achieve a perfect fit between two circles than two rectangles. The edge of the door is tapered to fit into a concave surface in the doorway. Vault doors are typically about 3.5 in. (9 cm) thick; the doors at Hiroshima were 6 in. (15 cm) thick.

▼ The mechanism of a combination lock. The slots must be aligned before the safe door can be opened.

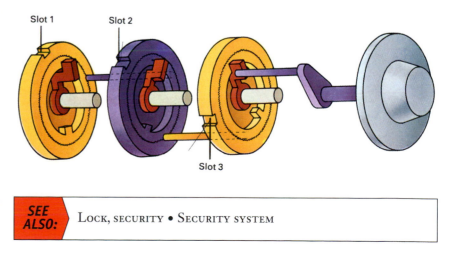

Slot 1 Slot 2

Slot 3

SEE ALSO: LOCK, SECURITY • SECURITY SYSTEM

Sailboard

The first steerable sailboard was made by the U.S. inventor Newman Darby in 1964, but the shape of this craft had more in common with conventional boats than boards familiar today. In 1969, a U.S. businessman, Hoyle Schweitzer, and an aeronautical engineer, Jim Drake, produced the sailboard on which current designs are based. Their original board consisted of a normal surfboard with a triangular sail attached to a mast and stretched with a wishbone-shaped boom.

The board

Today, there is a wide variety of sailboard designs. In many respects the sailboard is a water wing, except that the water traverses its length longitudinally. One of the most common mass-produced designs consists of a polyethylene shell filled with polyurethane foam. This combination forms a resilient board that is ideally suited to withstanding the rigors of sun, sea, and hard use, but it is relatively slow to respond. Lighter and more responsive boards are made using a glass fiber shell filled with polyurethane foam and strengthened with strips of carbon fiber and a layer of aluminum honeycomb. Expensive competition boards are made of a shell of a carbon fiber composite without any internal filling. Kevlar is also used to make sailboards. This material is five times stronger than steel without the metal's weight but is also extremely expensive. In general, the lighter the board, the more expensive it is likely to be.

For efficiency, sailboards must be shaped to offer the least area to the sea (wetted area), and longer boards must be equipped with a small keel, or daggerboard, to provide the lateral resistance essential when sailing into the wind. At the rear of

◀ The outer shell of this sailboard is made of polycarbonate sheet and low-friction Makrolon. It is lined with a layer of carbon-reinforced glass fiber to provide stiffness, a layer of high-density polyurethane to provide structural stability, and a polyester mat layer. The foam is then injected under pressure.

▼ The Klepper 320 sailboard has a number of features that make it particularly suitable for high-performance sailing in strong winds.

the board, a skeg (fin), similar to that used on surfboards and analogous to the dinghy's rudder, is used to provide directional stability. Without it, even the most experienced boardsailor would find directional control difficult, with the board's rear end fishtailing from side to side slowing progress drastically.

Generally, boards built with an accentuated rocker (the curvature from stem to stern) give high performance, but some people may demand greater stability. Boards used for regatta sailing have a deep hull similar to a dinghy's, and those used for wave jumping feature a distinctly upturned nose.

The mast

The universal joint about which the mast pivots is one of the most important features of the whole board, being not only vital to its performance but also to the safety of the sailor. Essentially one of two types, the joint or pivot will be either purely mechanical, where the mast is fixed to it with a pin, or it will be one of the flexible types made of a resilient rubber or nylon. Positioned firmly while sailing, the pivot must be able to be pulled free in an emergency so as not to trap the sailor in the event of an overturn. Even if a boardsailor loses control, only the mast and sail will lie in the water as a capsized dinghy would. Once back on the board, the sailor can easily right the mast with a tug on the uphaul, a sheet (rope) attached to the mast for this purpose.

Most sailboards have a mast about 14.75 ft. (4.5 m) long. Glass fiber, aluminum (18 gauge,

anodized for saltwater protection), and alloy are the most popular materials. An aluminum mast is about 7 lbs. (3 kg) in weight. These materials allow the mast to flex a little in strong winds, or else the mast would most likely snap, but an excessively flexible mast would result in significant power losses. Carbon fiber is sometimes used because of its great strength and light weight.

Metal masts are usually one-piece constructions with parallel sides. Glass fiber masts, on the other hand, are usually tapered. Although the thinner top makes the mast less strong, it can lend a beneficial whiplash effect. Glass fiber masts are usually used with all-purpose boards.

The wishboom

The wishboom, so named because of its appearance, is the brake, accelerator, and tiller of the sailboard. Unlike a dinghy, the wishboom completely encircles the sail; the sailor controls the board by grasping one side of the boom or the other, depending upon which tack he or she is on. Grip is an essential feature of the wishboom; a slip of the hand easily leads to complete loss of control, so the aluminum bars are rubber sleeved and shaped to be within reach in all conditions. At 7 lbs. (3 kg), the wishboom is light enough to allow freestyle tricks to be exploited once the basics have been mastered.

The sail

Completing the rigging is the sail. The sail's design depends on its purpose. Wave jumpers and those who like heavy-weather sailing look for strength, while those seeking to exploit light winds in a race will look for the flexibility necessary to make full use of the lightest breezes. Sail area ranges from about 59 to 70 sq. ft. (5.5–6.5 m²). Most sailors need a set of each of these sizes to be equipped for the conditions they will encounter. Sails of smaller area—45 sq. ft. (4 m²)—are often used where there is plenty of wind.

The diversity of styles in boardsailing is vast. Freestyle, wave jumping, racing, and long distance are all forms of the sport practiced with ever-growing popularity. Long-distance sailing has led to the interesting development of a variosail. Forced by the lack of a conventional boom about which to reef the sail in an adverse weather change, designers turned to the zipper to provide them with a previously unforeseen flexibility. Now sections can be added or removed at will.

Materials used in sailboards vary to the same extent as in dinghy sailing, but resilience and strength are two prime qualities sought by the sailmaker. ICI's Terylene sailcloth dominates, with windows set into the sail to provide visibility.

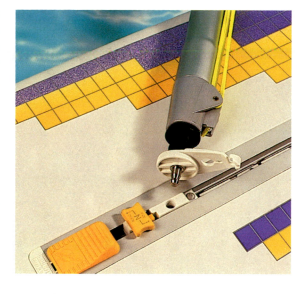

◄ A Klepper sailboard fitted with a mast track, which offers the sailboarder a choice of five different mast positions so that perfect trim can be achieved in all wind conditions.

Steering

Where the sailboard crosses the boundary between surfboard and dinghy is in its movable mast. Slotted into the board around the center point, the mast is held in place by a universal joint. The sailor hangs onto the wishboom; there are no stays. The universal joint allows the sailor to move the mast fore or aft at will and this ability combined with movements of the body is all the control a boardsailor has.

Whether the board luffs up—steers into the wind—or bears away—steers away from the wind—is governed by the relationship between the board's center of effort and the daggerboard's central point of lateral resistance.

The center of effort is the notional center of all the wind force upon the sail, the location of this point varying with the wind's angle of attack. With the sail tilted forward, the center of effort moves forward of the center of lateral resistance, and the board bears away. With the center of effort behind the center of lateral resistance, the board luffs up.

Once the basic art of steering is mastered, the boardsailor is ready to use the wishboom fully by tacking (changing direction), a natural extension of steering. Tacking requires manual dexterity combined with physical agility, and these skills are prerequisites for a successful boardsailor. As the board points into the wind, the sail empties and flutters, bringing the board to a gradual halt if the tack is not executed quickly enough. At this point, the sailor simply walks around the front of the mast, grabs hold of the other side of the wishboom and tilts the mast backward to bear away in the new direction.

SEE ALSO: BOAT BUILDING • CARBON FIBER • GLASS FIBER • SAILING • WAVE MOTION

Sailing

◀ A yacht takes part in the Antigua Race Week. Before such an event, crews train extensively to bring boats and rigging to peak trim for racing.

In the context of this article, to sail is to travel on water using the power of the wind for propulsion. Whereas such travel is now mainly confined to sport and leisure, sails were once the source of propulsion for the great explorers of the 15th and 16th centuries, such as Christopher Columbus, Francis Drake, and Vasco da Gama.

The history of human navigation probably started many tens of thousands of years ago, when people learned to keep themselves and their belongings afloat on water using logs, bundles of reeds, or branches to provide buoyancy. These early vessels would drift with the currents or, at best, could be propelled using primitive paddles.

After the discovery of paddles, it would soon become obvious that the wind could be as powerful an opponent to muscular propulsion as could be the currents and waves, frequently forcing an undesirable leeward, or downwind, drift. That humans learned fairly early to use this drift to advantage is clear from vase paintings and clay models of Egyptian origin, variously dated by archaeologists to be 7,000 to 11,000 years old.

By 3000 B.C.E., downwind sailing using square sails to catch the wind was an established means for the waterborne transport of people and goods. Contemporary depictions show vessels whose sails hung from a horizontal spar, or yard, that could be set at various angles to the wind by means of ropes attached to its end. The square

format of early sails was consistent with early technologies for weaving fiber or reed and resulted in a sail that could be easily hung, raised, or furled onto a simple spar. Furthermore, when tethered at its lower corners, a square sail is naturally blown by the wind into a near-optimum curvature for downwind sailing, also allowing some angular variation from this course.

The technological development of sailing vessels has always been a compromise between demands for speed, cargo-carrying capacity, and maneuverability. Combined with the influences of local traditions and different availabilities of materials across the world, that compromise resulted in a tremendous variety of boats—by no means all of which were entirely successful.

The most primitive sailboats were able to use wind power only while the wind was blowing approximately in the intended direction of travel; for the remaining time, sailors had to resort to rowing for propulsion. Obviously, the greater the range of angles from which sails can exploit the wind, the greater the proportion of time that voyages could proceed under sail and the faster and easier the progress in the intended direction.

Prevailing winds

Long-distance navigation became much easier as sailors became more familiar with the prevalence of distinct wind directions in certain parts of the globe. In a belt that extends to a few degrees either side of the equator, the hot climate causes air to rise, drawing in cooler air from the Northern and Southern Hemispheres. Earth's rotation causes those air currents to drift westward, resulting in a tendency for wind to originate from the northeast in the Northern Hemisphere, and from the southeast in the Southern Hemisphere.

These winds, which became known as trade winds for their usefulness to seagoing traders, act from around 10 degrees either side of the equator. In the belt around the equator called the doldrums, air rises rather than traverses the surface. This region became notorious for its sometimes prolonged periods of calm, which could be dangerous for sailors with limited supplies.

The rising air currents at the equator form part of a global convection system and are complemented by falling air currents over the cold regions around the poles. Winds therefore spread out from the poles, and Earth's rotation adds an eastward shift to their direction. This effect results in the typical northwesterly winds of the Northern Hemisphere and southwesterly winds of the Southern Hemisphere. (A term such as *northwesterly* refers to the origin of a wind, not the direction in which it blows.)

Given a knowledge of the prevailing winds, sailors could plan routes that were favored by the predominant wind conditions. In this way, they reduced the proportion of time for which they would need to drop anchor to hold station during periods of adverse wind directions.

Windward sailing

A great advance in sailing occurred when sailors discovered how to sail into the wind. This practice required a change in sail mounting, from one that held the sail square across the boat to one that could hold the sail closer to the centerline. In this position, a side wind can drive the boat forward, while the profile of the boat and the rudder position hold the boat on course. Sailing almost perpendicular to the wind is called reaching.

If, while reaching, the rudder is turned to steer the boat farther into the wind, the boat is propelled at a slight angle toward the wind. Thus, gradual windward progress can be made by following a series of paths, first one way across the wind direction and then the other, always getting a little farther upwind—a process called tacking.

The advantages of sailing closer into the eye of the wind were considerable. The ability to sail closer to the wind than trading adversaries made for faster cargo deliveries than those of competitors, and hostile craft could often be outmaneuvered irrespective of their weaponry.

The design requirements for good windward sailing started to be understood only in the 19th century, and sailboat design has advanced significantly in this respect since then. Modern racing yachts, for example, have windward performances far superior to those of the fast clippers of mid-19th century, even though their performance at 90 degrees to the wind is only slightly superior.

Developments in sailboat design

The particularly successful sailing vessels of the past can be assessed in terms of their windward-sailing performance. Historical evidence suggest that the ability to hold a steady course with square sails was first exhibited by the Norse long ships on their phenomenal North Atlantic voyages between the 7th century and the 10th century. These ships, which ranged in length from 70 to 270 ft. (21–82 m), had hull profiles that even today are considered to have impressively low drag characteristics. Their sail rigging was the first to use bowlines and spars to tighten the luff—the windward edge of the sail—and ensure that the sail remained correctly shaped at low angles of wind incidence, a prerequisite for effective windward sailing.

The builders of early Chinese junks used bamboo battens to stiffen the lower edges of their square sails. These junks also featured low silhouettes and good design characteristics below the waterline, their builders having developed the

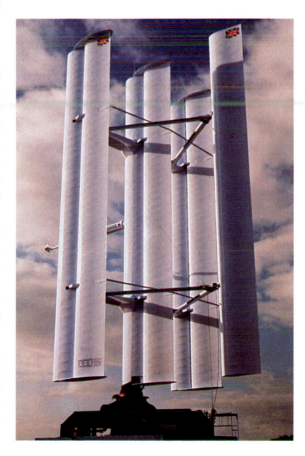

◀ Some modern sail designs make radical departures from the flexible sheets of conventional sails. The form of these rigid vertical airfoils is closely related to that of aircraft wings, and the same mechanism that provides lift for aircraft generates a horizontal force in this case.

efficient central rudder many centuries before European boatbuilders. These design advantages contributed to the preeminence of the Chinese as overseas traders for many centuries.

The first sail in which the yard was used at such an angle to the mast that it acted as a stiff leading edge was the lateen sail, whose name derives from the word *Latin*. Lateen sails can be set closer to the wind than is possible with square sails, and their introduction contributed much to the technique of windward sailing. The first use of the lateen sail was believed to be on Arab dhows in first century C.E., and the sail design was later introduced for vessels of the Mediterranean region and Iberian peninsula from the 9th century to the 13th century. Among the vessels that benefited from the high windward efficiency of the lateen sail were Venetian vessels and Portuguese caravels, which took part in the exploratory and merchanting voyages of the peoples of those regions.

The chain of development went on to include the 17th-century Scandinavian *jacht* and the Massachusetts schooner, which were direct forerunners of modern ocean racers. In this gradual

▶ Schooner and Bermuda sail combinations evolved from the lateen sail—a single triangular sail suspended from a yard arm angled so as to stiffen the leading edge of the sail.

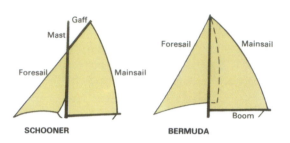

development process, the lateen sail evolved into a more manageable combination of two sails: a foresail, whose leading edge was sharpened by replacing the oblique yard by a permanently set sail luff, and an aft, or mainsail, suspended on a beam called a gaff, which took the place of the aft portion of the yard of the lateen sail.

Further developments reduced the tendency to capsize by eliminating the gaff to lessen the topside weight. The result was the modern Bermuda sail, whose foresail and mainsail both hang directly from the top of the mast. The windward efficiency of the Bermuda combination is now ascribed to its large aspect ratio: the ratio of the height to the length of a sail.

Mechanics of sailing

For any vehicle to move, it must have a means of generating a driving force that can at least balance the forces that resist its motion, and a sailboat is no exception. In the case of a sailboat, the main driving force comes from the aerodynamic action of wind on its sails and rigging, and the main resistance to motion comes from the hydrodynamic action of water on the hull and rudder.

The aerodynamic and hydrodynamic forces can each be split into a drag force that acts in the direction of the flow of air or water relative to the sailboat and a side force that acts perpendicular to that direction. How these interact to result in forward motion is best explained by considering the case of a sailboat moving at constant velocity. In this condition, all forces must be in balance, since there is no acceleration. Furthermore, there must be a balance in the turning forces that influence the vertical inclination of a sailboat, otherwise the sailboat will be liable to capsize.

Aerodynamic forces. As shown in the box at left, the force produced by the action of wind on a sail acts at an angle to the wind direction. According to the above definition, this force can be considered to be the resultant of a drag force that acts in the direction of the wind and a side force that acts perpendicular to that direction. The angle of the resultant force relative to the side force is known as the drag angle of the sail, or ε. As will become clear later, good windward sailing requires a small value of ε, implying a small drag force relative to

SAIL AERODYNAMICS

Aerodynamics determines how a sail uses the energy content of a moving air current to produce a force that can drive a sailboat. The resultant force of a whole sail is the sum of all the forces acting over each part of the sail, and at any point, that contribution to the resultant force acts at right angles to the surface of the sail. For a square sail set to face the wind, the origin of the force is easy to conceive: it is the difference in pressure between the windward and leeward faces of the sail. For a triangular sail set at an angle to the wind, the origin of the force is more complex but still originates from a difference in pressure between the two faces of the sail.

As can be seen below, the inner surface of the curved sail catches some wind, which exerts a pressure on the sail as it is deflected by the windward surface. Also, air passes more rapidly around the outer surface of the sail as it has farther to travel than across the inside of the sail. According to Bernoulli's theorem, the faster flow rate of the air on the outside of the curved sail reduces its pressure. This effect contributes to the difference in pressure between the two surfaces and therefore to the total force on the sail. As the angle of the sail to the wind direction decreases, the force due to the Bernoulli effect dominates, thus explaining why triangular sails with stiffened leading edges are so effective when sailing into the wind.

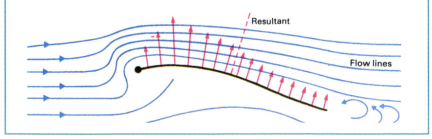

the side force. It is achieved by specifying thin spars and rigging to reduce air resistance and by setting the sail with a tight luff and shallow camber, or curvature, to maximize the contribution of the Bernoulli effect—which acts in the direction of the side force—to the resultant force on the sail.

Hydrodynamic forces. When a motorboat sails in a straight line, there is a resistance to it cutting through water caused by a phenomenon called viscosity, which is due to the tendency of the particles in a fluid to stick together. This force acts in alignment with the centerline of the motorboat as long as the motorboat follows a straight course.

In the case of a sailboat following a windward course, the rudder points the bow of the boat slightly windward of the course direction. When thus maneuvered, the hydrodynamic force shifts toward the windward direction as a result of the asymmetrical flow of water around the hull. The angle of the resultant force relative to the side force—and perpendicular to the course direction—is known as the drag angle of the hull, or ∂. Once again, good windward sailing requires a low value of ∂, which is achieved by a streamlined profile, often in combination with a centerboard that projects from the keel and acts like a vertical underwater wing to boost the side force due to the Bernoulli effect in water.

Balancing the forces. When sailing at a steady velocity, the resultant of the hydrodynamic forces must be equal and opposite to the resultant of the aerodynamic forces. When this condition applies, it is possible to relate windward sailing ability to the two drag angles, ∂ and ε, because ∂ is the angle between the centerline of the boat and the course direction, while ε is the angle between the centerline of the boat and the direction from which the wind originates. Thus, the angle between the course direction and the origin of the wind is the sum of ∂ and ε, so a sailboat that has low drag

▶ This crank is used to hoist the mainsail. As the mainsail is lowered, the boom in the background turns to take up the slack in a process called reefing. The mainsail can be reefed to reduce its surface area during stormy weather.

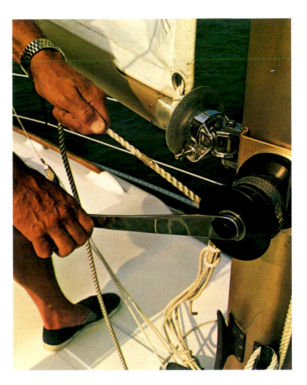

angles can sail close to the wind. The same boat can sail less close to the wind by loosening its sails to increase the drag angle.

Turning forces. A complicating factor in the mechanics of sailing is that the aerodynamic resultant force acts at some point above the deck, while the resultant hydrodynamic force acts in the opposite direction below the waterline. This combination results in a turning force, or torque, that would blow the vessel over if there were no opposite torque to balance it.

For this reason, the center of gravity—the point where downward force of the weight of the boat appears to act—must be below the center of buoyancy—the point at which the upward force of buoyancy appears to act. If the side forces cause the boat to heel clockwise as viewed from the bow, for example, the center of gravity shifts to the left of the centerline, while the center of buoyancy shifts to the right, resulting in a counterclockwise torque that balances the clockwise torque due to the side forces.

In order to maintain strong side forces, the boat must remain as close to vertical as possible. This aim is achieved by striving for the greatest possible height of the center of buoyancy above the center of buoyancy. Then the righting torque—the turning force that tends to keep the vessel close to vertical—increases steeply with the angle of heel. Good righting stability is achieved by combining a deep, heavy keel with light topside equipment, such as spars and rigging, and by designing the hull so that its center of buoyancy, which depends on the cross-sectional profile, is as close to the waterline as possible.

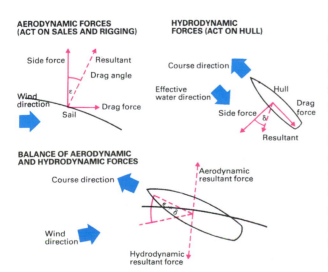

AERODYNAMIC FORCES
(ACT ON SALES AND RIGGING)

Side force — Resultant
Drag angle
Wind direction ε
Sail — Drag force

HYDRODYNAMIC
FORCES (ACT ON HULL)

Course direction
Effective water direction — Hull
Side force — ∂ — Drag force
Resultant

BALANCE OF AERODYNAMIC
AND HYDRODYNAMIC FORCES

Course direction — Aerodynamic resultant force
Wind direction — ε — ∂
Hydrodynamic resultant force

◀ A yacht sailing at about 45 degrees into the wind will have an aerodynamic force acting at 90 degrees to the wind and a drag force along the direction of flow. Similarly, hydrodynamic side forces and drag forces act on the hull. The resultant hydrostatic and aerodynamic forces are balanced. The net effect is a driving force into the wind.

Modern developments

Modern developments use new equipment and modeling methods to test and optimize sail and hull designs, the majority of which are essentially traditional. As a rule, sails and hulls are designed separately, since the testing and evaluation of all variables becomes immensely complex for combinations of sails and hulls. In effect, the testing of an integrated yacht design would require the resources of both aerodynamic and hydrodynamic laboratories and would need more measurements than required for an aircraft and ship together. It is not surprising, therefore, that such a full and costly program is rarely performed for an end product that is essentially recreational.

Models of sails and rigging are tested in wind tunnels in the same way as aircraft models are tested. Force sensors measure drag, side force, and the position of the center of effort—the point on which the combined effect of the sails and rigging acts—for various values of windspeed, angle of incidence, and heel angle of the sail. The forces measured on the models are then scaled up to predict the forces to be expected at full scale. Similarly, models of hulls are tested in towing tanks and flowing-water tanks. Again, drag and side force are measured using force sensors, as is the center of effort—the point at which the hydrodynamic forces seem to act on the model. Once again, these values are scaled to predict the forces to be expected for a full-sized hull.

Measurements of hull and sail characteristics are most often used to check for possible advantages of small variations in existing designs. Less frequently, they are used to evaluate radically different design solutions, such as multiple hulls or rigid, vertical airfoils, for example. One great advance of the 20th century was the introduction of computer control and servomechanisms to adjust the rigging of sails on the basis of parameters such as wind direction and strength.

New materials

In common with many other areas of technology, sailboat design and construction has benefited from the introduction of new materials, such as

SAIL-ASSISTED MOTOR SHIPS

Launched in 1980, the *Shin Aitoku Maru* was the first commercial ship to use sails to supplement its diesel engines and thus reduce its demand for fuel. The sails are rigid cylindrical sections rather than the more conventional triangular sails, and computer control ensures that they are always set at the best angle to extract power from the wind.

A second control system compares the actual speed to the required speed and adjusts the output of the diesel engines to make up for any power shortfall due to lack of wind or adverse wind direction. By virtue of its great degree of automation, the *Shin Aitoku Maru* was claimed to be operable by a crew of only eight people.

In 1995, the Danish Ministry of the Environment and Energy sponsored the Knud E. Hansen company of naval architects and marine engineers to perform a study of

◀ This is the Japanese vessel *Shin Aitoku Maru*. Its sails are the two shield-shaped objects mounted on masts. One of the supports is just visible at the top of the sail nearer to the bow of the vessel; the supports move under computer control to turn the sails so that their inner surfaces face the wind.

past sailboat and sail-assisted propulsion projects, including that of the *Shin Aitoku Maru*. The aim of the study was to decide whether sail-assisted motor boats could ever be economically viable (despite fuel savings, the increased construction and running costs of such vessels have impeded their widespread adoption by international maritime freight carriers).

The initial results of the study were not promising: on the basis of the premise of a five-sailed vessel, 219 yards (200 m) in length and with a dead weight of 55,100 tons (50,000 tonnes), the overall cost of freight would increase by around 10 percent, despite significant reductions in fuel consumption. However, the same study stated that the construction and running costs would be likely to diminish with further refinement and simplification. This trend should be expected to reduce and possibly eliminate the excess cost of sail-assisted shipping relative to conventional shipping. Moreover, the study predicted fuel savings of around 27 percent on routes where favorable wind conditions prevail, such as the Atlantic Ocean, and of up to 50 percent where the specially designed hold could accommodate cargo more effectively

than conventional cargo ships could. This saving corresponds to an estimated saving of 5,300 tons (4,800 tonnes) of fuel oil, with the associated reduction in emissions of carbon dioxide, a greenhouse gas, and various harmful nitrogen and sulfur oxides, which contribute to acid rain.

The use of wind power in combination with sail power is by no means limited to freight vessels: Windstar Cruises currently operates four vessels that combine sails with other forms of propulsion. The largest of these vessels—the 617 ft. (187 m) *Wind Surf*—has seven triangular, polyester sails with a maximum surface area of 26,881 sq. ft. (2,497 m^2). These sails furl and unfurl under computer control, providing around 60 percent of the total thrust. Additional thrust is generated by a diesel-electric propulsion system, whose two propulsion motors have a combined maximum power output of 4,935 horsepower (3,680 kW).

Other potential sources of propulsion from wind include kites and unpiloted air vehicles, or UAVs. It has been calculated, for example, that the Boeing Condor I—a powered UAV with a wingspan of 200 ft. (61 m)—could extract up to 10,000 lbf. (44 kN) of towing thrust from trade winds.

carbon fiber, glass-reinforced plastics, and new polymers for sail fabrics. Some material substitutions have improved performance, while others have improved the durability of sailboats.

Sails need to be made from fabrics that are strong, lightweight, and fairly stiff. They must have smooth surfaces to keep drag to a minimum and must be resistant to moisture, bacteria, and the ultraviolet component of sunlight, while being impermeable to wind and invulnerable to mechanical fatigue. Vast improvements in most of these properties have been made by replacing natural fibers with synthetics, such as Dacron polyester. These synthetic fibers are made into synthetic sailcloth by weaving and hot calendering (passing through heated rollers).

Rigging requires lightweight materials that have good tensile strength. Hemp ropes were replaced first by iron then by galvanized-steel and finally stainless-steel cables. Spars need stiff lightweight materials that are resistant to corrosion, so wooden beams have been replaced by aluminum alloy tubes, for example. Hulls need corrosion-

resistant materials suitable for forming into smooth, lightweight skins of great strength and impact resistance, so aluminum alloys and glass-reinforced plastics often replace wood.

Other sailing technologies

The principles behind sailing are also used in other activities. They are most obvious in windsurfing, where a frame-mounted sail provides a side force and the windsurfer leans back to surf at an angle in the water, providing the reaction force that would arise from the hydrodynamics of a sailboat's hull in the case of a sailboat.

Ice boats often use vertical airfoils in place of sails, and their hulls are mounted on skating blades. The reaction force is provided by outriggers that press on the ice as the "boat" heels over. Such vehicles can reach speeds of up to 50 mph (80 km/h) in a reasonably stiff breeze.

SEE ALSO: AIRCRAFT DESIGN • BOAT BUILDING • FIBER, SYNTHETIC • GLASS FIBER • MARINE PROPULSION • SELF-RIGHTING BOAT

Salt, Chemical

A salt is a chemical compound that consists of positive ions other than hydrogen (H$^+$) or oxonium (H$_3$O$^+$) ions and negative ions such as chloride (Cl$^-$) ions. The formulas of salts are such that the positive charges balance the negative charges, so there is no overall electrical charge.

The name of a salt consists of the cation name followed by the anion name, so the salt that has formula NaCl—representing a one-to-one compound of sodium ions (Na$^+$) and chloride ions (Cl$^-$)—is called sodium chloride, and NH$_4$Cl is ammonium chloride. The ammonium ion (NH$_4$$^+$) is the only common nonmetallic cation.

The type of anion in a salt has a major influence on its chemical properties, so salts tend to be grouped together by anion—the chlorides, nitrates, and sulfates are groups of salts with their own distinctive chemical properties, for example. The names of anions are derived from the name of the parent acid, so nitrates are related to nitric acid, and sulfates are related to sulfuric acid.

With the exception of hydroxide and oxide, anion names that end in -*ide* tend to indicate anions with no oxygen: fluoride (F$^-$) and sulfide (S^{2-}), for example. Anions whose names end in -*ate* or -*ite* tend to contain oxygen. For similar ions with different numbers of oxygen atoms, the anion with less oxygen takes the name ending in -*ite*. Examples include sulfate and sulfite (SO$_4$$^{2-}$ and SO$_3$$^{2-}$), nitrate and nitrite (NO$_3$$^-$ and NO$_2$$^-$).

Formation

Salts form when an acid reacts with a base. The reaction is commonly accompanied by the formation of water, as is the case when sodium hydroxide (NaOH) reacts with hydrochloric acid (HCl) to form sodium chloride:

$$NaOH + HCl \rightarrow NaCl + H_2O$$

When the base is a carbonate, such as sodium carbonate (Na$_2$CO$_3$), a strong acid will release carbon dioxide from the carbonate:

$$Na_2CO_3 + 2HCl \rightarrow 2NaCl + H_2O + CO_2$$

Salts also form when a reactive metal dissolves in an acid, so zinc forms its sulfate with sulfuric acid (H$_2$SO$_4$) and releases hydrogen as a gas:

$$Zn + H_2SO_4 \rightarrow ZnSO_4 + H_2$$

Other methods are specific to certain types of salts. For example, ammonium salts may be formed by passing ammonia gas through a dilute

▲ This plant produces a salt—ammonium phosphate—by a neutralization reaction between ammonia gas and phosphoric acid. The product is used in fertilizers and for the cultivation of yeast.

solution of the appropriate acid. Each ammonia molecule (NH_3) accepts a hydrogen ion from the acid as it forms an ammonium ion.

Structure and solubility

In the solid state, all salts are crystalline: their ions form an ordered three-dimensional structure called a crystal lattice. In such structures, the immediate neighbors of any ion are ions of the opposite charge, so each sodium cation in sodium chloride is surrounded by six chloride anions, and vice versa. Electrostatic attractions hold crystal lattices together, and these attractions are so strong that they keep the solid lattice together when a salt is warmed, preventing melting until high temperatures are reached. Sodium chloride melts at 1474°F (801°C), for example. (In a few exceptional cases, notably with ammonium salts, chemical decomposition disrupts the lattice at relatively low temperatures.)

The forces that hold a crystal lattice together must also be overcome when a salt dissolves. In many cases, the attraction between water molecules and ions outweighs the attractive forces in the lattice, and the salt is soluble in water. When lattice forces outweigh the affinity between ions and water molecules, the salt does not dissolve.

As a rule of thumb, salts that have particularly small cations or particularly large anions with low charges tend to be soluble. Examples include the salts of the alkali metals—all sodium and potassium salts are soluble, for example—and salts that contain nitrate or hydrogen carbonate (HCO_3) anions. In the latter case, the great sizes and small charges of the anions render their salts soluble.

Types of salts

Salts can be broadly divided into three categories: simple salts, double salts, and complex salts. Simple salts contain a single metal ion and a single anion. Familiar examples include sodium chloride (common salt, NaCl), sodium hydrogen carbonate (baking soda, $NaHCO_3$), sodium carbonate (washing soda, Na_2CO_3), copper sulfate ($CuSO_4$), and potassium nitrate (saltpeter, KNO_3—a constituent of gunpowder).

Double salts contain two types of metal ions. Among the most important examples are the alums, which are sulfates that contain chromium ions (Cr^{3+}) or aluminum ions (Al^{3+}) together with an alkali-metal ion, usually sodium or potassium. From a commercial point of view, the most important alum is potassium aluminum sulfate—potash alum, $KAl(SO_4)_2 \cdot 12H_2O$. This salt is used as a mordant in dyeing processes—it helps bind dye molecules into the fabric being dyed. The solid salt always contains 12 water molecules per formula unit, and they are an integral part of the crystalline structure of alums. For this reason, they are included in the formula of the salt.

Complex salts are salts in which one of the ions comprises a metal atom bound to one or more other chemical groups. Such an ion is called a complex ion, and it remains as a distinct entity when the salt dissolves. Potassium hexacyanoferrate (III), $K_3Fe(CN)_6$—used as a fertilizer and in some dyeing processes—contains the complex hexacyanoferrate (III) ion, $Fe(CN)_6^{3-}$, for example, while tetraamminecopper (II) chloride, $Cu(NH_3)_4Cl_2$, contains the complex tetraamminecopper (II) ion, $Cu(NH_3)_4^{2+}$.

Salts of weak acids and bases

Some salts exhibit acidity or alkalinity when they dissolve in water. This is because the associated base or acid has a strong tendency to remain in molecular form, so its ions tend to rob hydrogen or hydroxide ions from water molecules to reform the molecular acid or base. Examples are ethanoate (CH_3COO^-) and ammonium ions:

$$CH_3COO^- + H_2O \rightarrow CH_3COOH + OH^-$$
$$NH_4^+ + H_2O \rightarrow NH_3 + H_3O^+$$

While the molecular forms of ethanoic acid (CH_3COOH) and ammonia (NH_3) have no impact on the pH value of the solution, hydroxide ions (OH^-) register as alkaline and oxonium ions register as acidic on a pH meter.

◀ In the foreground, a solution of cobalt (II) chloride ($CoCl_2$) produces crystals as it cools. In the background, crystals of sodium hydrogen selenite ($NaHSeO_3$) are drying.

 SEE ALSO: Acid and alkali • Alkali metals • Chemistry, inorganic • Dyeing process • pH measurement

Salt Production

Common salt, sodium chloride ($NaCl$), is widely distributed throughout Earth's crust, and every gallon (4.5 l) of seawater contains about 4 oz. (113 g) dissolved in it. Huge deposits of rock salt, or halite, formed by the evaporation of seawater in geological periods exist in many parts of the world, notably in the United States, Canada, Mexico, Russia, and Europe.

Rock salt deposits are worked by well-used mining techniques, and if the salt is sufficiently pure, it can be used without further purification. Mining is usually done by the room and pillar method, which ensures that substantial rock salt pillars are left for support.

In a typical salt mine, the working height is approximately 25 ft. (7.6 m), with the working faces being around 50 ft. (15 m) wide according to the local conditions. The face is undercut to a depth of 12 ft. (3.7 m) using a heavy-duty rock-cutting machine and then drilled to a standard pattern with a mobile hydraulic rotary drilling carriage. The face is then charged with explosives and short-delay detonators. Firing the explosives produces a heap of over 1,000 tons (900 tonnes) of well-fragmented rock salt, which is then transported to an underground crushing plant. From the crusher, a further system of conveyor belts takes the processed rock salt to the base of the mine shaft, where it is hoisted to the surface.

When mined, the purity of rock salt is generally greater than 97 percent and for many uses requires only crushing and grading. If pure salt is required, the mined material may be dissolved in water to form brine, which is then evaporated by one of the methods described below. Alternatively, the salt may be extracted directly by drilling boreholes down into the salt deposits. Water is then pumped down the boreholes to dissolve the salt, forming brine, which is pumped back up to the surface for evaporation.

Evaporation techniques

Salt is produced from brine by evaporation in long, shallow pans. Heat is supplied by steam pipes near the bottom of the pan or directly to the bottom using hot gases from a fire. Salt crystals formed in the brine fall to the bottom of the pan, where they are removed by a scraper system. The salt produced by this process is in the form of characteristic flaky crystals and is known as flake, or grainer, salt.

Brine may also be evaporated in open ponds using the heat of the sun. The brine is usually run first into large concentration ponds with a surface

◄ Salt production in the Canary Islands. Concentrated brine is run into crystallizing pans where evaporation by sunlight results in the deposition of various grades of salt.

area of up to about 50 acres (20 ha), where impurities such as clay and sand and the less soluble salts such as calcium carbonate and calcium sulfate, separate out. The concentrated brine is then run through a series of smaller crystallizing pans, where salt of varying grades is deposited.

Vacuum evaporation

A typical vacuum plant for salt making consists of a series of three or more closed vertical cylindrical vessels with conical bottoms. Each of these vessels, or effects as they are generally called, has a steam chamber, or calandria, either totally submerged in the brine to be evaporated or externally connected. The calandrias contain a large number of vertical tubes through which the brine can be circulated, an arrangement that exposes a very large surface area. This system is most efficient for transferring the heat of the steam to the brine.

The condensation of the steam from the boiling brine in each vessel produces a reduction in pressure, and as a result the brine boils at temperatures lower than would be the case at ordinary atmospheric pressures. The salt crystals that form are taken from the bottom of the vessels and pumped in the form of a slurry to filters, which separate the salt crystals from the brine.

 SEE ALSO: Mining techniques • Salt, chemical • Vacuum

Index